PETER C. SWANN

AN
INTRODUCTION
TO THE
ARTS OF JAPAN

BRUNO CASSIRER

OXFORD

7580

BM8J (SWA)

PRINTED IN ENGLAND FOR
BRUNO CASSIRER (PUBLISHERS) LTD., OXFORD
BY LAWRENCE BROS. (W-S-M) LTD., WESTON-SUPER-MARE AND LONDON
DISTRIBUTED BY FABER AND FABER LTD., 24 RUSSELL SQUARE, LONDON, W.C.1
BLOCKS BY FINE ART ENGRAVERS LTD. AND
HALF-TONE ENGRAVING CO. LTD.

TO MY WIFE
WITH SINCERE
THANKS

ACKNOWLEDGEMENTS

A BOOK of this nature is the outcome of so many experiences, opportunities and so much help that it is impossible to make a comprehensive acknowledgement. However, certain people and institutions played a particularly large part. Dr. William Cohn initiated me into Eastern art and guided my first steps. A scholarship from the Scarborough Committee enabled me to study in America and Japan. In Japan itself, many scholars helped and guided me: Professors S. Mizuno and T. Nagahiro, Dr. S. Shimada, Messrs. S. Noma, R. Kaneko, Y. Yamanobe, and above all, Nishikawa Shinji, a good friend and my frequent companion on many journeys to see Japanese sculpture. Without his help, wide knowledge, and sympathy to a troublesome foreigner I should have missed many of the opportunities which can make a stay in Japan memorable.

The staff of the National Museum in Tokyo were always of unfailing assistance and I wish to record my sincere thanks to Mr. M. Ishizawa, Curator of Fine Arts, through whose kind offices I obtained many photographs and through whom Mr. Tadashi Shimao most generously agreed to allow me to reproduce illustrations from *The Pageant of Japanese Art*, a work produced by his company which is in the best tradition of Japanese scholarship and fine art publications. To him and to the eminent photographer Mr. M. Sakamoto are due many of the reproductions which are the most important aspect of this work. Without their co-operation the book would have been impossible.

The Trustees of the British Museum, the Victoria and Albert Museum, and the Musée Guimet among others provided additional reproductions. The book owes a great deal to the enthusiasm of Mr. George Hill and to the taste and skill of Mr. E. S. Elsey-Double. Miss Jane Arthur undertook the onerous task of typing the manuscript. Finally, my thanks are due to my wife who, like many writers' wives, in one way and another suffered somewhat during the writing of the book!

CONTENTS

INTRODUCTION

FAMILIARITY with Japanese art in the west generally begins and ends with colour-prints. During the last seventy-five years they have won a place in our own artistic heritage. The contribution of the colour-print to late 19th century European painting has been universally recognized. In this respect, and unfortunately only in this respect, Japanese art is better known in the West than even Chinese art. The general art-loving public may also have seen a Japanese ivory carving, a late (and generally bad) piece of export porcelain or a charming lacquer object. Little else has reached Europe.

Apart from a few scholars like Langdon Warner, eminent critics have not concerned themselves with the whole range of Japanese art in the last thirty years. Why? There are two main reasons—a flood of Chinese art and the political unpopularity of Japan which culminated in the recent war. It is sad that the appreciation of an art should be influenced by political considerations but unfortunately this happens.

The neglect of Japanese art is the more surprising when one remembers that 20th century appreciation of the arts of Asia in general began with those of Japan. It is unfortunate that the Japanese art introduced to Europe at that time belonged to her most decorative period. The first exhibition of Japanese art in London was held in 1854. It aroused little interest. Yet, by the 1880's, through appreciation of the colour print, Japanese art was the rage of Europe. Then some years later, in this century, a flood of fine Chinese art overwhelmed the West. Many Westerners were shocked to find that what they had eulogized in Japanese art had been influenced by and even directly inspired by earlier, though not necessarily finer, Chinese models. This produced a reaction born of disillusion in which *all* of Japan's artistic achievements were decried as pale reflections of earlier Chinese masterpieces. It appeared that Japan's art was no exception to the rule—which in our time had become a popular conception—that all Japanese achievements were imitations. Western critics, in discovering and exploring the monumental art of China, began to ignore the very real and often unique contributions of Japanese art. Japan was not even given its due as the world's greatest storehouse of Chinese art, for indeed no complete understanding of Chinese art can be reached without a study both of the Chinese treasures so lovingly preserved in Japan and of Japanese art itself.

The aim of this book, therefore, is to try to re-assess Japanese art in the light of our vastly expanded knowledge of all the arts of the East.

Laurence Binyon in 1923 said that the Japanese " have added new elements, and in some particular respects have surpassed the older nation, though in other respects they have never attained the same level." Is this a fair summing up? No answer to the question can be provided without a consideration of the ceramics, textiles, metal work, and lacquer of Japan as well as its painting and sculpture. In the same way no book on Chinese art would be complete if it ignored the bronzes and ceramics of that country. All visual arts are deeply rooted in the crafts, and Japanese artistic taste often found in them its most characteristic forms of expression. The distinction between art and craft has nowhere been finer than in Japan. Unlike China, in Japan the crafts were never scorned or considered inferior. Many famous painters worked also as potters or as designers of lacquer ware. Indeed, this freely accepted attitude that all art is one is a most refreshing feature of Japanese art in general.

There have been many books which have tried to interpret a nation's art in terms of its psychology, not always successfully. Yet the survey of the art leads naturally to interest in the characteristics of the people. The Japanese have very mixed qualities. Tender and romantic, kind and sensitive, they can also be brutal, impetuous, cynical, and treacherous. Convinced of the superiority of their own traditional way of life, they have never hesitated to adopt and to try to adapt, whatever they think advantageous and ' successful ' in that of other nations. This instinct has often, as at the present time, led them into difficulties which spring from a lack of understanding of the foundations upon which others have built their achievements. Their facility in the mastering of new techniques, whether Chinese or Western, has led to frequent crises in which often only their innate aesthetic taste has saved them. Facility so easily produces superficiality and the Japanese have not always avoided the trap which their ready skill laid for them.

The Japanese have a word ' *shibui* ' which can only be inadequately translated as ' good taste.' It has come to mean ' quiet,' ' restrained,' ' refined,' ' tasteful,' ' subdued,' ' cultivated,' and it conveys the Japanese ideal of taste. It is easy for the art historian, dwelling among the beauties of the past, to be appalled by the products of 20th century western life in Japan where they contrast so hideously with what is left of the old Japan. But to dwell upon this ugliness is as false as it is to represent Japan in the rosy terms of the tourist poster, as a land of fanciful scenes of cherry blossom, gaily kimono-clad ladies, and the haunting sadness of Madame Butterfly. The whole world has moved on and we have all suffered the same misfortunes.

Painting and sculpture must form the basis of any appreciation of Japanese art but the real taste of the Japanese is equally found in many an unexpected corner—in the minute garden whose apparently careless natural charm is in fact the product of the most careful thought, in the arrangement of a bowl of flowers, in the faultless architectural balance of a room, in the vigour expressed by a few lines of calligraphy, in the sensitivity of an evocative line of poetry. Above all, it is to be found in the shrines and temples carefully preserved through the centuries. These much-visited treasure-houses of ancient art provide a constant reminder of past glories. Their beauty and their contents are deeply ingrained in the popular artistic sense.

The Japanese know the history of their art better than any other Asian people; museums are excellent and intensively active; more records have been preserved than in other lands; Japanese scholars have been more industrious than those of other Eastern nations and their attributions are usually accurate. The Japanese people have a genius, almost a mania, for conservation. Art objects from the very earliest times which in China have long since disappeared have in Japan been carefully protected—occasionally, as the student anxious to see them will have found—with almost maddening caution. Japanese standards of beauty may differ from ours—therein lies much of their interest; their approach may be quite different, which gives the Westerner an opportunity to open his mind and form his own judgments. And it is for the Westerner that this book, only an introduction in every sense, is intended.

No introduction to a nation's art can ever be satisfactory. It must ignore many vexed questions, leave doubts unvoiced, simplify or avoid many problems. It must perforce leave out more than it includes. This book will share in full measure all these failings—and add some of its own. Long lists of artists, genealogies of schools, and chronologies of works are not included. It attempts merely to fill in the broad outlines of Japanese art by reference to a number of representative and outstanding works almost all of which are illustrated. The hope is only to stimulate an interest and fill a gap.

The history of Japanese art is a very long one. At the very beginnings of Japanese civilization there were made superb examples of neolithic art, long before the first great cultural impact on Japan—that of China. Such influences have sometimes obscured the native Japanese artistic spirit but they never entirely obliterated it. As N. G. Munro said, " the artistic talent of later Japan was rooted in the pre historic past." To this very distant past we must now turn.

● Towns.   ■ Kiln sites.

MAP OF JAPAN

SHOWING PRINCIPAL PLACES MENTIONED

IN THE TEXT

CHAPTER I

JAPANESE ART TO THE 6TH CENTURY

THE art of stone-age man is perhaps the most difficult of all arts to appreciate and judge. Our reconstructions and interpretations seldom help to elucidate much of its meaning. The obvious danger is that of modern man over-intellectualizing the motives of his stone-age ancestors, of reading into them his own more complicated or rather more sophisticated outlook. But the pattern of the development of neolithic art in Japan is fairly clear.

Before considering Japan's earliest art, however, it is important to understand a little of the native Japanese religion which has come to be known as *Shintoism*, ' The Way of the Gods.' Its origins and development are so vague that adequate summary is difficult. First it is essential to distinguish the elaborate state cult which was built up for political reasons and the deep-rooted ritualism which springs from a simple animistic creed. The former had comparatively little influence on art while the latter has deeply affected the Japanese character and thus has coloured the whole Japanese approach to art.

The very vagueness of *Shintoism* has been a source of its power. It has given it a resilience which has enabled the native beliefs to survive the impact of more advanced, compelling religions such as Buddhism. Through the centuries its influence has waxed and waned but the native gods have never been completely neglected. To this day its most important ceremonies and festivals are scrupulously observed. The main *Shinto* shrine at Ise, for example, was founded in A.D. 478. Since the 7th century the whole shrine has been completely and exactly rebuilt on an adjacent site every twenty years, the present set of buildings being no less than the fifty-ninth reconstruction.

Shintoism is rooted in the rich Japanese mythology. According to this, the race is descended from the gods. Such mythological origins, are, for instance, related in the *Kōjiki* and *Nihongi*, 8th century compilations which, though under strong Chinese influence, include much indigenous material. They command as much respect nowadays in Japan as does the Book of Genesis in the West. But the more simple and fundamental beliefs of the cult have influenced the Japanese spirit very deeply. Sansom defines *Shintoism* as " a religion founded upon a conception, a vague and unformulated conception, of the universe as composed of a myriad sentient parts." Thus everything in nature, the awesome as well as the friendly, the beautiful, the unusual and even the everyday things have their divinities and share the quality of being *kami*. This word originally meant ' superior ' but has come to mean ' divine.' The Emperor derives much of the respect which he commands, and which he has preserved through many difficult times, from the belief that he is the chief intermediary between the spirits and his people. In times of strain the Japanese people will always return to their native gods—and thus also to the Emperor.

Japan is a rich and fertile country and Ashton points out that *Shintoism* is a religion of love and gratitude rather than of fear—in particular, gratitude for the bountiful gifts of a kindly nature. It is the awareness of the myriad spirits in nature combined with an

1

appreciation of nature's kindness which has given the Japanese a sense of the beauty and friendliness of their picturesque islands. This has affected the artist as well as the peasant. Although one can exaggerate the influence of *Shintōism*, it is safe to say that it has left a deep and distinguishing mark on the innermost sensitivities of the Japanese people, and finds its earliest expression at the very beginnings of Japanese art in the neolithic period.

Archaeological excavations of neolithic sites in Japan have revealed two types of culture fairly evenly distributed. They are distinguished by their different techniques of pottery making. In one type (Fig. 1), called the *jōmon* (lit: coiled rope) the heavy, earthenware pots were made with coils of clay. During the period in which this type of pottery was produced, the inhabitants of Japan began to change from a nomadic, hunting and fishing culture to a more settled civilization. In the second type, called the *Yayoi*, after a neolithic site of that name, the pottery is of a much more advanced technique. Where the two types occur together, the *jōmon* is found on a lower level and therefore appears to be earlier. Some scholars claim that the remnants of the Ainu people living to-day in Hokkaidō belong to the same stock as those who produced the *jōmon* culture (sometimes called 'proto-Japanese') while the *Yayoi* people, who came later, certainly had more recent and closer contacts with the mainland. Other scholars, basing their studies on skeletal remains, claim that the two peoples are the same and that the differences are simply due to evolution. It seems that the *Yayoi*, from about the 1st or 2nd century A.D. introduced more advanced agricultural techniques, a knowledge of bronze- (and soon afterwards iron-) casting, and evolved a more intricate tribal organization. The union of the *jōmon* and *Yayoi* stocks produced the Japanese people. Archaeologists are extremely cautious about dating either of these cultures beyond saying that the stone-age lasted from about the 10th century B.C. to the beginning of the Christian era. Some scholars,[1] however, place its beginnings much earlier, in the 3rd millenium B.C. Local differences in the state of development and the dispersion of these two cultures create many perplexities for the investigator.

Recent discoveries of *jōmon* type pottery have enabled Japanese scholars to divide this first long period into three sub-periods according to the degree of skill revealed in the manufacture of their pottery. Some two hundred small clay figurines have been discovered which belong to the two later sub-periods. The imagination which inspired them, the workmanship and the variety of decoration place many of these without doubt among the most outstanding examples of neolithic art yet discovered anywhere in the world (Fig. 2). Japanese scholars see in them a development during which their style gradually becomes more conventionalized and, in the last period, more and more imaginative and ornate. Their geographical dispersion shows that they were first made in the central part of Japan and spread northwards. Many examples are fertility symbols of the mother-goddess type, resembling neolithic figurines found throughout the world at a similar stage in man's development. In Japan, the desire seems to have been not only for human fertility but also for the increase of all life; this may explain why these figures do not show the usual features of pregnancy often associated with many early figures.

There is no reason for thinking that the example reproduced in Figure 2 is a fertility symbol. It comes from the earlier period and, measuring ten inches in its truncated form, is among the largest yet found. The flat figure is burnt brown, its blackish shoulders decorated with an impressed pattern. Its symbolism or meaning can hardly be surmised but the powerful modelling, tense attitude and striking facial expression reflect the haunted

---

[1] V. Elisséeff in *Destins du Monde*. Vol. 1. Paris, 1957.

1. *Pottery vessel* of *Jōmon* type.
Height 14¾ inches.
Tokyo National Museum.

2. *Clay Figurine* of *Jōmon* type.
Excavated in Yamanashi Prefecture.
Height 9⅞ inches.

imagination of a primitive people. Probably the figure was made to propitiate some important spirit of the kind which abounded in the life of neolithic man. Some Japanese experts say that the fantasy seen in these figures springs from man's joy in creation but there can have been little 'joy' in the spirit which animated the creator of this figure. Terror or, at best, magic would perhaps better describe the force which moved its maker. It requires no great stretch of the imagination to see even in this early figurine a deep-seated Japanese taste for the fantastic and horrific which repeatedly appears in the art of subsequent ages—and which is seen in a very developed stage in the masks of later periods (see Figs. 19, 38). Later *Shintō-ism* may well have become a friendly religion but there is much that is terrifying in its earliest manifestations. It is interesting to see even in such primitive Japanese art, a relatively polished technique and a decorative sense which is highly developed in comparison with those of the arts of other parts of the world at a similar stage in the development of their inhabitants. This skill and style remain features of Japanese art throughout nearly two thousand years, and presage a most original culture.

From about the 3rd to the 6th centuries A.D. the picture of early Japan becomes clearer. This phase is called the Old Tomb Period (*Kō-fun Jidai*) from the man-made earth mounds covering the stone burial chambers of important people. Some of these are of gigantic proportions; that of the Emperor Nintoku, who died *ca.* A.D. 400, is 90 ft. high (Fig. 3) and, with its moats, covers an area of 80 acres near Osaka. The size of these tombs indicates that the social organization of the tribes had developed from a patriarchal family system to a system of small communal states. Many of these burial mounds have remained untouched owing to the sanctity which surrounds all things imperial; this understandable respect is a great obstacle to the archaeologist. The mounds are magnificent sights rising in quiet, undisturbed majesty from the small, flat, cultivated fields which surround them— the still water of their moats adding to the atmosphere of inviolability they radiate. What treasures do they contain? Early Japanese and imported Korean and Chinese art? Bronzes, jades, and even gold jewellery would probably be found in them. Certainly, by this time, the crafts flourished for there are later records from which we can surmise that considerable trade guilds existed. But, though the impossibility of excavation at present may be tantalizing, it is just this reverence for the past which has preserved these mounds intact, like so much else of Japan's cultural heritage. How much the poorer we should be if this spirit had never existed!

The Old Tomb Period coincides with the later part of the *Yayoi* type culture. As contacts with the mainland increased, so more objects such as bronze mirrors and jade objects entered Japan where they were admired and treasured. Koreans emigrated to the islands bringing with them a deeper knowledge of Chinese culture. It must be remembered that the Chinese had occupied part of Korea and that one Chinese outpost survived there into the 4th century A.D. Japan, unlike China, had a very short and undistinguished bronze

3.   Aerial View of the *Tomb of Emperor Nintoku* near Osaka.

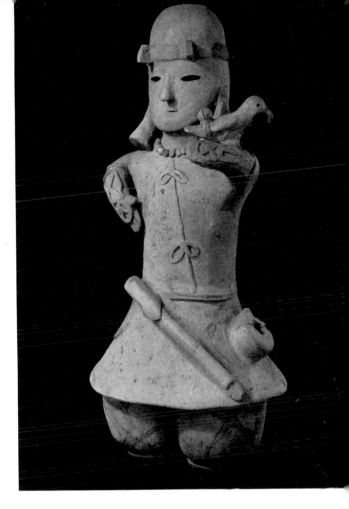

5. *Haniwa* figure of *Warrior with Falcon*.
Excavated in Gumma Prefecture. Old Tomb period.
Height 2 feet 6 inches.

4. *Bronze Bell (Dōtaku).* Yayoi period.
Tokyo National Museum.

age. Close and easy cultural contacts with the mainland only developed towards the end
of China's great bronze age (end of 1st millenium B.C.) at a time when the finest bronze
work was already forgotten and China was moving into the iron age. A number of bronze
implements such as spear-heads and bells (Fig. 4) are found in Japan but they do not
compare in quality or in quantity with the Chinese products of the Shang and Chou
periods (*ca.* 13th–3rd centuries B.C.).

The most characteristic product of the late *Yayoi* culture are the unique *haniwa* figures
which the early Japanese set up in circles round the foot of earthern burial mounds to
retain the earth (Figs. 5, 6, 7, 8). *Hani* means ' clay' and *wa* ' circle,' i.e. ' clay objects
arranged in circles ' and the individual pieces vary in size from 20 to 40 inches. Many
are only simple, undecorated cylinders which, for all their simplicity, give evidence of considerable ceramic skill. But by far the most interesting are models of human figures,
animals, houses, etc. Together they throw much light on the life, dress, and customs of a
time which was by no means as primitive as it might at first appear. The inspiration for the
models of human figures undoubtedly comes from ancient China and some writers have

6. *Haniwa* figure of a *Horse*.
Excavated in Saitama Prefecture. Old Tomb period.
Height 2 feet 9 inches.
Tokyo National Museum.

7. *Haniwa* figure *Head of a Woman*.
Excavated in Osaka Prefecture.
Old Tomb period.
Height 7½ inches.

8. *Haniwa* figure *Head of a Monkey*.
Excavated in Ibaraki Prefecture.
Old Tomb period.
Height 10¾ inches.

suggested that, as in China, figures were made as substitutes for the human sacrifices which in very early times accompanied the burial of important people. However, the Japanese did not begin to make models of human beings until the beginning of the 5th century A.D., many centuries after the Chinese had discontinued the custom and it is unlikely that they had any connexion with human sacrifice. One interesting artistic comparison can be made with two rare neolithic pots now in the Museum of Far Eastern Antiquities, Stockholm

(Fig. 9), which come from the Kansu area in China and probably date to almost two thousand years before the *haniwa* figures. It is impossible to prove any direct influence but the modelling is strikingly similar. It is not even possible to say whether the *haniwa* figures evolved from the simple cylinders. Their interest lies in their effective modelling, which owes something to their technique of manufacture. They are made in a shape which is basically a hollow cylinder. This allowed the fire to reach all parts more evenly, while the perforations for the eyes and mouth allowed gases to escape and thus avoided cracking. These technical expedients contributed to the plastic effect. Above all the *haniwa* were the products of simple craftsmen working in haste on the occasion of the death of an important individual. This speed resulted in rapid, sure modelling and an extreme economy of means. The two *Dancers* illustrated in Figure 10—perhaps intended to represent a man and a woman— seem to be singing as they dance and the treatment of the arms as well as the haunted expressions are reminiscent of some of the *jōmon* figurines. Certainly they belong to the same spirit-fraught world of magic and superstition. The impression of arrested movement, so fitting to an art of the grave, imparts a ghostly quality to many of these figures. The expressions created by the empty eyes and open mouths would have deterred at least a timid grave-robber—if such a man existed. The wistful monkey's head (Fig. 8) with its appealing look and eloquent, watchful twist, must rank among the world's masterpieces of animal sculpture of any age.

The men, women, houses, ships, and animals represented in these terra-cotta models belong to a world increasingly conscious of and inspired by China, but not as yet completely overwhelmed by it. Here, in these early centuries A.D., the original Japanese artistic talent speaks clearly and directly—perhaps more understandably to us in the 20th century than at any other time since it first expressed itself some fifteen hundred years ago. It was to be many centuries before this Japanese spirit in the arts was able to break once more through the heavy overlay of a more sophisticated, alien Chinese world. Perhaps it never again appeared with such pure, naïve charm and such eloquent simplicity.

9. Fragment of a *Neolithic pot*.
West China.   Second millenium B.C.
Museum of Far Eastern Antiquities, Stockholm.

10. (Right).   *Haniwa* figures of *Dancers*.
Excavated in Saitama Prefecture.   Old Tomb period.
Heights 18 inches and 11 inches.

CHAPTER II

THE ASUKA OR SUIKO PERIOD[1]

A.D. 555–646

THE introduction of Buddhism to Japan in the middle of the 6th century brought about an almost unbelievable change in the life of the Japanese tribes—a change even more revolutionary than the introduction of western culture and techniques in the 19th century. The Japanese, until then a comparatively primitive people, adopted in a remarkably short time the religion, and with it the complete culture, of a nation infinitely more advanced than themselves. The will and imagination which enabled them to do this are admirable. Nevertheless, in their admiring, unquestioning adoption of things Chinese they sometimes overlooked the fundamentals of Chinese achievements to grasp only the glittering externals. From this momentous introduction of Chinese Buddhism and its effect on Japanese life springs the too-often repeated criticism that the Japanese only reflect other cultures and somewhat palely at that. The judgment is by no means altogether sound.

The Chinese themselves had taken their Buddhism in the first centuries A.D. via Central Asia from its birth-place in India. From China it spread to Korea which, from about the first century onwards, had cultural contacts with Japan, and it was from there that the Japanese obtained their introduction to this profound and stimulating religion. In this way the Japanese acquired their Buddhism third- or even fourth-hand. It is a tribute to their native intelligence and energy that they both desired it, and could grasp it so rapidly. The masterpieces that China, even with her long artistic tradition, was inspired to create under the influence of the Buddhist faith, are a matter for wonder; the achievements of the Japanese, building only on a genuine enthusiasm, vigour, and taste, are even more surprising.

Like all religious art, Buddhist art cannot be understood without some knowledge of the religion and its founder. As with the life of Christ, that of the Buddha is full of events which have inspired centuries of artists both in his home country and across the vast areas of the Far East into which Buddhism penetrated. It should be remembered that, in its finest hour, Buddhism had more adherents than any of the world's religions has ever claimed. Its art from India to China, Siam to Japan, is one of the glories of man.

Like Christ, the Buddha was an historical figure but born nearly six centuries before Him and the story of his life is permeated with mythology. His father, Suddhodana, was a wealthy chief of a small aryan tribe called the Shakyas in the city of Kapilavastu, north

[1] Asuka is the name of the place in which the capital was situated during these years. The whole period is alternatively often called Suiko from the name of the Empress Suiko (593–628) whose reign was the most brilliant of the whole period.

India. His family name was Gautama but the son is usually known by the name Shakyamuni. Tradition tells of his great physical beauty and high intelligence and many other signs of his destined greatness. In spite of the advantages of birth and wealth, being surrounded with every form of luxury, his spirit was troubled and inner happiness seemed to elude him. Even a beautiful wife and a handsome young son failed to bring him content- ment. On three occasions when he happened to ride out of his castle, he met in the form of human beings, three of the principal reasons for sorrow—old age, sickness, and death. According to the scriptures, the gods sent these apparitions to remind him of the purpose for which he was born. They awoke his determination to discover why living beings suffered and thence how to escape the pain on which the world seemed to be built. During his meditations on these problems, on the fourth occasion when he left his castle, he met a homeless ascetic. The calm features of this man showed that here, at least, was one seeking a solution to the problem of pain inherent in the transience of all things. Determined that he too would seek in similar solitude deliverance for himself and all mankind, the Prince slipped quietly away from his castle in the middle of the night. The stories of what is called ' The Great Renunciation ' and the events leading up to it such as his four exits from the palace are often depicted in Buddhist art. The life of pleasure which he formerly led and his birth in the Lumbini Garden are frequently shown. He is said to have been delivered from his mother's side while she supported herself by holding on to the branch of a tree. One of the most frequent representations is the scene of his departure from the palace in which heavenly beings support his horse's hooves in order to prevent any sound reaching the sleeping household. Another popular scene shows him in the forest bidding farewell to his white horse which kneels before him and to his lamenting groom. His victories over the forces of evil inspired countless artists and, of course, his death, as he lay surrounded by mourning disciples, is as often represented as that of Christ on the Cross.

The Prince, after leaving his home, set out on the second great period of his life in which he sought truth in the traditional Indian way as a homeless ascetic. The stories of his temptations in the wilderness have something in common with those of Christ. After some years of study he decided that he could not find the solution to his problems in any of the Brahmanical teachings which emphasized the need for man to spiritualize his inner self. This, he felt, was only a balm and not a radical cure of man's sorrows. Man was still bound by the chain of birth and rebirth from which escape was impossible.

He then decided to win salvation through the traditional method of austerities, hoping thereby to free his soul from his body. Reducing his food almost to nothing, the Prince wasted away nearly to the point of death. But this means, too, failed him and he took food to regain strength before entering into his last trial—that of the most profound meditation. Under the Bodhi tree at Bodh Gaya he sat during one final night of the most testing temptations, enduring and repulsing the repeated onslaughts of Māra and his evil company of demons. As dawn broke, he achieved enlightenment, saw the innermost secrets of birth, death, and rebirth and the final way of escape. At this moment he became the Buddha, ' The Enlightened One.'

The third period of his life was spent in spreading his teaching throughout the north- east of India. His following grew rapidly, miracles as astounding as those of Christ are recounted and he was recognized as the founder of a new sect within the old Hindu tradition.

At the age of eighty his end drew near. With his sorrowing disciples around him he entered into his final ecstasy and passed into *pari-nirvana,* the final release, ' the complete extinction of selfhood as well as the material on which it is built.' His body was burned and the relics divided—their fate over the centuries was as chequered as that of the fragments of the true cross. In 1956, the 2,500th anniversary of this event was celebrated throughout the world.

After the death of the Buddha, his teachings spread still further. Certain of them have had the most far-reaching importance in the history of Asia. Their subsequent development as a religion, especially in the forms accepted in China and Japan, deeply influenced the arts of these countries. Buddhism flourished in India for over 1,500 years till the coming of Islam (10th–12th centuries) and it survives to this day in Ceylon, Burma, Siam, Tibet, and Nepal not to mention the countries of the Far East. It spread like fire through central Asia and to China and Japan where it set alight the imagination of a people ripe for a spiritual awakening.

The Buddha's doctrine evolved in various schools which, about five hundred years after his death, formed two main divisions, the *hinayana* or 'lesser vehicle' and the *mahayana* or 'greater vehicle.' In *hinayana*, although the laity also shared in the benefits of Buddhism, the tendency was to stress the life of the secluded monk as the way to salvation. The great difference between this and the *mahayana* was the elaboration in the latter of the concept of celestial *bodhisattvas*. These were mortals who, because of merit gained in past lives, were entitled to become Buddhas and enter *nirvana*, but, through compassion for suffering humanity, delayed the final consummation. Thus the *mahayana* greatly increased the numerous assembly of heavenly and ghostly beings. It was mainly the *mahayana* form which reached China and Japan and the *bodhisattva* concept which appealed to their peoples. They eagerly adopted and developed Buddhas of the past and future, guardians, demons, angels, *bodhisattvas* in particular, and all the visual aids to belief so attractive to the lay mind. One of the strong points of this *mahayana* Buddhism was an extremely accommodating outlook which enabled it to absorb, often without conflict, the native beliefs of the countries which it reached. Thus Chinese *taoism* and Japanese *shintoism* coloured the Buddhism of China and Japan respectively. Just as the native doctrines of these foreign countries were accepted into Buddhist beliefs, so the native gods also found themselves enrolled among the ranks of the Buddhist divinities. All this was achieved by peaceful means for, of all the world's great religions, Buddhism must rank among the most unwarlike. The pacifist outlook of the religion made it attractive to rulers anxious to have a quiet, easily manageable population. This same aspect of Buddhism worked against the faith when a king had military aspirations and resulted in occasional but serious persecutions of the believers.

The time of the official introduction of Buddhism into Japan is given as A.D. 532, the year in which the King of a Korean kingdom presented the Japanese Emperor with a number of Buddhist ritual objects including a statue of Prince Shakyamuni. This, of course, is nothing more than a convenient date, for Buddhism must have been known in Japan prior to that year through the numerous cultural contacts with Korea which had started as early as the 1st century A.D. Buddhism is said to have been introduced into Korea by two Chinese priests in A.D. 372 and already in A.D. 405 a Korean had come to the Japanese court to teach the Chinese language. The transition through Korea must have been very rapid.

In spite of a desperate semi-religious, semi-political opposition, it took less than fifty years for Buddhism to establish itself even more firmly in Japan than in China. The progress of the faith was particularly fast after Prince Shōtoku, sometimes called ' the

Buddhist Constantine,' acting as regent for his widowed mother, encouraged the spread of the faith by official edict. Henceforward many monasteries were built, manned with priests and furnished with all the trappings of the faith.[1] No conversion, except perhaps that of Java by Islam, can ever have been more rapid, more complete and more sincere. Almost overnight the Japanese accepted from the missionaries of the Greater Vehicle a spiritual revolution which had swept through India, central Asia, China, and Korea. In art this revolution found expression in a mixture of elements from the plastic art of the Hellenic world, Iranian elegance, and the sensuous sweetness of Indian Gupta art.[2]

Japanese scholars do not agree on many of the details of the earliest sculptures which, despite their delicate materials, have escaped destruction. Although early Buddhism in Japan was comparatively simple with few divinities and little of the complicated iconography which makes statues of later periods more difficult to understand, their diversity of type and the disappearance of their mainland prototypes has created considerable problems. There is no doubt, however, about the origin of their inspiration.

In the 5th and 6th centuries in China there were created the vast cave temples at Yün-kang and Lung-mên. This happened under the devout rulers of the Northern Wei dynasty (A.D. 386–532) who had been completely won over to Buddhism. The Wei were a northern tribe, which had conquered a large area of Inner China, and under their patronage hundreds of cave temples were carved from the living rock with myriads of statues, both large and small. They are one of the artistic wonders of the world. The work of literally thousands of skilled sculptors over a long period went into them—a vast monument to a burning faith. Almost certainly, sculptors who had worked or been trained there found their way to Korea and to some of the southern Chinese states such as the Liang (A.D. 502–556) thus spreading Buddhist art far and wide. In the South the absence of good rock cliffs made cave-temples a rarity, and the talents of the artists were directed into bronze casting. Bronzes are portable, and such works were exported over the rest of the Far East, into Korea and eventually into Japan. In Japan, likewise, there are no caves suitable for temple carving and even good stone is rare, whereas wood is plentiful. So, as well as bronzes, many fine wood sculptures have survived in Japan, whereas in China such work has largely disappeared.

Among the earliest sculptors known by name in Japan is a Korean-Chinese immigrant, Tori, whose family came to Japan in A.D. 532. He gave his name to the earliest school of Japanese sculpture, the Tori School. A number of figures in this style have been preserved, the most important being his famous bronze *Shakyamuni Triad* dated A.D. 623 which can still be seen in the Hōryū-ji Monastery near Nara (Fig. 11). The dominant influence of late Northern Wei sculptural styles (Fig. 12) is clearly seen in this work which is the most easterly manifestation of types formed at Yün-kang and Lung-mên. The drapery is symmetrically arranged in clear-cut folds which fall richly but very formally over the pedestal; there is a certain lack of proportion in the limbs; the so-called 'archaic smile' on the lips brings a little animation to an otherwise impassive face. The body is heavily swathed in robes and there is a high degree of stylization in the whole composition. But, in addition to the strong Chinese influence, one can already recognize in this triad a sense of rhythmical design, which was to become one of the characteristics of Japanese art. The faces are heavy and full with a high bridge to the nose, a long cylindrical neck

[1] 46 temples had been built by A.D. 640. Sansom, *A Short Cultural History of Japan.* London, 1946. p. 147.
[2] R. Grousset, *Le Japon.* Paris, 1930. p. 14.

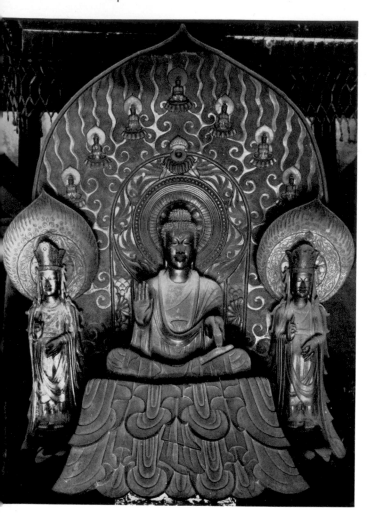

11. *Shakyamuni Triad* by Tori Bushi.
Bronze. Asuka period.
Height Seated figure 2 feet 10 inches.
Attendants 2 feet 11¾ inches.
Hōryū-ji, Nara.

12. Seated figure from a Chinese cave
temple. Stone. Northern Wei
period (Early 6th century).
Courtesy S. Mizuno.

and generally well-proportioned features. Such figures, like those in the caves, are obviously intended to be seen only from the front. The expressions are calm, highly stylized and convey both dignity and mystery. The superb casting matches the majesty of the concept. The regularly arranged drapery seems to have absorbed much of the sculptor's energies. But it is in the elegant back-ground motifs that its maker felt really at his ease and free to escape from the strict canons laid down for the central figures. There is a high degree of spiritual detachment and other-worldliness in the work, especially in the faces. The artist's concept of the gods is still that of supra-human beings. It is unfortunate that the angels which orginally surrounded the halo are now lost.

Another early work, the *Guze Kannon* (Fig. 13) in the Yumedono or ' Dream Hall ' of the Hōryū-ji is attributed by some Japanese scholars to the same Tori school. But there are notable differences. Although it has the appearance of a bronze statue, it was in fact carved from a single piece of camphor wood and then covered with gold leaf. Its magnificent state of preservation is due to its having been treated through the ages as a ' secret statue ' visible to the worshipping public only on very rare occasions. The face which is infused with a new warmth and tenderness shows a most striking development. The modelling in general is more plastic and the whole figure somewhat less stylized, though the full possibilities of wood as a sculptural medium have hardly yet been realized. The attendant figures of this image have a similarity to the *Tori Triad* but the whole conception is lighter, more graceful and certainly more sympathetic. The figure is taller, more humanly proportioned and the face begins to show more personality. Some historians have suggested that it is a portrait of the great Prince Shōtoku whose support for Buddhism in early times was so momentous. One might say that in the *Tori Triad* the artists seem to stand at the end of a tradition while in the *Guze Kannon* they are at the beginning of a new one.

The technique and workmanship in both works is of the highest quality. Throughout Japanese art there are seldom signs of first halting steps or of the unsteady hand of the beginner. Japan was presented with the spectacle of an art completely formed in China; and her great achievement was to recognize that art, to join in its production with tremendous creative energy, and to develop it in new ways which China never surpassed.

Korea was not the only source of Japanese knowledge of Chinese art. Different influences spread from different centres on the mainland to satisfy the inquiring mind of the Japanese. Thus, from the earliest days in Japan, there were at least three different schools. To distinguish between them is often hard, and opinions differ among the Japanese about the attributions of surviving works. A well-marked style, different from those of the *Tori* school and the *Guze Kannon*, is seen in the *Kudara Kannon* (Fig. 14). Kudara is the Japanese name for the Korean kingdom of Paekche from where the figure or its creator are said to have come to Japan. Some Japanese see in it a relationship with the *Guze Kannon*. But the statue has such individual qualities that it is best considered as a unique work. Ultimately its inspiration may have come from a different part of China, perhaps from the south rather than the north, and from a period slightly later than the Northern Wei. In this long, slender figure the limbs are again out of proportion but in exactly the opposite way to that of the *Tori* bronze. The elongation gives a grace and lightness to the whole concept. The figure is conceived far more in the round and the drapery which curls forwards instead of sideways produces an effect very different from the frontality of the *Tori* bronze. The three dimensional impression is much stronger. There is a far greater feeling of movement in this tall figure than in the squat *Tori* bronze. The lateral movement

13. *Cuze Kannon*. Wood.
Asuka Period.
Height 6 feet 5½ inches.
Yumedono Hall, Hōryū-ji, Nara.

14. (Right). *Kudara Kannon*. Wood.
Asuka period.
Height 6 feet 10½ inches.
Hōryū-ji, Nara.

15. (Opposite page). *Miroku* (Maitreya). Wood.
Asuka period.
Height 4 feet 4½ inches.
Chūgū-ji, Nara.

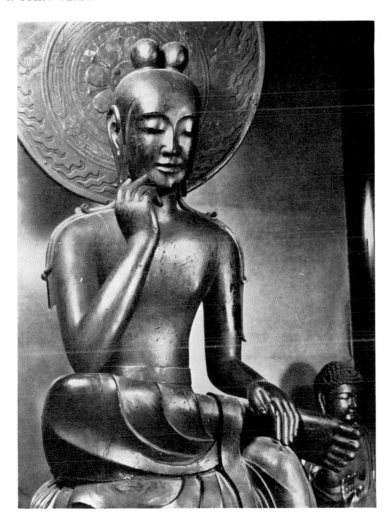

of the body gives it a most pleasing grace. The drapery is lighter and the figure less heavily swathed—in fact the sculptors have transformed all the heaviness of the bronze into lithe, willowy elegance. Instead of the thick, stylized expression of the *Tori* image, we have here a calm, inward, almost mysterious spiritual look of contemplation. The *Tori* bronze is an imitation of stone originals which were meant to be seen from below in dimly lit caves. Translated into bronze and, brought down from their niches, they lose much of their power. In the *Kudara Kannon* the sculptor, a Korean whether working in Korea itself or in Japan, has found in camphor wood the material best suited to his talents and he has responded to its possibilities. In support of its Japanese origin some Japanese scholars have pointed out that the camphor tree did not grow in Korea when this statue was made.

The spectator still looks up at the figure but it no longer stands high in a niche on a wall. It has been brought down almost to ground level, and it remains elevated above humanity solely by virtue of its proportions, which keep it, as it were, at a mysterious

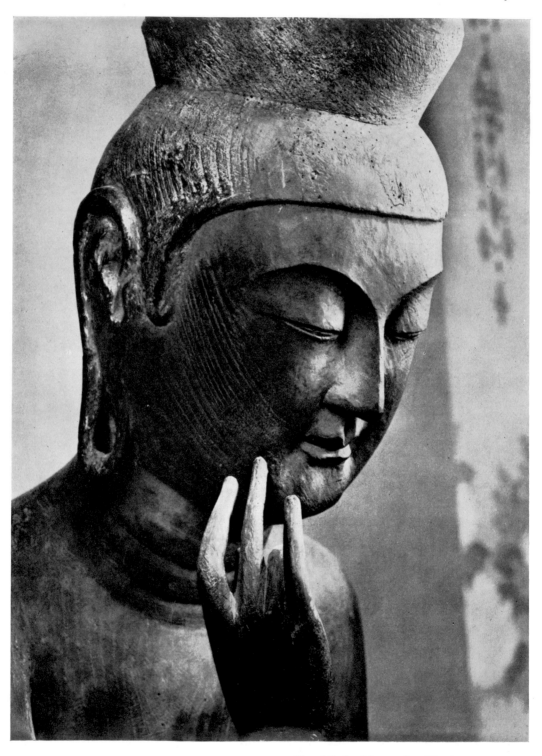

16. *Miroku* (Maitreya). Wood. Asuka period.
Height 4 feet 1 inch. Kōryū-ji, Kyoto.

distance. The sculptural idiom of this statue forms a complete contrast to that of the *Tori* style. The drapery is in very low relief with large undecorated areas; the artist is conscious of the body beneath the robes though not yet compelled by any desire to model it in detail. In all respects the figure reflects a new simplicity and austerity in Buddhist religious feeling. This extraordinary image, unique in far eastern sculpture, exercised little influence on subsequent work. From this time onwards a different trend in Buddhist artistic thought took the sculptors in the direction of a more solid representation of the body. The *Kudara Kannon* represents a noble but isolated vision.[1]

On the latest style of the Asuka period, the authorities again differ. It is represented by two superb works of deep religious inspiration. Their subject is *Miroku* or ' the Buddha of the Future.' One is in the Chūgū-ji Monastery near the Hōryū-ji (Fig. 15) and the other in the Kōryū-ji Temple near Kyoto (Fig. 16). The former is sometimes described either as a Kannon or as a portrait of Prince Shakyamuni while the latter is sometimes called the ' *Kudara* ' *Miroku* to suggest that this too is of Korean origin. These statues raise problems which will probably never be solved. Both are wooden figures seated in meditation expressed in terms of calm and repose with one leg crossed over the other, hand to chin and upper body uncovered. What immediately distinguishes them is a new sense of physical beauty which nothing else in the art of the time leads us to anticipate. It is difficult to imagine a more complete mastery of the simple wood which the artists chose for their medium. The warmth and mellowness of the material as well as its sculptural possibilities have been fully exploited to infuse not only the faces but the whole bodies with tenderness. In the Kōryū-ji figure even the grain of the wood itself has been skilfully brought out to give an added elegance to the face. Sculpture is here raised to a level of intimacy rare in the early art of the East. Any tendency to over-soften the features has been counteracted by giving sharp edges to the nose and a strong cleft to the chin. The bottom half of a strikingly similar 6th century stone statue was found in Kyungju, Korea. Small bronze statues of similar pose and feeling are also well known, notably some statuettes which formerly belonged to the Hōryū-ji but were given to the Emperor (Fig. 17). S. Matsubara has pointed out the significance of some fine white marble examples from 6th century China (Fig. 18) but none of them have the refinement of these works in which their carvers have followed Chinese or Korean prototypes but infused them with a sensitive, melting quality which is tender without being weak, lyrical without being sentimental. They show Japanese religious art and craftsmanship at its purest, neither completely overwhelmed by foreign influences nor carried away by the realism and virtuosity which in later periods so often diluted the strength of the artists' vision.

These *Miroku* statues differ from both the *Kudara Kannon* and the Tori school works. Although the Kōryū-ji *Miroku*, from its similarity to Korean works, is often said to be of Korean origin, the Japanese spirit reveals itself in a degree of sensitivity and warmth which the Koreans never reached. The sculptor has liberated himself from the conventions of the other styles. The heaviness of the features has gone and the Japanese have given free play to their appreciation of surface textures and facial expression. The human intimacy found in these statues is absent from similar works of the mainland. The delicate gesture of the slender finger lightly poised near the chin, the low simplified crown, the

---

[1] An excellent facsimile copy of this statue in the British Museum, was ordered by Binyon when he was in Japan.

lack of ornaments and the detached contemplation of its dreamy, half-closed eyes contribute to a figure of sustained lyrical and spiritual inspiration. Very early the Japanese learned the fundamental artistic truth that nobility can only be expressed through restraint.

From this early period, too, date some of the carved masks for use in the *gigaku* performances held in the temples (Fig. 19). These were ceremonial posturings accompanied by music. The masks, which seem to belong to another world with an imagination quite different from that which the previous art of China and Japan would lead us to expect, may originally have been copied from Chinese prototypes but none of these have survived. The Japanese examples are thus unique in eastern art. The earliest of these masks formerly belonged to the Hōryū-ji, that treasure house of early Buddhist art, but the temple presented them to the Imperial collection in the late 19th century and they are now kept in the National Museum, Tokyo. They show the same imaginative sense which inspired some of the pre-historic art of Japan, immensely enriched by the new worlds of Buddhism and

17. *Miroku*. Bronze. Asuka Period. Height 11⅛ inches. Formerly in the Hōryū-ji, Nara. Presented to the Emperor and now in the Tokyo National Museum.

18. *Seated Buddhist Figure*. White Marble. Dated A.D. 544. Height 1 foot 9¼ inches. Shūdō Museum, Tokyo.

19. *Mask for Gigaku Dance.*
Wood. Asuka period.
11¼ by 8¼ inches.
Tokyo National Museum.

Chinese culture. This love of fantasy, seen so clearly here, combined with a genius for the expression of personality are two of the most powerful and individual features of Japanese art. They show themselves constantly throughout its history and distinguish it from that of the Chinese in which personality is generally overpowered by the grandeur of their conceptions. Nobody could claim that the Chinese, for all their achievements, were ever great portraitists, while the Japanese seem always to have been attracted by what is individual. They have resisted the Chinese impulse to create types. Each age produced its portrait masterpieces. Sometimes they have carried them to a point where quick fantasy lead them into an eccentricity bordering on the grotesque. The Japanese sense of humour is a welcome aid for the uninitiated Westerner in his attempt to appreciate this Far Eastern art.

Though this period is chiefly notable for its sculpture, a few specimens of its *paintings* have also survived. From the earliest times Japanese painting has differed from that of the Chinese, although there are many obvious similarities. In both countries the painters use the same materials—paper or silk to paint on, a very sensitive brush, with black ink in all its nuances and water colours. They are influenced by the art of calligraphy which uses the same brush and ink and tends to emphasize line and outline at the expense of shading. Shading, as we know it, is hardly ever used in the east. The colouring is flat and generally even. The subjects, too, are often the same—landscapes, flowers, figures, animals, religious, and genre scenes, etc. Wherein, then, lies the difference between the painting of China and Japan?

Without any doubt the Japanese artist, even when painting as close as he can to the Chinese style, generally imposes his personality on the pictorial arts. The Japanese tend to see painting much more as decoration than the Chinese. For the latter it is one of the most exalted means whereby a man can express his spirit. The Japanese appreciation of decorative values comes not only from a love of colour and an eye for a beautiful surface but also from a fundamentally less philosophical approach to painting. From very early times the Chinese have accumulated a vast literature on the theory and philosophy of painting while the Japanese have been comparatively little concerned with such problems. Where the Japanese break away from their Chinese teachers they can rise to great heights. Where they try to ape them too closely they often justify the criticism of being shallow copyists. When borrowing directly from the Chinese they are inclined either to over-sweeten or to over-emphasize. They tend to empty Chinese painting of just those qualities which make it sublime. What the Japanese lose in depth of artistic inspiration they some-times try to gain by a sensationalism in composition in which virtuosity takes the place of sensibility. In the decorative arts the Japanese have produced some of the most original work the world has ever seen but—with a few notable exceptions—subtlety in painting is not their strong point.

The nature of Japanese writing as opposed to the Chinese also had its influence on the painting of the two peoples. The brushstroke as used in calligraphy is the basis of all eastern ink painting. The Japanese script, especially where it uses the native syllabary rather than Chinese characters, is smoother, softer and far more cursive than the firm Chinese characters. The abbreviated native *hiragana* syllabary characters with their rounded forms and running lines have influenced Japanese painting in the direction of a softer, more flowing line. The ink too tends to have less power, less depth and resonance than in a Chinese ink painting. Even to-day if a painter in Japan wants good ink he tries to find the Chinese product.

The study and appreciation of eastern calligraphy and brushwork has hardly begun in the West but generally it is possible for a Westerner, after a little experience, to tell the difference between the softer or the consciously exaggerated brush of the Japanese and the more powerful, inwardly comprehended stroke of the Chinese. The media of far eastern painting express spiritual values so sensitively that it takes a very skilled Japanese to be able to pass himself off as a Chinese painter. To our confusion, however, some have succeeded. And in any case it can rightly be claimed for the Japanese that, in their own way, they are just as original in painting as the Chinese although this originality is expressed in spiritually less exalted terms.

There is an additional reason for this. In Japan painting never became the exclusive domain of the scholar as so often it did in China. In this sense it has a broader base than in China. The influence exerted by the accomplished craftsman on Japanese painting gives it a resilience not always found in Chinese painting. The artisan-painter in Japan is less fettered by tradition and therefore often more vigorous than the scholar-painter in

China. The Japanese, it is true, are at times tempted to sacrifice too much to the ultimate decorative effect but they are often saved by a sense of design which in all periods shows itself as perhaps the most highly-developed in the world. When not trying to follow Chinese modes too slavishly, the Japanese painter can be completely individual and spontaneous.

In trying to trace the beginnings of the pictorial arts in China scholars often produce as evidence the animated hunting scenes cast in low relief or incised on bronze vessels. Similar artifacts can be quoted for the early painting of Japan, where metal mirrors or early bronze bells called *dōtaku* (Fig. 20) in a similar way show simple pictures of every-day scenes. These lively match-stick figures, even though they bear little relationship to later Japanese painting, place the emphasis on that line and movement which are the foundations of all far-eastern painting.

The treasury of the Hōryū-ji owns the earliest extant paintings of the Asuka period. Here, near the *Tori* bronze *Triad*, is kept the small sanctuary known as the *Tamamushi* or ' Beetle Wing ' Shrine, so called from the use of irridescent beetle wings under metal openwork to decorate the edges. On the pedestal are painted scenes from the lives of the Buddha in his various incarnations. The one illustrated (Fig. 21), perhaps the most famous of all, is that in which he is shown giving his own body to feed a starving tigress and her cubs—a scene which illustrates his great compassion for all living creatures, animal as well as human.

These paintings are in red, green, and yellow lacquer on a black background—a technique unusual in the east and one which comes nearest to western oil-painting. The archaic method of depicting successive phases of an action on a single surface has its advantages; by showing the Buddha's disrobing, his fall into the pit and his death, in a semi-circle, the artist was able to produce an impression of vivid action and to satisfy his unschooled public by completing his story. The absence of comparable contemporary Chinese works makes it very difficult to date the painting with any certainty but the very beginning of the 7th century might not be a rash estimate. The schematic rocks and bamboos are like T'ang engravings and suggest an already well-developed landscape tradition going back perhaps as far as the Han Dynasty in China. Certainly, in this simple but exquisite scene there is that sense of drama which the Japanese enjoy to the full.

20.   Detail of Bronze Bell.   (See Fig. 4).

22. Pottery of Sue type with ash-glaze.
Diameter (mouth) 5½ inches. Tokyo National Museum.

21. (Left). Painting on a panel of the Tamamushi or
" Beetle Wing " Shrine. Lacquer on wood. Asuka period.
25½ inches by 14 inches. Hōryū-ji, Nara.

What pottery of the period has survived shows that this craft was little more than a
continuation and development of the *Sue* wares which originated in the late *yayoi* period.
The powerfully shaped jar shown in Figure 22 was thrown on the potter's wheel; the neck
is quite skilfully made but the body is heavy and clumsy. Its main attraction is the dark
green ash-glaze which runs naturally down the body. We cannot date the vessel accurately
but similarities with Korean wares have led Japanese scholars to place it in the period just
before Nara. The craft of pottery making was unfortunately slow to react to Chinese
models and there is little to suggest that the Japanese were keeping up with the progress
being made on the mainland of China. There was nothing in Japan as yet to compare
with the *yüeh* type pottery or the pre-seventh century tomb-figures of China.

A specimen of metal-work of the Asuka period deserves particular mention. This is a
gilt-bronze banner—a detail of which is shown in Figure 23. The whole object, which
again belonged to the Hōryū-ji, is over fifteen feet in length and the section reproduced
shows heavenly beings or *apsarases* playing musical instruments or making offerings.

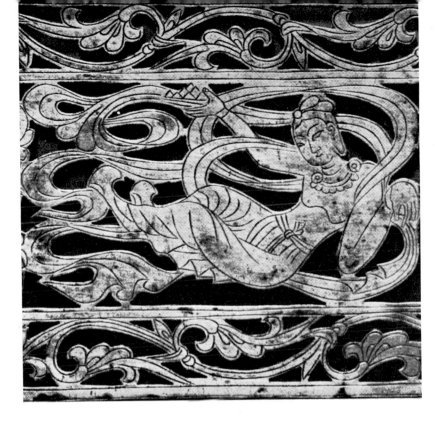

23. Detail of *Gilt Bronze Banner*.
Length of whole banner, approx. 15 feet.
Hōryū-ji, Nara.

24. Stone *Flying Angel*
Possibly from the Lung-mên Caves.
Chinese. Northern Wei period.
(Early 6th century).
Victoria and Albert Museum,
London.
Width 24 inches.

A band of arabesques of honeysuckle whose origin scholars have traced to ancient Greece surrounds the lively figures. This very large work was produced by piercing sheets of bronze and the designs were then incised on one side. The style of the figures is pre-T'ang and reflects the elegance of some of the Chinese cave-temple carvings (Fig. 24). The design of the billowing robes is particularly effective; its assymetrical arrangement contrasts with the regular arabesques to make a lively, free pattern. The workmanship recalls that of the paintings and metalwork on the *Tamamushi* Shrine.

As a result of the damp climate in Japan, most of the earliest textiles have disappeared without trace. In parts of China where the climate is very dry, fragments of textiles have survived from the two centuries before and after Christ. We can only gain some idea of early Japanese textiles from more durable materials such as pottery or sculpture. We know little about the work of the earliest times other than that knowledge of weaving probably came from China in the *Yayoi* period together with other cultural improvements. The Korean craftsmen who reached Japan in the 4th and 5th centuries must have included some who were skilled in the craft and there is evidence to suggest that the Japanese court made them very welcome. Some of the *haniwa* figures evidently represent people of high rank and the clothes they wear are of a complicated style and made of material with simple but elegant designs.

A remarkable number of textile fragments have survived in Japan from the Asuka and Nara periods in a variety of techniques—figured silk, brocades of many types, silk gauze, embroidery, dyeing by various methods. In the Chūgū-ji, a nunnery adjacent to the Hōryū-ji, are fragments of two Asuka period banners made in A.D. 622 (Fig. 25) depicting the rebirth of Prince Shōtoku in Paradise. The colours of the embroidery done on purple silk gauze are still remarkably fresh and the needlework itself is very fine. The designs are free and lively, the figures in particular have a remarkable vitality.

The variety, quality, and sincerity which these earliest Buddhist-inspired arts of Japan show are a remarkable illustration of the way the Japanese could master and absorb this rich, new culture despite the fact that they were far removed from its centre of dissemination. In the Nara period which follows, the Japanese were to be exposed to the full force of Chinese civilization.

25. Fragment of an *Embroidered Silk Banner* depicting the *Rebirth of Prince Shotoku in Paradise*. Asuka period. Chūgū-ji, Nara.

CHAPTER III

THE NARA PERIOD

EARLY NARA OR HAKUHŌ
645-712

LATE NARA OR TEMPYŌ
712-794

THE Japanese were not content for long to accept their knowledge of China second-hand through Korea and Korean immigrants. In A.D. 600 they sent their first national embassy with cultural objectives to the Sui court of China itself. From then until 894 not less than seventeen others followed. What the visitors saw there must have impressed them even more than the rumours of China's greatness and the reports of the Koreans. In these embassies the Japanese accepted treatment as a subordinate nation. The cultural domination of Japan by China culminated in what is known as the Taika Reform of A.D. 645 when the country instituted far-reaching administrative changes in an attempt to adopt the complete administrative and social system of the T'ang dynasty, which had succeeded the short-lived Sui in A.D. 618. Unfortunately, the country, though spiritually willing, was not ready socially, economically, or politically to support such a long-term, wholesale emulation of a country with vastly greater resources and older traditions. It is remarkable that the changes achieved as much as they did. In addition to the dazzling grandeur of the T'ang political and cultural scene, the Chinese ideal of a centralized monarchy controlling a vast and obedient empire made a strong practical appeal to the rulers of Japan. It held out the tempting possibility of controlling some of the more independent clans outside the capital area. But this was a problem which the Japanese could not solve simply by adopting an alien code. It would be possible to write the history of the next thousand years in terms of the various efforts the central authority made to overcome the independence of the local lords.

In 710, the Japanese established their capital city at Nara. They modelled it as closely as possible on the Chinese metropolis of Ch'ang-an, one of the wonders of that and any age. Such a large-scale imitation can have but few parallels in the history of the world. Individual palaces like Versailles have been copied but seldom a whole city. Modern Nara does not resemble the ancient city very closely, but to walk round parts of it is to recapture some of the atmosphere of 7th century China. Old temples still stand in their open spaces, discreetly separated yet near enough to create the solemn impression of a compact holy city untouched by the centuries. Many of the ancient sculptures are preserved in their original homes having withstood the passing of more than a thousand years with unbelievably little damage.

In its finest hour the city must have presented a glorious spectacle: four miles square with wide if muddy streets, great monasteries set in their parks, and palace buildings between them all tiled and brightly painted. But this glittering façade hid a more sordid reality. The countryside had been stripped of wood for the temple buildings. In the scattered villages the inhabitants had much to fear from the sullen aboriginals and even more from bands of armed robbers. The peasantry were badly housed, scantily clad and poorly fed. By comparison, the brocade-clad nobility lived like gods. In China, in theory if not always in practice, the lowest in the land could through diligence reach the highest rank; but Japan ignored this important feature of their Chinese model. Education was reserved for the more exalted classes and the lot of the poor was hard.

Culturally the main effort was spent in a sincere struggle to understand and absorb Chinese Buddhism and, to a lesser degree, Confucianism. It is important to appreciate that by the time Buddhism arrived in China in the first centuries A.D. Confucianism had already had centuries in which to establish itself. In Japan, however, the two arrived together and, although the Japanese paid lip-service to the admirable tenets of Confucianism, it was Buddhism which fired their imagination. In this they were only following the Chinese tendency of the time. Buddhism was then the more vital force. It appealed to the spirit rather than to the intellect and to the common man as much as to the upper classes. Confucianism was a somewhat dry, ethical code more attractive to the scholar and the ruling classes. The egalitarian aspect of Confucianism and the concept of ' The Mandate of Heaven,' whereby an evil ruler forfeited his right to the throne and could be supplanted by a popular uprising, made no appeal to the Japanese aristocracy. They believed not only in the divine right but in the divine origin of the Emperor. There could be little flexibility in such a fundamental concept. Whereas in China there was room for the rise of great dynasties popularly supported and universally esteemed, in Japan the imperial power was generally only delegated to whoever happened to be strong enough to force his will on the Emperor. This tended to rob the *de facto* ruler of that sense of ultimate responsibility without which government becomes at its best bare opportunism and at its worst ruthless exploitation. The ruler's aim was often only to maintain his power and politics easily degenerated into a merciless struggle for power. The hope that the quietist tenets of Buddhism might calm the leaders of unruly clans was not realized. In subsequent centuries Japan suffered badly for her failure to reach the more subtle Confucian springs of Chinese culture. In the realm of art it is possible to attribute the Japanese weakness in Chinese-style landscape painting partly to a lack of Confucian training which, like Taoism, urged man to seek unison with nature. This is the philosophical root of much Chinese painting and its absence in Japan contributed towards the fundamental differences between their two arts.

Nevertheless, what the Japanese lacked in depth of understanding was balanced by their energy and enthusiasm. A sign of the tremendous vitality of this early age is clearly seen in the rapid creation by a comparatively undeveloped society of a large and skilled class of artisans capable of producing works of art on a scale and of a quality which compares well with those of China. Many foreign craftsmen had come to Japan, taught the Japanese and intermarried with them, thus becoming an integral part of their thriving society. As the Japanese craftsmen came to age and independence so, by selection and emphasis, they began to put their stamp on Japanese art.

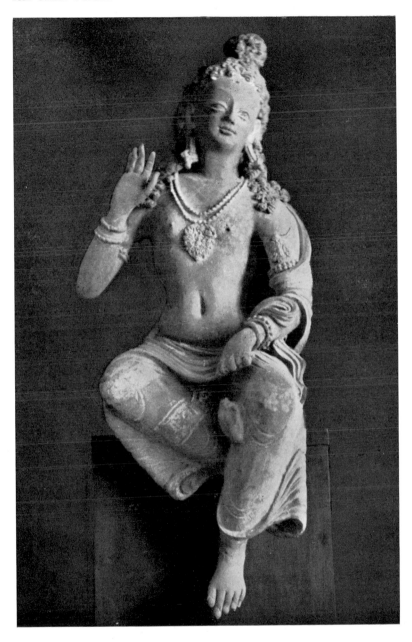

26. *Bodhisattva from Fondukistan* (Afghanistan). Stucco.
ca. 7th century A.D.
Height 2 feet 3 inches.
Photograph courtesy George Butcher.

27. *Shō Kannon.* Bronze.
Early Nara period.
Height 6 feet 3 inches.
Yakushi-ji, Nara.

28. *Gakkō Bodhisattva.*
One of the attendants to the main Yakushi
Buddha. Bronze.
ca. A.D. 720. Height 10 feet 3 inches.
Yakushi-ji, Nara.

29. Detail of the companion figure
to Fig. 28 in the Yakushi-ji, Nara.

In their direct contact with T'ang China, Japan not only came a step closer to the ultimate source of Buddhism but it also took this step at a time when China itself was closer to India. China, we must remember, was as anxious to have intimate contacts with the Indian well-spring of Buddhism as were the Japanese to learn from China. Many Chinese pilgrims from the 5th century onwards overcame great hardships in their travels across Central Asia to India where they studied at the fount of Buddhist learning. There and en route they saw examples of Buddhist art in the full flood of late Gandharan and Gupta styles.

The origin of the styles of Buddhist sculpture introduced into China and developed there presents a very complicated problem and no easy answer can be offered. Some scholars claim that they came from the north-west Indian Gandharan styles which contained a great deal of Hellenistic influence. Others have suggested a central Indian origin from the great Gupta dynasty which reached its height ca. 375–490. Discoveries in central Asia, on the other hand, have shown that along the northern and southern routes to India which skirt the Tarim desert considerable Buddhist colonies flourished in Khotan, at Karashahr, Kucha, and Kashgar. Chinese contacts with these Central Asian kingdoms and settlements were frequent. The military power of the Northern Wei state compelled these colonies to pay tribute and even to send Buddhist teachers with all their religious equipment.

As far as Gandharan art is concerned, it appears that there were two marked styles—an earlier Gandharan style influenced by Hellenistic modes and a later Gandharan style which was strongly oriental in its approach. A characteristic of the later style is the use of stucco and clay which enabled the sculptors to model far more freely than is possible in stone (Fig. 26).

It may be possible in time to establish the existence of a Central-Asian style which received strong influences from later Gandharan sculpture, from Central India (especially in painting) and from Iran. The basically sensual forms came from India, the complicated crowns and floating ribbons are probably of Iranian origin while the drapery owes much to Gandharan prototypes. In Central Asia these styles merged and were then probably introduced into China. All we can say is that the Chinese styles were the result of mixed influences brought to China by a complicated route and there developed along individual lines.

The most typical expression of the tradition brought from India and central Asia as interpreted by the Chinese and taken over by the Japanese is the gilt bronze *Kannon Bosatsu or Shō Kannon* (Fig. 27) in the Yakushi-ji (The Temple of the Buddha of Healing) in Nara. No records exist to help in dating this statue accurately. On stylistic grounds it could be placed in the early Nara period. The body beneath the robe is more evident and at the same time more graceful than in works of the preceding period. It begins, but only just begins, to have the warm living quality which we associate with Chinese T'ang sculpture. The curves and lines of the flesh are still smoothed over in a tentative manner; the pose is still rigid. The constricted waist, full chest and transparent ' wet ' clothing reflect faithfully the far eastern interpretation of Indian or central Asian modes. Traces of the Yün-kang and Lung-mên styles persist in the flaring skirts but these create an impression of a lifeless, almost automatic anachronism.

The *Gakkō Bodhisattva* in Figure 28 which is sometimes called the finest T'ang sculpture to survive, shows this style as fully developed some forty or fifty years later, ca. 720. It belongs to the same temple, the Yakushi-ji, and is one figure of a triad with a seated

30. *Buddha Head*, Bronze. Early Nara period. Height 3 feet 6 inches. Kōfuku-ji, Nara.

Yakushi Buddha in the centre. A tremendous change has taken place in this half-century. All the remaining stiffness of the earlier work seems to have melted. The stance is now completely relaxed with the hips strongly bent. What is called in Sanscrit the *tribhanga* or ' thrice bent ' pose removes the last traces of rigidity from the portrayal of the human form. With the indolent sway, the tension disappears and the new T'ang qualities of monumentality and majesty are joined to sensuality. The flesh is rounder and fuller, as if studied with pleasure from a well-covered model. Movement now enters Japanese sculpture. The body is sharply distinguished from the heavy, freely flowing drapery which hangs about it. The outlines of the torso flow with a more generous movement as if in sleepy sensuality. The last traces of the archaic smile have gone and more human characteristics are designed to impress our senses.

It is interesting here to turn back a few decades to the large bronze head (Fig. 30) discovered in 1937—all that remains of a huge bronze statue some 16 ft. high which originally stood in the Yamadera Temple completed in 685. The head dates to about the same time. Here the human modelling inspired by the late Gandharan heads is seen at its best. The sculptural terms used to portray an idealized humanity require no knowledge of Buddhism for their appeal. Japanese scholars are sharply divided on the influences which contributed to this head. Some claim that it shows fully developed T'ang elements, others that it is under very early T'ang influence. Certainly it comes from a time before the rich modelling of T'ang sculpture began to appear in Japanese art. But, as in the Kōryū-ji *Miroku*, the lyrical approach and the tender expression are essentially Japanese. The unfailing sense of form and the clear-cut simplicity, which form one side of the Japanese aesthetic tradition, are in this head shown in one of their earliest manifestations. A most convincing calm radiates from the features which recall the moving power of the Asuka period masterpieces and yet look forward to the vivid portraiture of late Nara times.

The change brought about by the introduction of the rich T'ang styles in the 7th century can be exaggerated. Popular traditional types persisted and, as the Yamadera head shows, much remains of the simple reverence of the Asuka period. The Japanese craftsmen sometimes clung to their earlier visions of the Buddha as a gentle, benign divinity, but more often they exercised their skill in depicting an elegance demanded by a society whose tastes were becoming more sophisticated and applied themselves to the problems of representing the complicated iconography which came with T'ang sculpture. Thus in works of the period they sometimes seem to be more absorbed in the complicated trappings such as glittering haloes and precious jewellery than in the sincere faith which the Gods were supposed to radiate.

One of the most perfect examples of the happy unions of Asuka and early Nara styles is seen in the Hōryū-ji *Kannon* popularly known in more recent times as the *Yumetagae Kannon* (Fig. 31). ' Yumetagai ' means ' to change dreams ' (from inauspicious to auspicious omens). Here a balance is held between the voluptuousness of the T'ang and the quiet simplicity of the Asuka styles. The slight, almost imperceptible sway of the figure, more forwards than sideways, gives a sense of gentle movement. The sloping shoulders and sensitively carved arms have a flower-like quality. The lotus base is a later restoration but the original must have been very similar; the whole rhythm of the statue echoes the graceful lines of its petals. The crown, with a *Miroku Buddha* in the centre, balances the proportions of the head. In both the crown and the jewellery which hangs on the breast,

31. *Yumetagae Kannon.* Bronze.
Early Nara period.
Height 34¼ inches. Hōryū-ji, Nara.

32. *Gakkō Bodhisattva.*
Clay. Late Nara period.
Height 5 feet 10½ inches.
Tōdai-ji, Nara.

the sculptor has resisted the temptation to indulge in an iconographical *tour-de-force*. The drapery of the skirt shows delicate restraint and even the bottle in the left hand, said to hold the elixir of immortality, has not been over-stressed. The gesture of assurance in the right hand is not too obvious. Yet in spite of all the gentle rhythm of this most gentle of ' Compassionate Bodhisattvas ' there is no loss of power. The face has the humanity and inspired faith of the Yamadera head but in the lips there is the sweet, worldly softness of the T'ang models seen in many Chinese clay tomb figures and in the few paintings which have survived. The eyes though almost closed dominate the face. They appear to express the characteristics of forgiveness, forbearance and the attainment of truth through contemplation—the simpler concepts of Buddhism which attracted the early Japanese adherents to the faith. The figure is a calm introduction to the thunderous majesty of the late Nara or Tempyō period masterpieces.

The late Nara period (712–794) is sometimes called the Tempyō period from the Tempyō era (729–749), the most important twenty years within it. Many historians, both Japanese and Western consider it to be the golden age of Japanese sculpture, a period when complete technical mastery combined with the deepest inspiration created the finest works in the history of Japanese sculpture.

In the 150 years which had now passed since the introduction of Buddhism, the religion had made tremendous strides. It had become more accessible to all classes and provincial temples and nunneries had been opened to bring the message to all parts of the country. The central treasury had paid for the building and furnishing of many new temples and the direction of religious matters was concentrated in Nara. Buddhism held the position of a national religion, and a vigorous court in the capital encouraged, financed, and protected it. Everything in the Nara period was done on what seems to us an almost megalomaniac scale. The Japanese seem to have devoted their full energies to spreading the faith.

Contacts with the Chinese became ever closer, and embassies sometimes five-hundred strong visited the T'ang court bringing back with them paintings and sculptures from the very centre of Chinese civilization. No actual example of one of these imported sculptures has survived but certainly by now the Japanese were thoroughly familiar with the art of the religion which they had adopted and they began more confidently to impress upon it their own native characteristics.

What are these native characteristics ? Some Japanese scholars say that they are ' neatness and prettiness ' but that hardly does justice to the magnificent images of the late Nara period any more than it would characterize the sculptures of Chartres. Perhaps the outstanding quality of the work of this period comes from the Japanese fascination for surface and texture which at its most sensitive infused their works of art with a rare living quality. Another important characteristic of the period is the attention to line. This can produce the grand sweeping outlines of an early *Yumedono Kannon*, though it can also lose itself in the fussy trivialities of a T'ang-inspired but over-decorated Bodhisattva. In Tempyō art, the artists held line and decoration in masterly balance, and subordinated both to the deep religious idealism which inspired them. The statues have a solidity and fullness which we do not see in the art of other periods. The Buddhism which gripped the nation allowed nothing of the sentimental sweetness of later Buddhism. To look at the sculptures of the period is to be moved by the living force of their creator's beliefs—sometimes tender, sometimes terrifying. But mild or austere, at rest or in violent motion, they are imbued with sincerity and conviction. By comparison, many of the later sculptures look like empty shells. Here is an idealism and a religious art which can compare with any in the world.

In the late Nara period there was a great advance in the already highly developed Japanese ability to give personality to faces. The striking portraiture of the period may have been due in part to the use of new materials capable of finer expression. This was the great age of clay and dry-lacquer statuary. The *Gakkō Bodhisattva* or *Bonten* in the Tōdai-ji, Nara (Fig. 32) shows the same calm inwardness as the *Yumetagai Kannon* discussed above, but the modelling of the face, though still idealized, brings out a human individuality—an impression which is increased by the close attention to the hands, drapery, and hair. The deep chest and broad shoulders, by their disproportion with the head, increase the living quality of the work. The *Gakkō Bodhisattva* shows the 'classical' style in Japan at its most mature—the divinely inspired human sculpted in terms which surround it with an atmosphere of sanctity and serenity. Most historians state that idealism is the fundamental characteristic of the art of this period. Here, at least, it is founded on a very striking appreciation of human qualities.

Clay as a material for Buddhist sculpture was well-known in Central Asia and in China. There its plastic qualities had been explored since the first centuries A.D. at least. Chinese historians tell of a great art of monumental clay sculpture but, apart from the provincial works of Tun-huang, little has survived to provide evidence of its splendours. It is, however, a most fragile material and it seems almost miraculous that in Japan so many fine early pieces have survived in perfect condition. In these clay sculptures a happy compromise is reached between T'ang richness and Japanese simplicity. The faces, indeed, often look more like portraits than idealizations. The directness of their appeal and the intimacy they create is rarely, if ever, found in the sculpture of China. The makers of these statues approached their subjects more as equals. Their confidence is reflected in every feature. The problems of expressing personality as well as religious faith fascinated them.

There is some confusion about the identity of the *Gakkō (Moonlight) Bodhisattva* and its companion the *Nikkō (Sunlight) Bodhisattva*. It seems that originally they stood in another temple whence they were brought to the Tōdai-ji, 'The Great Eastern Temple' in Nara. Iconographically they appear to be *ten* or *devas*—'Divine Beings.' These were often gods of other religions such as Hinduism and Brahmanism who were incorporated into the Buddhist pantheon of the *mahayana* or Greater Vehicle. If they were 'Sunlight' and 'Moonlight' divinities they would usually be shown with a sun or moon among their iconographical attributes. The *Gakkō* figure, according to many authorities, is probably *Bonten*, the *Brahma-deva* of the Hindus, the supreme god, creator of all things. The Buddhists early assimilated him into their pantheon as the ruler of the human world. The two figures must originally have been brilliantly coloured with painted and patterned robes and golden hair. The painting has now mostly fallen away to reveal the plain clay beneath. Apart from this, the figures are extraordinarily well-preserved; even the robes where they pass round the necks still have their sharp edges. This is remarkable for the damp Japanese climate is most harmful to clay images.

The four heads reproduced in Figure 33 give an idea of the heights of expression to which this clay sculpture could rise. They show how close the Japanese had come to the finest art of the T'ang period. In this type of sculpture they may well have surpassed the T'ang. All four heads are stern, if not violent, in expression; their furrowed brows and piercing eyes are made even more vivid by the use of obsidian inlays for the pupils, a further move

33. *Four Heads* of Late Nara period clay statues.   Reading left to right:
    (a) Meikira Taishō, Height 5 feet 6 inches.   Shinyakushi-ji, Nara.
    (b) Shūkongō-shin, Height 5 feet 7¾ inches.   Tōdai-ji, Nara.
    (c) Kōmoko-ten, Height 5 feet 4 inches.   Tōdai-ji, Nara.
    (d) Jigoku-ten, Height 5 feet.   Tōdai-ji, Nara.

towards realism. They fix the worshipper with their forbidding gaze or stand ready to strike down the offender. T'ang tomb figures of *lokapāla* go far in this direction but the Chinese with their emotional reticence would probably have been somewhat less effective in communicating the fury of these threatening figures. Symbolic of divine energy, they are the classical forerunners of a stream of images which flowed down into the 19th century; they show the Japanese gift for expressing movement and energy which appears in every material from bronze to ivory and in every size from the monumental temple guardian to the lilliputian *netsuke* (see Figs. 167, 168).

This type of statue reflects a new phase of Buddhist thought. In addition to the essentially friendly earlier statues with their impassive and contemplative attitude, we find these images which are intended to convey terrifying ideas of punishment for sinners. It is not known which sect inspired them; none of those then popular appear to have stressed this violent side of Buddhism which, generally speaking, belongs to a later period. But as communications improved and T'ang contacts reached out with more ease and security into central Asia, so new doctrines flowed quickly into China and thence to Japan. We must remember that Japan was in touch with the heart of Chinese civilization in the capital and could respond quickly to new innovations. Certainly this ferocious aspect of Buddhism appealed to the Japanese mentality and offered a tempting challenge to the sculptors.

As the Japanese steadily mastered the basic techniques of sculpture, so too they enlarged their repertoire of images and the range of materials they employed. In addition to bronze and clay, they began to use dry-lacquer in two techniques. These were the hollow dry-lacquer (*dakkatsu-kanshitsu*) and the wood-core dry-lacquer (*mokushin-kanshitsu*). In the former the figure was modelled out of three to six layers of hemp cloth impregnated with lacquer over a light, hollow frame. In the latter, they applied lacquer to a solid, roughly-shaped wood-core and the master added the final refinements of modelling in the more plastic material. The hollow dry-lacquer technique involves difficult processes which possibly accounts for its being abandoned after this period when the artists discovered the full plastic possibilities of wood. Its products have the advantages of being light and impervious to insects but are very delicate. It is assumed that the method originated in China and that, since hollow dry-lacquer statues were easily transportable, they could be brought to Japan without difficulty. Western museums, notably in America, possess about ten examples from the T'ang dynasty, none of which, however, compare in quality, not to mention state of preservation, with the Japanese masterpieces. As far as we can now judge, it was in Japan that the technique reached its highest development. As happened on other occasions it seems that the Chinese invented and the Japanese perfected. The magnificent examples preserved in Japan, especially those of the Kōfuku-ji at Nara, now kept in the city's National Museum, give a clear indication of a great art most of which is lost to us.

We can see this unusual technique at its best in two sets of statues—the *Eight Guardians* and the *Ten Great Disciples of Shakyamuni*. The whole set of the former has survived but only six of the latter. They can be dated A.D. 743. The three-faced, six-armed figure in Figure 34 represents *Ashura*, 'A Spirit of Spirits,' a benevolent being who protects the Buddha. The appealing face of this statue has a quite un-Eastern aspect and nothing comparable exists in Eastern art. The clear, boyish countenance with its serious, penetrating eyes radiates an almost discomforting frankness. The straight lines of the body are somewhat sketchily treated and all attention is concentrated on the handsome face. Apart from its esoteric Indian features—six arms and three heads—the figure is easily

34. *Ashura*. Hollow dry lacquer.
Late Nara period. Height 5 feet. Kōfuku-ji, Nara.

intelligible, the faces reflecting a deep, religious faith. Here again the Japanese gift for portraiture, individuality of expression, and accurate, sensitive modelling has placed its stamp on a model ultimately Indian and transmitted through early T'ang China. The Japanese, like all people who accepted Indian religious ideas and the art which went with them, have from time to time become fascinated by such many-headed, many-armed deities which sprang from the fertile Indian imagination to people the rich pantheon of *mahayana* Buddhism. But it is open to question whether these figures ever appealed as strongly to the Japanese as to the Indians. The Japanese were probably less attracted by the systemization which is characteristic of Indian religious thought. There is a certain confusion of purpose in the carefully developed features as compared with the sketchily indicated arms. The Japanese fondness for the grotesque provides many examples of how they were always ready to exploit the possibilities of fantasy but it was a fantasy which generally sprang from a sense of humour or drama, as in the masks, or from simple imaginative emphasis, as in the terrifying deities. Iconographic peculiarities involving physical abnormalities appealed to them only momentarily, and the *Ashura*, for all its symbolism, remains essentially an individual human figure.

The soft, sensitive modelling possible with hollow dry-lacquer was not always so successfully employed. The large *Vairocana Buddha* (Fig. 35) in the Tōshōdai-ji at Nara, for
example, appears to the westerner more as a T'ang style *tour-de-force* in the dry-lacquer
technique than a moving creation of religious faith. The *Vairocana Buddha* or, as the
Japanese call it, the *Birushana Buddha*, became popular as a main deity in this period.
This is the Buddha whose light shines everywhere; it was considered the essential body
of Buddha-truth, the eternal Buddha from which all the other Buddhas are supposed to
emanate. Only two statues of *Vairocana* exist in Japan, the other being the great bronze
Buddha in the Tōdai-ji. But subsequently a derivation of this figure, the *Dainichi* or
'Great Sun Buddha' became very popular. The dry-lacquer *Vairocana* is beautifully
proportioned, and with its Thousand Buddha nimbus behind achieves an impressiveness
in keeping with the subject. But the features, for all their stern dignity which the Japanese
greatly admire, are somewhat gross and the figure lacks the sincere inspiration and the
gentle modelling of other statues of the period.

The same temple also houses what has often been considered the finest example of
portraiture to survive from this early period. This is the seated figure of *Priest Ganjin*
(Fig. 36), a Chinese prelate who, at the invitation of Emperor Shōmu, came to Japan in 753.
In the course of his six efforts to reach the islands he lost his eyesight but he lived to teach
the faith and to found the Tōshōdai-ji. He died in 763. According to tradition he brought

35. *Vairocana Buddha.*
Hollow dry lacquer. Late Nara period.
Height 10 feet.
Tōshōdai-ji, Nara.

Chinese workmen with him who made the *Vairocana Buddha*.   His portrait shows all the possibilities of hollow dry-lacquer modelling.   Sharp lines are softened by lacquer which smoothes over all transitions between feature and feature, body and drapery.   The drapery is not too closely studied and the thin frame of the ascetic is only briefly suggested by gentle swellings where the bones show through the skin.   Here is restraint used most effectively. Our attention is immediately drawn to the poignant, sightless eyes, turned inwards in deep contemplation, and to the very sensitive mouth with its almost martyr-like expression. Seldom has a finer representation of saintly faith and meditation been produced in art. It is difficult to see whence comes the power of this statue; the features are not in themselves strong or distinctive and every line is muted.   But the artist, said to have been Ganjin's own pupil, has given them a radiant calm and sense of serene security which comes of inner triumph.   His interpretation enriches the whole of the art of the Nara period.

36. *Priest Ganjin*.
Hollow dry lacquer.
Late Nara period.
Height 2 feet 7½ inches.
Tōshōdai-ji-, Nara.

37. *Jūichimen (Eleven-headed) Kannon.*
Dry lacquer.
Late Nara period.
Height 6 feet 10½ inches.
Shōrin-ji, Nara.

38. Mask for Gigaku Dance.
Height 11⅞ inches.
Tōdai-ji, Nara.

The most famous wood-core dry-lacquer statue is the *Jūichimen Kannon*, the ' Eleven-headed Bodhisattva of Compassion ' owned by the Shōrin-ji Temple, Nara (Fig. 37). Each of the small subsidiary heads is intended to represent a different aspect of the divinity, while at the very top is a Buddha head which symbolizes the final enlightenment. The plastic treatment of the body is entirely successful and the swirling drapery moves natural-istically; many of the details such as the hand are exquisite, but the elegant lines of free-moving T'ang modelling have here been made heavier. The face is full and solemn and the work has great strength and vitality.

The wood-core dry-lacquer method seems only to have been a passing phase; gradually the carved wood-cores were more accurately modelled until the final lacquer coatings became unnecessary and the Japanese artists returned once more to wood in which their genius always found its most congenial material.

To turn from this to the masks of the period (Fig. 38) is to see Japanese humour and technical mastery running riot. The dances in which these masks were used were performed in temples on great occasions, and the most splendid of these must have been the con-secration, in 753, of the Tōdai-ji Temple in Nara. The example illustrated here was used on that memorable occasion and has been preserved in the temple itself. The meaning of these *gigaku* dances or posturings has never been explained and no examples of the masks have survived in China. It is always assumed that they came from China but the evidence is lacking. They may equally well be a spontaneous production of a postulated southern strain in the Japanese race; for such masks are a characteristic of many southern peoples. It is as if the solemn development of early Eastern sculpture had for a moment been inter-rupted by these masks with their infallible sense of caricature and exaggeration. In the flickering light of pine torches their grotesque power was then, as now, most exciting. The strong mark these masks left on Japanese artistic taste is seen in countless reflections in many kinds of material through the succeeding ages. The craftsmen who produced them obviously enjoyed their moments of relaxation from the more serious tasks of circumscribed religious sculpture and they show the spontaneity and quick observation, the sophistication and wit of a very mature people. Nothing could be farther from the lifeless products of patient copyists. They act as perfect foils to many of the noble figures which sit so impass-ively within the temple halls. Could it be that this is the portrait of a monk? It is the travesty of a figure that belongs to all times and every religion—the sharp, prying nose and good humoured brow, the cheeks and eyes wrinkled with laughter. Might it not represent the popular but not over-intelligent priest, the ineffectual overseer and the butt of every-body's jokes? If Nara could thus throw off its heavy ecclesiastical atmosphere it cannot have been a dull place. These occasional glimpses into the amusements of a perceptive artisan reveal a peculiarly attractive side of Japanese art which has only recently disappeared. The Japanese sense of fun is more acute and comes to the surface in art much more readily than that of the Chinese. It is interesting that, although as a people the Chinese have a far readier sense of humour than the Japanese, it seldom appears in their art. The reverse is true of the Japanese. The ability of artists to cause a smile is an endearing characteristic of almost all periods of Japanese art.

Paintings are of course, far more easily transportable than sculpture. The monks who visited China could bring back models (either copies or originals) and one might, therefore, expect painting to reflect its Chinese origins more immediately and more faithfully than sculpture. It is, indeed, often difficult to say whether an early painting was done by a

39. *Portrait of a Woman.*
Detail from a screen.
Ink and colour on paper.
First quarter of 8th century.
4 feet 1½ inches by 2 feet 2 inches.
Shōsō-in, Nara.

Japanese or a Chinese artist but the tendency recently has been for Japanese scholars to claim that more and more early works of art are native products rather than Chinese importations. An interesting non-Buddhist example of this can be seen in the detail of a portrait of a woman in Figure 39. This comes from one of six paper screens *Beauties under Trees* now preserved in the Shōsō-in (Cf. p. 50) three of which have seated and three have standing figures. Only the underpainting of the body remains but the face, lightly coloured and with lips indicated in a more brilliant red, preserves its original appearance. When placed in the Shōsō-in real feathers were attached to the body itself in imitation of a dress style said to have been popular in China at that period, but these have long since fallen off to leave only the outline. We may assume that this picture shows the typical mid-T'ang type of feminine beauty as seen also in a thousand Chinese tomb figures preserved from that time—a plump matronly body, full face and thick tresses of hair, tiny delicate features set in rounded cheeks. All the elements of Far Eastern figure painting are here fully formed—the emphasis on flat planes and outline and the so-called calligraphic line, a vivid sense of movement and a lack of modelling. In the last resort it is impossible to say whether this painting is in fact Chinese or Japanese but elements of Japanese taste

40.   View of the Hōryū-ji Compound showing Kondō or ' Golden Hall ' and the Five Storied Pagoda.

can be claimed for it—an alive, personal quality, a sentimentality and softness which are absent in what we understand by T'ang painting of such figures if we can judge from the little that remains of them. Above all the face seems to have more personality and animation and the figures more freedom of movement than the Chinese. But all this is speculation and we shall probably never be able to say more of this painting of an elegant lady under a tree than that it dates from the first quarter of the 8th century when the civilization of the T'ang saw its most brilliant age.

   Such few relics of mid-Nara painting are valuable for the light they throw on the arts of China and Japan in that early period. But they are over-shadowed by the greatest example of early eastern religious wall-painting, the murals of the Hōryū-ji.[1] Of these, the art historian T. Naitō remarked, " Indeed, it is not too much to say that they represent the highest achievement of Mahayana Buddhist painting and the peak of the development of Far Eastern art." In 1949, exactly ten years after Naitō's death, the temple's Kondō or Main Hall (Fig. 40) which contained these paintings was burnt out in a disastrous fire, and the paintings were scorched to little more than black and white outlines. The disaster can only be compared to a loss say of the Giotto frescoes. It must also be remembered that they were painted on the walls of one of the East's most treasured monuments, for the

[1] *Wall Paintings of the Hōryū-ji Monastery* with an introduction by Ichimatsu Tanaka, Benridō. Tokyo. 1951.

Kondō itself was among the oldest and architecturally most important buildings in Japan. Fortunately, just before their destruction a publishing firm had successfully photographed them in colour and we therefore have a good record of their original appearance.

There has been long controversy about the age of the building and the murals which it contained. Modern scholars have concluded that the original Main Hall was burnt down in A.D. 670 and then rebuilt as nearly like the original as possible. They claim that the paintings could not have been done after A.D. 741 and most likely were painted about 710.

Not only the date of these figures has been difficult to determine but also what deities they represent. Four wide panels contain trinities and eight narrow panels contain single figures. The theory now held is, that the four large central panels depict four Buddhas who were particularly popular objects of worship at that time, *Amida, Yakushi, Shakya-muni,* and *Miroku*.

The tradition of wall paintings is, of course, an Indian one of long and impressive lineage. Outstanding examples have been preserved at such sites as Ajanta and Bāgh in central India. Such eminent scholars as Stein, Pelliot, Grünwedel, le Coq, Kozlov, and Otani have surveyed the route by which Buddhism came into North China, across the Pamirs and the Taklamakan desert, and they discovered many wall-paintings in Turfan and Tun-huang at the gate to central Asia and at other places along the route. These are mainly provincial works and cannot compare in quality with the twelve Hōryū-ji frescoes. Who did them with such mastery in this outpost of the Buddhist religion remains a mystery. Even their source of inspiration is disputed. Naitō, for example, claims that they spring directly from the paintings of Ajanta in India while the French scholar, Jeannine Auboyer, and Benjamin Rowland deny this and find their models in Central Asia and Northern China. This would appear to be more probable.

The majestic figures were outlined in strong red lines. A type of shading, a most unusual feature in Far Eastern art, was used but more for emphasis than for volume. This, like the draperies, is ultimately inspired by Indian painting. Cave Temple I at Ajanta, dated 5th–6th centuries, gives an idea of how strongly the Indian manner of painting bodies, facial expressions, and transparent clothing influenced all Buddhist artists from Central Asia to Japan. The Japanese, however, have stilled and spiritualized the figures, simplifying the riotous compositions which the Indians enjoyed and could handle with such complete confidence. This simplification is seen in its earlier stages at sites like Turfan in central Asia and in Tun-huang but the conclusion of the movement, a fitting climax to the art of Nara, is found in the Hōryū-ji. No comparable wall-paintings of this period have survived in China but from literary records it appears that their style may have owed much to that introduced into China by a Central Asian painter with the Chinese name *Wei-chih I-sêng* who, according to the historians, used brush-strokes " appearing like iron-wire bent into shapes." The heat of the fire, although it destroyed the colours, brought out parts of the drawing hitherto not visible and these give support to a theory that, as in India, stencils were sometimes used for the outlines.

The detail shown in Figure 41 is the head of a *Kannon Bodhisattva,* the attendant to a seated *Amida Buddha.* Even in these reproductions of works which have been fading for twelve centuries, one can see that they share with some of the early sculptures that earnestness and confident sincerity which characterize Japanese religious art. How skilfully the painter has slightly turned the head to look down kindly at the worshipper! How well it balances and softens the steady frontal gaze of the central Buddha. How brilliantly the red and gold crown and the necklaces of rubies and emeralds must once have shone, the emeralds catching up the green in which the hair is depicted!

As a people newly converted, the Japanese were always ready to give a warm welcome to some new missionary or learned priest from China and they eagerly awaited the latest artistic developments from the mainland. Each one must have appeared more astonishing than the last. Local artists must have seized on everything that was new and exciting and they worked hard to do justice to them. The picture we have is one of a whole society with single-minded faith devoted to the creation of a beautiful, pious city. Even to see, four years ago, the Japanese craftsmen rebuilding the Kondō as an exact replica of the one destroyed was to sense that same energy which built the city and which has perpetuated Japan's artistic heritage through the ages.

Another survival from the 8th century are the fragments of a painted scroll depicting scenes from the lives of *Shakyamuni*. It is entitled 'The Illustrated Sutra of Causes and Effects in Past and Present' (*E-Ingakyō*) and is dated A.D. 735 (Fig. 42). The pictures illustrate the text given below them. As the somewhat hack work of a Buddhist copying bureau which aimed at disseminating the faith by simple pictorial means they do not pretend to be profound or even highly-skilled works of art on a level with the Hōryū-ji wall paintings, but their form is interesting since it foreshadows the Japanese *e-makimono* or painted hand-scrolls of later times (Cf. p. 74 ff.). These somewhat naïve little scenes, though of inferior artistry, recall the paintings on the Tamamushi Shrine (Cf. p. 23).

41. *Kannon Bodhisattva.*
Detail from the wall paintings of the Kondō, Hōryū-ji, Nara.
Whole mural 10 feet 10 inches by 8 feet 6 inches.
Early Nara period.

相 河 提 所 離 汝 告 路 尋 空 作 共 我 生 顛
八 注 即 著 苦 便 我 由 光 中 是 不 今 厭 倒
十 詣 使 寶 之 可 怖 恒 而 光 念 淨 在 離 緃
種 佛 航 履 法 來 我 河 去 明 時 中 此 心 橫

42. Detail from the *E-Ingakyō* (Illustrated Satura of the Causes and Effects in Past and Present).
Ink and colour on paper.   8th century.   Height 10½ inches.

Like them, they depict outstanding events in Shakyamuni's lives. There is little or no characterization in the faces and all other elements are expressed by the simplest means. The landscape features are highly schematized in a manner which adds much to the charm of the composition and are important for the evidence they give of early pre-T'ang landscape styles. The artists completely disregarded natural proportions but attempted simple perspective and three-dimensionality. Fragments exist of two sets of these pictures and probably large numbers of them were made at the time. They employ the same conventions to tell their stories: a group of people, a pavilion or a walled castle, a few dwarf mountains or some rocks and trees. There is no attempt to give more than the barest essentials necessary to set the scene. But for all their brevity they show a strong dramatic feeling and a skilful narrative sense. Their very forthrightness has the same appeal as some of our medieval landscapes. If these were the inconsidered, mass-produced works of a bureau, how much more must we regret the many lost treasures of T'ang Chinese and T'ang-inspired Japanese art.

The greatest artistic event of the late Nara or Tempyō period was a national undertaking to construct in the Tōdai-ji Temple at Nara a giant seated Buddha figure in gilt bronze some fifty-three feet high. This huge monument to the religious fervour of the people illustrates how deeply Japan was steeped in the faith. But it was an ambitious enterprise which heavily taxed the resources of a rapidly expanding nation, already fully-stretched to build other temples and to stock them with their equipment and religious finery. The clumsy, ugly figure as it now exists bears little resemblance to the original which has suffered greatly from fires and bad restoration. But the size alone of this *Daibutsu* or Great Buddha, within a room which, although considerably smaller than the original one,

43.   *Rubbing* of a design on one of the lotus leaves forming the base of the Giant Buddha.   Bronze.
Late Nara period.   Tōdai-ji, Nara.

is still the largest wooden building under one roof, gives an indication of the breath-taking sight it must once have presented.   Only a few of the huge lotus petals which form the base of the statue and which are incised with graceful designs (Fig. 43) show the splendid workmanship of its creators, who, in casting this colossus, were following the tradition of the giant stone and clay Buddhas of Bamiyan in Afghanistan and of such Chinese sites as Yün-kang.   We can only imagine the excitement of the bronze casters of the *Daibutsu*, as section upon section this great figure grew towards completion, if we compare it with that of the builders of our great cathedrals, as they rose tier upon tier into the sky.

Auspicious omens marked the end of the work—perhaps the most fortunate being the discovery of a gold mine in Japan which enabled the gilding of the huge figure to be completed.   The statue was dedicated amidst scenes of pomp and fervour in a splendid ' eye-opening ' ceremony when with a large brush the eyes were painted in.   Four years later, in A.D. 756, the Empress gave the complete household equipment of her late husband to the Tōdai-ji Temple.   The thousands of objects included in the gift were stored in the Shōsō-in, a huge log-cabin raised on great pillars, which was built in the forest near the temple to house them.   This, the oldest surviving ' museum ' in the world, has stood there almost untouched through the succeeding twelve hundred years, preserved only by the sanctity surrounding the royal house and by the inviolability of the imperial seals on its doors.   Experts open it with the greatest reverence once a year for the traditional airing and many of its objects are not yet fully catalogued.   As one would expect of this sino-phile court, the majority of the objects are of Chinese origin—musical instruments, armour as shining as on the day it was made, medicines, glass, pottery, and all the trappings of an imperial household.   To walk round this vast storehouse and, with the aid of a torch, peer at a few of the objects so carefully preserved there is a most eerie and moving experience.

However, not all the objects found in the Shōsō-in are of Chinese origin and some of the contemporary native works which it contains show how rapidly the Japanese were mastering the techniques required to copy the treasured Chinese models. This is particularly true in the field of ceramics. The most frequently encountered type of Chinese T'ang dynasty pottery is characterized by a three-coloured glaze of green, brown, and cream on powerfully yet sensitively shaped vessels. Thousands of these have been excavated from tombs in China and most museums contain splendid examples. Some of this pottery has been found in Japan and, whereas it was once usual to refer to it as yet another importation, Japanese scholars now assert—with some archaeological evidence to support their claim—that, though modelled faithfully on the Chinese, it is Japanese made. Green-glazed titles from temples of a slightly later period show that the Japanese could possibly have made such pottery. The bowl in Figure 44, unearthed in Ibaraki, Osaka Prefecture, is an excellent example of the ware. It is confidently potted, sturdy in shape, but the smooth, well-fitting lid gives it distinction and elegance. This simple bowl, the result of a most accomplished technique, shows the eagerness of the Japanese to learn not only the religious but also the secular arts of their Chinese teachers. The difference between this and earlier wares provides in its humbler way, as eloquent an indication of the great leap forward taken by the Japanese as do the more elevated arts of painting and sculpture previously described. A Chinese *yüeh* jar now in the Imperial collection, was preserved in the Hōryū-ji since the Nara period and the Japanese were thus not deprived of examples of the best ceramics

44. Pottery Bowl with Three coloured glaze. Late Nara period. Height 6¼ inches.
Tokyo National Museum.

45. (Left). *Bodhisattva Playing a Flute*. Detail from a panel of a cast bronze lantern. Late Nara period. 3 feet 10½ inches by 1 foot 5½ inches. Tōdai-ji, Nara.

46. (Right). *Octagonal Mirror Box*. Lacquer on leather decorated with gold and silver. Nara period. Diameter 8¼ inches. Shōsō-in, Nara.

that China could produce. F. Koyama claims that they were imitated in Japan which provides an indication that the Japanese had very skilled techniques at their command at this early time.[1]

In metal-work, the Japanese joy in their newly-found freedom of expression and in the seemingly endless possibilities that Chinese art and techniques offered is no less remarkable. A youthful Bodhisattva on one of the panels of a cast-bronze lantern (Fig. 45) which stands outside the Tōdai-ji Temple seems to move freely to the music of his own flute. His celestial robes billow with graceful ease across the lattice-work, their curves taken up and reversed in the scrolls at the edges. The folds of the robes have an impish carelessness admirably suited to the boyish face and the whole composition has a pertness emphasized by such happy touches as the way in which the scarf, coming up from the right of the head, curls upwards and then down behind the halo.

Lacquer, it will be recalled, was used on the Tamamushi Shrine (see p. 23). Historical records provide evidence of the importance attached to the encouragement of the craft. A legal code published in 701 mentions the establishment of an Office of the Guild of Lacquer Workers and encouraged the cultivation of the lacquer tree. " Each farmer

[1] " The Yüeh-chou Celadons Excavated in Japan " *Artibus Asiae*, Vol. XIV 1/2. pp. 26–42.

employing six hands and over should, during the ensuing five years, plant eighty lacquer trees on his ground, those employing four hands, seventy trees and those employing three hands, forty trees." Where an area was particularly productive of lacquer, taxes could be levied in the material. Lacquer found its most exalted use in the making of religious sculptures but this was only a passing phase and it is with respect to its secular decorative uses that we shall be mostly concerned.

The Nara period was a time of apprenticeship and experiment for Japanese workers. Lacquer was applied to leather and hemp but these methods proved unsatisfactory and were soon abandoned. The octagonal *Mirror Box* (Fig. 46) from the Shōsō-in, however, is a rare example of the lacquer on leather technique and of a type of decoration in which gold and silver were mixed with glue and then painted on. This was a forerunner of the *makie* technique (see later) in which gold and silver dust were sprinkled on wet lacquer. Despite the clumsiness of the method, however, the design is very skilful. It is probable that this

47. (Left). Detail from a fragment of warp brocade. Decorated with large blossoms, arabesques, and birds on a green background. Nara Period. Tokyo National Museum.

48. (Right). *Deer Under a Tree*. Stencil dyeing on hemp. Late Nara period. 4 feet 11 inches by 1 foot 10 inches. Shōsō-in, Nara.

E

box, like the majority of Shōsō-in objects, came from China but again no Chinese examples have survived. In design it reminds one of Chinese silver work—in particular the lively birds descending on a pond filled with imaginary flowers called by the Japanese *hosoge* ' flowers of precious appearance.' The simplification of the wings and feet of the birds and the arrangement of the flowers are indications of a style which, in its maturity, suggests a Chinese rather than a Japanese origin.

The development of the textile industries kept pace with those of all the other arts. Just as the legal code of 701 encouraged the lacquer workers, so also it provided Government protection for the production of textiles. These laws established a Bureau of the Palace Wardrobe, an Office for the Guild of Needleworkers, the Guild of Weavers and a Palace Dyeing Office. Craftsmen from the Guild of Weavers were sent to the more outlying provinces to teach weaving. Splendid robes of brocade, cut after the latest Chinese fashion, became the favourite dress for the nobility. The clergy also demanded fine textiles and their exactions must have pressed heavily on the peasant manufacturers of silk, thus increasing the burden placed on them by the equipment of the temples then springing up.

The detail in Figure 47 is an example of early warp brocade in which the pattern and background are produced by coloured warp threads. The six-petalled flowers amidst foliage with flying birds is a very accomplished design reminiscent of T'ang cast mirror backs. Later the warp type brocade gave way to a less technically restricting weft brocade capable of finer and larger designs.

Dyeing also was popular during the Nara period. Examples of Batik, tie-dyeing, and stencil dyeing have survived. A fine example of stencil dyeing is the screen with *Deer Under a Tree* (Fig. 48) from the Shōsō-in. Like many T'ang dynasty Chinese textiles the design is of Sasanian-Persian origin. Considering the difficulties of the technique, this material is a remarkable example of the sensitive fingers and innate sense of design which distinguish all Japanese craftwork.

The violent expansion of culture and civilization during the Nara period was not without its dangers. The country had less than one-hundredth of the resources of China and the peasant population in the area of the capital was bled white to supply the manpower and money needed for the megalomaniac palace and temple schemes. It is understandable that many sought escape, some by emigrating to more inaccessible regions, others by entering the privileged ranks of the army or better still those of the religious orders. Many joined the roving bands of the vagrant class. In the last decade or so of the Tempyō era, which ended in 767, the national treasury was diminished by half through the extravagant expenditure of the priest-ridden court on buildings and gifts. The Japanese economy was not capable of supporting the vast schemes which Chinese inspired ambition had conceived. Imagination outran the purse, but the vitality and skill of the Japanese cannot be questioned. A desire to do too much with too little has led many a state to bankruptcy but has also produced some of the greatest monuments of the world's art.

CHAPTER IV

THE EARLY HEIAN PERIOD

794–876

KŌNIN 810–23. JŌGAN 859–76[1]

EXTRAORDINARY as the creation of Nara may appear to us, the decision which the Japanese now made to desert its splendours and to build an entirely new capital at Nagaoka seems almost incredible. Historians generally agree that it was strongly influenced by the desire of the court to escape from the growing power and ambitions of the clergy. One priest, Dōkyō, towards the end of the 8th century, had even become the lover of an empress and his aspirations to be made emperor were only foiled by the death of his mistress.

Removals on a great scale had many precedents, the custom having grown out of a belief familiar in many early civilizations, that a house was defiled by death. In early Japan, where a house was a comparatively simple building, such a move, whether of miles or yards, was a relatively easy matter. However, the shifting of a whole city, re-built in strict emulation of the finest that China had to show, was an undertaking which the Japanese would certainly not have contemplated without very good reasons. They must have envisaged considerable advantages from the change, for the treasury was already depleted and it required a tremendous effort entailing the labour of over 300,000 workers and the income from a whole year's taxation. It says much for the strength and discipline of the Japanese that they could accomplish it all without a major breakdown.

They had been working at Nagaoka for some ten years in preparation for the move, when just as suddenly the project was abandoned. Sansom, piecing together the many strands of intrigue in Japanese court life of the time, thinks that the cancellation was probably due to the fact that the noble in charge of building was involved in an intrigue over the succession and murdered. The principal conspirator, the Emperor's younger brother, met his end as a result of the murder. Misfortunes then befell the Imperial family and, despite all efforts to appease the spirit of the dead Prince, a succession of calamities ensued. The court, always very conscious of the spirits of the dead, may then have decided that it would be advisable to abandon the ill-fated Nagaoka site and choose a completely new one. Early in 793, after solemn divination, a new site was consecrated in what is now the city of Kyoto some five miles from Nagaoka. They named it—somewhat wishfully one feels—*Heiankyō* 'The Capital of Peace and Tranquillity.'

---

[1] The period is sometimes referred to by either of these two important sub-periods within it.

This time the Emperor did not wait for the new city to be finished but occupied his new palace in 793 while the work on the rest of the capital continued for another ten years. It was again laid out on the scheme of the Chinese capital of Ch'ang-an and modern Kyoto in some of its quieter corners can still convey a vision of the old Chinese metropolis. A dusty temple to-day fills the ordained square in the city grid amidst the huts for human habitation which have sprung up around it; a tree-lined canal looks just a little too artfully contrived to be other than man's handiwork, tiny streams which run alongside some of the less built-up roads bear witness to the ancient water system of the city.

In their religion, the Japanese in the new capital were still equally under the spell of T'ang China. New sects introduced from the mainland brought more complicated dogmas. In a country eager for innovations these rapidly took root and prospered, assisted perhaps by the fact that the older sects remained in their Nara strongholds, too content with their established positions to follow the court. It is easy to imagine the excitement that greeted the arrival of the new teachings in the capital. Apart from the intriguing doctrines they offered and the challenge they made to a people anxious to show their abilities, they provided opportunities to enter monasteries for recruits who could not find places in the older establishments. The most important of the new sects were the *Tendai* introduced by Dengyō Daishi in 805 and the *Shingon* introduced by Kōbō Daishi in 806–7.

The *Tendai* school came from its parent monastery on Mt. T'ien-t'ai (Japanese: *Tendai*) in China. This sect based its teaching on the celebrated Lotus Sutra, at the same time incorporating a number of native Chinese beliefs into the religion. It has been defined as a ' sort of monistic pantheism of which the central figure is the notion that the absolute is inherent in all phenomena, and that each separate phenomenon is but one manifestation of an unchanging reality.' Enlightenment for the follower of the *Tendai* sect would come as the result of a balance between studies of the scriptures, religious practices and contemplation. The main temple was set up on Mt. Hiei just outside Kyoto, and the court provided official recognition and finance to encourage the new sect in the teeth of what opposition the Nara clergy could muster. Perhaps the court hoped to establish greater influence over the new sect than it held over the older ones at Nara. Perhaps it felt that such religious rivalries might direct the energies of the Nara sects away from politics. From that time religious strife, often very bitter, became a feature of the Japanese scene. This, in its turn, enlivened the interest in the art which the new sects introduced. The uncompromising nature of *Tendai* suited the nationalistic atmosphere of the Heian period and Dengyō Daishi's temple, the Enryaku-ji, in its commanding position outside and overlooking Kyoto, prospered rapidly.

Kōbō *Daishi* or ' The Great Teacher ' Kōbō returned from China in 807 with a different interpretation of Buddhism which emphasized what became in Japan the *Dainichi Nyōrai* —the supreme, eternal Buddha from which all other Buddhas emanate. His sect, the *Shingon* means literally ' True Word ' referring to the magic formulae which were thought to represent the elements of the universe. As in the Indian *tantric* Buddhism from which it was derived, its adherents placed particular emphasis on incantations, spells, and magic symbols. These new teachings from China continually re-invigorated Japanese religious and artistic life. In a country as small as Japan their struggles seem to have become more acute, the issues clearer, and the fight for existence more desperate than in China.

Both the *Tendai* and *Shingon* gave an impetus to the movement to incorporate native *Shintō* gods into the Buddhist pantheon. Buddhist temples and Shintō shrines flourished side by side. That they felt a need to do this shows the strength and persistence of the native Japanese cult. The Great Illuminator *Dainchi* became identified with the Sun Goddess who was considered to be the ancestor of the Japanese people. The *Shintō* priests also were not slow to learn from Buddhist methods. *Kōbō Daishi* founded his temple on Mt. Kōya well to the south of Kyoto and away from the distractions and dangers of the capital. It still prospers there, a whole township of temples and halls deep in a dense forest of huge trees which produce an atmosphere of mystery admirably suited to the tenets of the sect.[1] Of the two eminent teachers Kōbō seems to have been the greater, admired and respected by the court for his urbane qualities and artistic talents, a ' Jesuit ' among Buddhist missionaries.

The court welcomed T'ang learning with the same unqualified enthusiasm with which it accepted Buddhist teachings. The poems of the great masters Po Chü-i, Li Po, and Tu Fu were chanted aloud and even their settings imitated to the last detail. They carefully studied the Chinese classics and Chinese occult theories. But the desire to communicate ideas rather than emotions can be the enemy of art. The necessity of illustrating a complicated iconography can deaden artistic sensitivity especially when that iconography is not a spontaneous, native product.

It has been said of the *Tendai* and *Shingon* teachings that " both sects emphasized esoteric doctrines of such complexity as to be hardly accessible to any but the trained clergy themselves, and they demanded a multiplication of elaborate, unfamiliar images and paintings and other symbols . . . formulas too often took the place of honest worship . . . there came into being icons to express the terrific as well as the benign aspects of the gods . . . there were also map-like hierarchies of greater and lesser gods set in their ranks about some central Buddha who was himself only one attribute of the single, pure and all inclusive ONE of the ancient Buddhism . . . there were wall paintings which showed whole paradises peopled with their divine inhabitants."[2]

A recently translated record of one of the contemporary Japanese seekers after the truth in China, a *Tendai* monk named Ennin,[3] tells how these travellers collected whatever they could carry in the way of new scriptures. They were particularly attracted by the *mandalas* or Buddhist map-like pictures of the cosmos (see p. 63). These were easily transportable and eagerly studied in Japan where one occult mystery seemed more attractive than the next. In all this, the Japanese showed their desire to keep up to date with developments in China—the same quality they showed regarding 20th century Western culture.

The Japanese sympathetically accepted the terrifying aspects of the belief in absolute divine power of this new *mikkyō* or Esoteric Buddhism and they deeply influenced their art. In sculpture they caused the attractive simplicity of the earlier period to disappear. The great sculptural objects of worship now became more than just superior human beings, ennobled by deep belief or softened by contemplation. Their effect on the spectator was now intended to be overwhelming and awe-inspiring; forms became heavy with symbolic meaning and divorced from reality. The worshipper could hardly have been intended to understand let alone to warm to his idol. The carvers made an attempt to provide something which would at once fascinate and subdue the more sophisticated nobles of the Heian court. Gone was the simple grace and freedom of the Kōryū-ji *Miroku*, the majestic

[1] Both sects established their temples amidst beautiful natural surroundings and both stressed the need for their worshippers to meditate in close contact with nature. This influenced their landscape artists.
[2] Langdon Warner. *The Enduring Art of Japan.* Harvard, 1952.
[3] *Ennin's Diary.* Translated by Edwin O. Reischauer. New York, 1955.

ideal of a *Gakkō Bosatsu*; their place is taken by a heavy, almost overpowering sensuousness. Strangely enough many Japanese see in these bulky statues an austere dignity which compensates for the loss of the simple realism and attractive candour of earlier works. They harmonize for them the traditions of Nara, the fully mastered techniques of wood carving and the mystic spirit of Esoteric Buddhism. Seiroku Noma considers the extent to which the realism of the previous period had been carried as vulgarity and sees in the new esoteric dogma a spiritualism which was needed to reinvigorate the sculpture, " to destroy the shell of stifling realism."

Two examples illustrate the sculptural tendencies of the period very well. The first (Fig. 49) is called in Japanese The *Nyōirin Kannon* or ' Kannon with the gem and wheel

49. (Left). *Nyōirin Kannon*. Wood. Early Heian period. Height 3 feet 7 inches. Kanshin-ji, Osaka.

50. (Right). *Yakushi Nyōrai* " The Buddha of Healing." Wood. Early Heian period. Height 5 feet 7 inches. Jingo-ji, Kyoto.

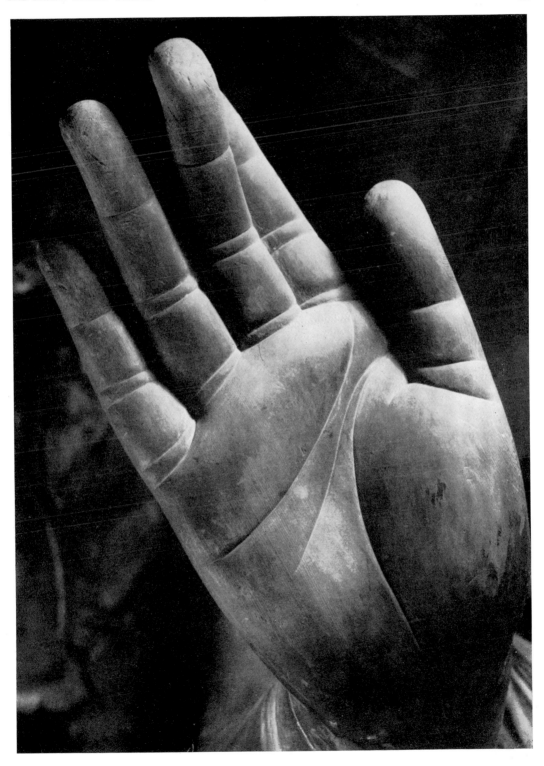

51.   Detail of the hand of a seated Yakushi Nyōrai.
Wood.   Shin Yakushi-ji, Nara.

52. Detail of a Wall Painting
from Bezeklik, Central Asia.

53. *Priest Rōben*. Wood. Early Heian period.
Height 41¾ inches. Tōdai-ji, Nara.

which satisfy all desires.' Four of the six hands hold a gem, a wheel, a lotus stem, and a
rosary (later restorations). This 'secret' statue is enshrined in the lecture hall of the
Kanshin-ji, Osaka which was built between 826 and 836 and the figure is said to belong
to that period. It is chiselled out of a single block of wood, a technique which was popular
at the beginning of the Heian period and which produced most of its great works. Despite
the rather heavy cheeks and the thick neck, the face has a certain charm and feminine
grace without any loss of the aloofness befitting an icon of these occult theories. The six
arms have a more reasonable arrangement than in many of these many-armed divinities
where they seem to be multiplied without any organic meaning, and only because the symbolism demanded them. In this *Kannon* the pose is relaxed and the body most sensitively
represented while still preserving those qualities which the Japanese say distinguish the

works of esoteric Buddhism—a ' solemn dignity ' and a ' sensuous vigour.'[1] The effect is enriched by the over-painting of the nimbus, figure, and lotus pedestal with fine designs which preserve their original colours. Elements of the Nara styles persist in this early Heian statue. The Westerner will appreciate the skilful carving of the whole statue and in particular of the lotus throne with its elegant ' rainbow coloured ' petals. The Japanese greatly admire the elaborate decoration which is a feature of the sculpture of the period.

Although the full impact of the new sects was not felt until the early years of the 9th century, the influence of esoteric Buddhist thought can equally be seen in the slightly earlier *Yakushi Nyōrai* in the Jingo-ji temple, Kyoto (Fig. 50), dated *ca.* 793. The modelling and drapery preserve elements of the late Nara clay styles, but the most distinctive feature is the peculiar heaviness of the shoulders and thighs, which is intended to depict the superhuman physical characteristics of the Buddha and ' instead of beauty of form, the aspiring spirit beyond form.' The expression of the face is forbidding and compelling, directed at the worshipper with a grimness which seems to contradict the gesture of ' have no fear ' shown in the right hand. No Chinese models to which these statues might be compared have survived; they were probably inspired by pictures which could easily have been brought back from places in China like Tun-huang or even from Central Asia by the priest travellers (Fig. 52). The connexion is suggested by the distinctive deep folds of a technique of carving drapery called ' rolling waves '—in which one rounded wave always alternates with a sharply cut fold. This heightens the unrealistic, rhythmical qualities of the modelling. It can produce a splendid, clear decorative effect but becomes often dry and monotonous. In short, the massive Indian- or Central Asian-inspired style seems peculiarly out of sympathy with Japanese sculptural ideals. It may be best to leave the last word on some of these statues with the Japanese critic who said that " they were too austere to be enjoyed."[2]

Fortunately the Japanese gifts for inspired portraiture had not died out under the impact of the new styles. The sculpture of the *Priest Rōben* (Fig. 53) made about 773 in the Tōdai-ji Temple, Kyoto and the *Shintō Goddess* owned by the Matsuno-o Jinja, Kyoto (Fig. 54), are both excellent examples of an unbroken tradition. The practice of making statues of *Shintō* gods was encouraged by Buddhist practice and most of the examples date from the end of this period and later. The Goddess, however, is an early example dated *ca.* 889–92. The carving is simple and heavy and imbues the figure with a solid dignity. The Buddhists, for their part, did not discourage these attempts by the *Shintō* followers since they were anxious to incorporate the native gods into the Buddhist pantheon as *avatars* or manifestations of Buddhist divinities. Yet, whereas the Buddhist gods of the period seem very unhuman, these *Shintō* divinities are only thinly-disguised human portraits. Unhampered by any desire to express the ' secret doctrines ' of the *Tendai* or *Shingon* sects, the sculptor felt free to portray a matronly figure of the time with her loosely hanging robe, high head-dress and gentle eyes directed slightly to one side. The result is a powerful figure which, in its solemn mass, reveals at once the force and limitations of single-block sculpture.

For all its weight and power, it is difficult to agree with some Japanese and Western critics that the early Heian is one of the finest periods of Japanese sculpture. Despite the appreciation of the possibilities of wood carving and the spiritual revival which came with the new Buddhism, the works of the period are not always attractive or convincing. They

[1] Y. Tazawa, *Pageant of Japanese Art.* Vol. III. Tokyo, 1953. p. 80.
[2] Seiroku Noma. *Japanese Sculpture* V. Tokyo, 1952.

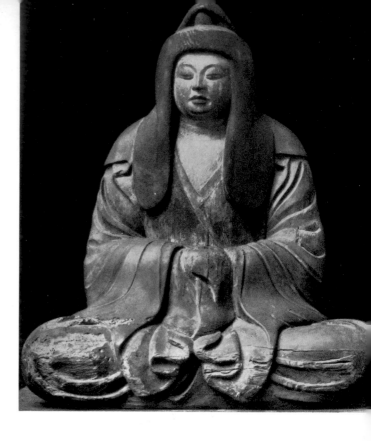

54. *Shintō Goddess*. Wood.
Early Heian period.
Height 2 feet 10¼ inches.
Matsuno-o Jinja, Kyoto.

seem to lie outside Japanese artistic traditions, as if their creators were not completely at home with the newly-imported sculptural ideas. As they interpreted them from drawings they may, indeed, not have understood them very clearly. The complicated iconography of the new sects emphasized one or another aspect of a divinity; a gesture of the hand or an attribute held in it seems to have become more important than the sculpture as an entity; the demand for iconographical accuracy often laid a dead hand on the artist's spirit. In all fairness it must be admitted that it may be difficult for the Westerner to appreciate the spell which esoteric Buddhist art is intended to cast over the spectator.

The problem raised by these sculptures is that of the fundamental approach of the Eastern artist in some periods to his work and of his aims in creating a Buddhist statue. The observations that Benjamin Rowland made on Chinese copies of Indian images apply also to Japanese products of this period. Prior to the T'ang dynasty the images made in China were not based directly on Indian models but on Central Asian models. But intrepid travellers and missionaries such as the Chinese Hsüan-tsang established direct contact with India. After many years spent there Hsüan-tsang returned to China (A.D. 645) to translate the sutras he had collected and to impart his knowledge to the people. He gave the first real conception of the Mahayana teachings to the Chinese. His work has rightly been compared to the "discoveries and the influence of the Renaissance humanists on the late development of classic learning in the West." But Hsüan-tsang was only one of many. The Imperial envoy Wang Hsüan-ts'ê is said to have brought back pictorial records of the holy places in India and replicas of important statues. For the Chinese, there was a definite merit attached to copies of famous images even if they were remote from the originals. Naturally, the more faithful the copy, the more of the magic of the original it would contain, and the more effective it would be as a religious representation. Nobody expected an artist to express his own personality in a work of art; he was more concerned with representing proportions accurately. This approach is visible in a number of early Chinese bronze figures which, perhaps for this reason, are not of outstanding artistic merit.

In the early Heian period the same restricting influences seem to be working on Japanese sculpture. Indo-Asian models suddenly seem to dominate the Japanese. Fortunately their inventive and independent spirit led them to tire quickly of these uninspired copies. Neither the heaviness nor the impassivity of their models completely satisfied their aspirations and they occasionally turned with relief to the *Shintō* deities in which they were not so restrained by the need to express iconographical formulae but which they would portray as figures of the ancestors of the race dressed in contemporary clothes.

What is true of sculpture in this period is true also of the paintings. Many more have survived than from earlier periods, and this suggests that, as an art form, painting acquired greater importance for the new sects. The more involved nature of *Shingon* and *Tendai* teachings could be better expressed by painting than by sculpture; much more subject matter could be compressed into a pictorial representation. The complex rituals demanded also more variety and change. One of the principal forms of painting was the *mandala*

55. Mandala. (Detail).
Gold and silver on
purple figured silk.
Nara period.
Kojima-dera, Nara
Prefecture.

56.   *Aka* ('*Red*') *Fudō*.
Colour on silk.
Early Heian period (?).
5 feet 5 inches by 3 feet 1¾ inches.
Myōō-in, Mount Kōya.

(Fig. 55), a complicated map-like type of painting in which whole cosmologies are represented in tabular form. These are often incomprehensible to all but the most erudite iconographical specialist. While admiring the fine line drawing of the individual figures and their impeccable draftsmanship. one cannot overlook a certain repetition and stiffness in both figures and compositions, which is characteristic of all strictly iconographical painting, but does not tend to produce inspiring works of art.

Of greater interest is another type of painting introduced during this early Heian period which expressed in broader pictorial form the same terrifying aspects of the new Buddhism that are seen in the sculpture. These are the *Fudō* pictures. A *Fudō* is one of the ' Five Great Kings ' who are supposed to protect the Buddhist world, and like the Guardians of earlier periods, are, of course, intended to deter the evil doer. The most famous, and indeed the finest, of the *Fudō* pictures is the *Aka*, or ' Red ' *Fudō* reverently housed in the Myōō-in, a temple of the *Shingon* sect on Mt. Kōya (Fig. 56). So sacred are these pictures that it is extremely difficult to obtain permission to see them. The *Ki* or ' Yellow ' *Fudō* in the Mii temple is perhaps the most inaccessible and the visitor must carry the highest introductions and references before, after a necessary interval for prayer, the priests will produce them from storage. Often the visitor will have to be content with seeing the 12th century copy of the *Mii* ' Yellow ' *Fudō* which is kept in the Manju-in, Kyoto.

The Japanese artists delighted in painting these grim portraits because they gave scope to their natural fantasy. Some authorities date the *Aka Fudō* slightly later than the early Heian period to which it has generally been attributed. It has even been placed as late as the Kamakura era. The assymmetrical arrangement of the figures, it is true, reveals an unexpected compositional advance on earlier works; there is a newly-found freedom in which the main figure no longer looks the viewer straight in the eyes but glares balefully out to one side. The Fudō's two young attendants are effectively placed together in one corner and not one on each side in the stiff traditional symmetry. The rugged mass of the landscape further heightens the impact of the scene. The brushwork of the whole work, and in particular of the face, is most vehement. The strong, rhythmical drawing conveys a feeling of tenseness and of threatening force. The sweep of the composition in one arc from the bottom left-hand corner to the top left-hand corner has the effect of a drawn bow-string and projects the intimidating impression. One of the attendant figures remains calm and friendly and thus, by contrast, admirably heightens the effect of the composition. The colour adds to the lurid impression.

Into the ceramic and metal-work crafts little new was introduced in the early Heian period. Both were hardly touched by the new sects. In ceramics, the techniques of highly-fired wares spread to a number of other kilns which, founded at this time, were to establish their reputations later—Bizen, Ōmi, Tamba, Ōwari, and Mino; the Seto kilns in Ōwari had a particularly illustrious career. Monochrome green wares have been unearthed which carry on the tradition of the three-colour glazes of the T'ang inspired pottery, and written records exist of the importation of the materials from which glazes were made. By this time Chinese *yüeh* type pottery must have been well known in Japan and pieces have been excavated which were buried in 904–5. These, it seems, the Japanese tried to imitate.[1]

[1] Fujio Koyama " The Yüeh-chou Yao Celadons Excavated in Japan," *Artibus Asiae*, Vol. XIV, 1/2. pp. 26–42.

CHAPTER V

THE LATE HEIAN OR FUJIWARA PERIOD

895–1185

THE late Heian or, as it is more often called, the Fujiwara period is perhaps the most important of all for an understanding of Japanese art and taste. Hitherto the arts of Japan had been strongly under the influence of China but during the Fujiwara centuries the native Japanese artistic spirit confidently asserted itself. This is evident in the traditional forms as well as in essentially Japanese innovations. In a broad sense it can be said that what the T'ang dynasty did for Chinese taste, the Fujiwara period did for that of Japan.

One of the factors which had led to the decision to move the capital from Nara to Kyoto had been the desire of the Court to escape from the suffocating grip of the clergy. But by this very move it played into the hands of certain members of the aristocracy. The most powerful of these noble families were the Fujiwara, an ancient line so established that, like the Emperor, they could claim kinship with the gods, though naturally not with quite such exalted gods. In these years, through a succession of weak emperors who were little more than puppets, the effective control fell into the hands of regents or advisors whose ambitions were even greater than those of the Nara church. This was the form of government presaged by developments in earlier times. Throughout the succeeding centuries the Emperor was preserved only as a figure-head, while behind his august person more ruthless men waged a bitter struggle for real power.

The politics of the period are extremely complicated. Court intrigues, challenges to the Fujiwara power, behind-the-scenes activities of retired emperors, and the warlike behaviour of the monks continually agitated society. The inhabitants of the Tendai monastries outside Kyoto and of the Kōfuku-ji at Nara often made the streets of the capital unsafe for the peaceful traveller.

The Fujiwara family, by marrying girls of their line to the emperors and princes, by placing their nominees in office, by obtaining tax-free estates, and by ruthlessly removing all opponents, steadily tightened their grip on the effective power. It proved unfortunate for the subsequent history of Japan that they further developed the system of hereditary administration which completely ignored the great Chinese concept of government through scholars who had proved their worth in open examination. It is interesting to speculate that this may have caused men, whose talents would otherwise have led them to expect high office in the state, to take to the arts instead. The status of artists may well have gained from the low condition of state service and the dangers of political life. Even some emperors found it wise to retire and devote themselves to the arts. This was a custom which the Fujiwara encouraged.

The life of the court at Kyoto was as refined and as sophisticated as any the world has seen. Its delicacy and sumptuousness almost defy description. It was a period in which, as Soper has said, the conventionalization of life begun with the move to Kyoto reached its highest degree not to be broken until the civil wars of the 1150's. Sansom has summarized the atmosphere of this sybaritic world: "preoccupied with art and letters, quick to criticize a weak stroke of the brush, a faulty line of verse, a discordant colour or an ungraceful movement; great connoisseurs in emotion and judges of ceremonies and etiquette; sentimentally aware of the sadness of this dew-like floating world, but intellectually unconcerned with its problems; prone to a gentle melancholy but apt to enjoy each transitory moment, and quite without interest in any outlook but their own." It was a world of calculated artificiality from which all unpleasant experiences of normal life were rigidly excluded. The isolation from foreign countries increased the atmosphere of artificial calm. No discordant note was allowed to disturb the precious, regulated harmony of noble life.

This is the elegant, profligate society mirrored by one of the world's greatest novels, the classic *Tale of Genji* written between 1008 and 1020 by Lady Murasaki. The story is familiar to the west in Arthur Waley's translation—the only criticism of which has been that it does the original more than justice. Despite occasional tedious passages, almost any page of the book will transport the reader to a world where sensibilities are almost too fine for our appreciation, where motives are so delicate that they hardly seem credible bases for human behaviour and where the fate of people great and small often hung by the slenderest threads. A love affair could be ruined by an unskilled piece of calligraphy or a carelessly tied ribbon, a man banished for a minute breach of etiquette.

The novel is a romance played against a brocade-like background. But, when reading it, one must remember that Lady Murasaki was a woman of the Court and her knowledge of life restricted by her sex and position. She shows mainly one side of the picture in which politics intrude only when they effect a sentimental love-affair. She talks little about the unceasing struggle for power constantly in progress behind the gaity and sadness of the flirtations which she records with such literary finesse. Savage feudal wars raged throughout the 11th and 12th centuries, and the vigour of the Japanese race was, for a time, spent in constant battles. While recognizing the suzerainty of the Emperor in Kyoto, the more powerful Japanese noblemen remained virtually secure and independent behind the massive walls of their huge fortified castles. Around them they gathered their hereditary fighting-men—the *samurai* or 'serving men' whose code of honour, *bushidō* ('The Way of the Knight'), governed their behaviour as rigidly as the code of chivalry did that of the medieval Western knight. Later propagandists exploited this Japanese feudal ideal to inspire every Japanese soldier down to the present day. The single-minded, blind devotion to their masters which the *samurai* were expected to show, and the all-important virtue of preserving their honour unto victory or death form the themes of a thousand stories and plays. These stories are generally built around the complications created by the inter-action of conflicting loyalties and emotions; the problems often become so tangled that suicide is the only honourable way out. One set of circumstances seems to be more involved, one solution more difficult—and to the Westerner often more unexpected—than the last. Behind them all, at its best, is a deep sadness, at its worst a contrived sentimentality.

68

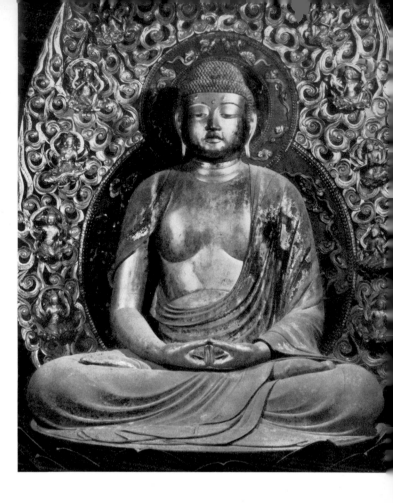

57. *Amida* by Jōchō.
Wood.   Late Heian period.
Height 9 feet 8 inches.
Byōdō-in, Kyoto.

The Buddhists of the time now quite frankly abandoned the attitude of humanity and pacifism which formerly distinguished them even in their moments of political scheming. The *Tendai* and *Shingon* monasteries henceforth accepted the feudal world of violence on its own terms and fought it with its own weapons.   Their warlike behaviour discredited them in the eyes of genuine believers among the population and politically made them dangerous allies for the Court. The emphasis of Buddhism began to change radically. The occult mysteries and stern discipline, the threats of hells to be encountered by the lecherous and voluptuous, all graphically illustrated in the arts, were hardly likely to appeal to a luxury loving nobility. The masses to which Buddhism would henceforth appeal could hardly understand them.

Towards the end of the period a new reforming sect, the *Jōdo* or ' Pure Land ' sect, known in T'ang China and introduced into Japan long before the Fujiwara period, began to gain widespread popularity through the zeal of a priest named Hōnen (1133–1212). This reaction against the abstruse *Tendai* and *Shingon* teachings provided a simple evangelical way to salvation through faith alone. It demanded of the believer only that he should sincerely invoke the name of the omnipresent Amida Buddha, the ' Lord of Boundless Light,' thereby securing final entry into paradise, the ' Pure Land.' Salvation by the mere repetition of the formula *namu Amida Butsu* was an attractive dogma which the older sects found difficult to combat. With that happy eclecticism found so often in the history of eastern religions, they sometimes tried to incorporate the new approach into their own more demanding or complicated teachings. The influence of Hōnen's views was particularly strong in the following Kamakura period but already in Fujiwara times it made itself felt.

Buddhist temples began to mirror as invitingly as possible the 'Pure Land' into which believers would be born and a new lightness and elegance appear in their architecture and decoration. The sculptors responded to the escapism and sentimentality of the age. Their statues for the temples reflect softer, more feminine ideals. The *Amida* statue (Fig. 57) in the Byōdō-in Temple at Uji examplifies the slender, well-balanced grace of Fujiwara sculpture. The massive bodies, the heavy faces with their stern expressions and the stiff drapery of the early Heian period are here modified to a more human scale and certainly to more elegant proportions. The body is placed in calm stability, the face is benign, and behind the whole figure rises a great nimbus with a characteristically rich, involved decoration which, by contrast, brings out the simple lines of the main figure.

This figure, in which the aspirations of a new generation of artists found expression, illustrates two important developments of the period. First, we learn the name of the artist who carved it—it is the late work of the famous sculptor Jōchō who died in 1057. Hitherto, Japanese sculpture had been almost entirely the work of anonymous craftsmen. Henceforward, and particularly in the next period, the individual and his school became increasingly important. During the Fujiwara period, under the patronage of eminent noble families, a number of master sculptors, some of whom were Buddhist priests, rose to fame. Jōchō, for instance, was patronized by Fujiwara-no-Michinaga, the powerful scion of the Fujiwara family during its most influential period. Prior to this time we know little of the ateliers which supplied the temples. The tendency now was for temples to open their own workshops for the creation of Buddhist images and the church occasionally paid high honours to the sculptors. Sometimes they even conferred religious ranks on them. It was but a short step from this to the sculptors liberating themselves from their artistic and financial depencence on the temples and setting up their own studios. There they also trained pupils to carry on their traditions.

In China we know very few sculptors by name. The emergence in Japan of artists like Jōchō marks the continuation of a movement begun long before in which they raised the arts to a recognized and even honoured occupation for men of outstanding ability. The results of this development were far-reaching. It gave the arts a new flexibility and a quicker response to current ideas; it made them more subjective and more varied. It also had important consequences for the crafts. Unlike in China, the Japanese never considered it menial for the individual artist to practise a craft. Lacquer, ceramics, metal-work, and textile designing gained greatly in later periods from this changed attitude and position of the artist (see later).

Jōchō, who set the pattern for Fujiwara and much of the subsequent sculpture, came from the studio of the Kōfuku-ji Temple at Nara, and, although he had his workshop in Kyoto, he continued to work a great deal in the old capital. This is of considerable significance for it meant that he was often in close contact with the early masterpieces of Nara times. Thus he must always have had before him the clearly-conceived figures which are the glory of that period. He is unlikely to have had much sympathy for the iconographic exercises produced in Kyoto and on Mt. Kōya by the *Tendai* and *Shingon* artists.

The second significant development of the time was the expansion of the demand for statuary. So great was this demand that the old laborious system of carving from a single block could no longer keep pace with it. The technical problem was solved by making

F

58. *Fugen Bosatsu.*
'The Bodhisattva of Universal Sagacity.'
Wood. Late Heian period.
Height 21¾ inches. Okura Museum. Tokyo.

59. (Right). Kichijō-ten. Wood.
Late Heian or Early Kamakura period.
Height 35½ inches.
Jōruri-ji, Kyoto.

statues from a number of separate pieces of carefully selected wood which were first roughly carved, then assembled, and finally finished by a master. The custom of masters finishing their pupil's work, later to become familiar in the painting ateliers of the West, was new in Japan at this time. The *Amida* in Figure 57 was made by this technique. It is immediately evident that the artist has paid greater attention to details—all of which are beautifully proportioned and assembled in such a way as to produce an idealized type. The calm pose with the hands in the gesture of meditation, the soft eyes and quiet beauty make visible on earth a serenity to be expected only in paradise. The *Fugen Bosatsu* 'The Bodhisattva of Universal Sagacity' in the Okura Museum, Tokyo (Fig. 58) and the *Kichijō-ten* in the Jōruri Temple, Kyoto (Fig. 59) are outstanding examples of the technique at its best. The latter is dated 1212 and chronologically belongs to the next period, but it preserves the sculptural style and aesthetic atmosphere of the Fujiwara age and provides a striking vision of its ideal of feminine beauty.

Both statues are highly coloured as were many of the works of the period. Gold is used in the *Fugen* statue following what is called the *kiri-kane* or ' cut-gold ' method by which very thin strips of gold leaf cut to simulate textile designs are applied to the surface. This takes the place of painted decoration. The technique is a purely Japanese invention, dating back to the Asuka period, and in Fujiwara times it was developed and used extensively. The *Kichijō-ten* is an extraordinarily rich and complicated piece of work—a *tour-de-force* of the assembled block system. The wealth of decoration somewhat impedes an immediate appreciation of the splendid rhythms in which the body is conceived. Originally it stood in a richly coloured shrine where the whole impression must have been more that of a painting than of a work of sculpture. Each section considered separately is a marvel of wood-carving—sleeves, jacket, sash, hands, and the many jewels—which in former times would have been made of metal—are carved in a masterly fashion. Such a complicated piece of work could never have been created by the single-block method. The hands in particular, always a strong point of Japanese wood-carving, are exquisite. The stance is regal and the face, though modelled in the simplest lines with an almost mask-like effect, conveys admirably the benevolence attributed to this goddess. Yet for all its queenly grace, it radiates a seductiveness which implies a complete relaxation of previous sculptural norms.

60. Portrait of *Prince Shōtoku as a Child of Seven*. Wood. Dated 1069. Height 23 inches. Hōryū-ji, Nara.

In spite of these highlights of the assembled-block technique, the dangers of mass-production inherent in such a method are obvious. As soon as a work becomes successful, the possibility of producing a great number of academic copies rapidly tends to stifle originality of thought. Repetition and conventionality robbed the technique of its advantages, and Jōchō's innovations were followed by his successors right down into the last century but with steadily decreasing power.

The Japanese genius for decoration and for beautifying surfaces also had its dangers. The *kiri-kane* method developed in this and the following period to an astonishing degree of skill. It was a technique which, if applied in excess could completely ruin a work by over-decoration. At first, however, it merely added lustre to the surfaces and realism to drapery reflecting the sculptural taste of the age. In later times it has been said that it was only this " fine angularity of shape produced by a knife on metal " which saved some of the works from sentimentality.

The Japanese never neglected their gift for portraiture. A good example is a sculpture of the often portrayed Prince Shōtoku. The statue, dated 1069, is now in the Hōryū-ji Temple (Fig. 60). This idealized portrait of the Prince ' Sage Virtue,' who was mainly responsible for the successful introduction of Buddhism in the 7th century, is supposed to represent him at the age of seven reciting a sutra. An inscription inside the statue records that it was the joint work of the sculptor-priest Enkai and the painter Hata Chitei. Another inscription, dated 1384, states that the hands and clothing were repaired in that year by a sculptor named Shunkei. The life-like quality and the intensity of the face are a remarkable achievement. The painted hair-line coming down in a severe triangle to cover the ears effectively sets off the fine young, sensitive features. Two unusual large loops of hair serve to frame the very long head which appears even longer through the high parting of the hair. The eye of the spectator follows the line of the red robe which hangs over the pedestal and the edges of the upper garment to the serene face strongly outlined by the black hair. The statue is beautifully coloured and housed in a simple black lacquered shrine. It is an intense and very impressive portrait which shows the confidence with which the Japanese were now working quite independently of their Chinese teachers.

The Fujiwara period, so important because of its achievements in sculpture, is also a decisive period in the history of Japanese painting. Its two hundred years saw the first real flowering of a native art which led, in the following period, to the creation of some of the most remarkable paintings of the Far East.

In the middle of the 9th century Buddhism in China suffered a serious persecution and towards the end of the century official relations between Japan and China were broken off. This in itself is an indication of a new Japanese mood of self-reliance, for before this period any such break with China would have been inconceivable. The Japanese quickly realized that the great period of the T'ang had passed and that Chinese power was dis-integrating. The sad last years of the T'ang dynasty must have shown a tiredness and faded quality which did not appeal to the energetic inhabitants of Fujiwara Japan. It was probably at this time that the Japanese for the first time fully understood the fundamental difference between their own aristocratic society and the more egalitarian system of China and the dangers to them inherent in the latter. The Japanese rulers, furthermore, probably did not want their subjects to witness the spectacle of the Chinese Imperial house in decay and eclipse. However, too much can be made of this break in diplomatic relations for monks continued to visit China quite regularly and Japan must have been informed of artistic developments on the mainland. This is borne out by the discovery in 1954 that a sculpture in the Seiryō-ji Temple, Kyoto was brought back to Japan in 987 by the Japanese priest Chōnen.

The elegance of the Fujiwara court encouraged the painters to relax from the forbidding outlook of early Heian art. The world of Prince Genji was more interested in the colour of a robe, the shadows on a brook, the shape of a pretty face, than in the grim aspects of a stern religious art. Its tastes are reflected in a movement away from the grandeur of the 9th and 10th centuries towards the supple tenderness of the 11th and 12th.

A triptych of *Amida and the Twenty-five Bodhisattvas* in the Dai-en-in, Wakayama Prefecture, of which a detail is shown in Figure 61 shows how this change affected Buddhist art. In this typical product of the friendly *Amida* sect, the Buddha is seated in the centre surrounded by numerous bodhisattvas forming a gay circle to welcome the faithful. No more does a grim Fudō threaten the unfortunate sinner from a canvas said to have been painted in blood. Here a jovial, shapely figure with laughing mouth and eyes plays a seductive song of welcome on the lute. The round-faced bodhisattva is dressed in colourful silks—red with a gold design on the knees and diaphanous printed gauzes which swirl rhythmically round the head and shoulders. A feeling of warm humanity pervades this riot of lovely colour. The gold decorations on the neck and arms simulate real jewellery intended to beautify rather than to symbolize. The head is slightly bent as if to keep time with the heavenly music which fills the air around. There is not a single austere line in

61. Detail from a Triptych.
Amida and the Twenty-five Bodhisattvas.
Colour on Silk.
Dai-en-in, Wakayama Prefecture.

62.   Detail from a Scroll painting *The Tale of Genji*.   Late Heian period.
Height 8½ inches.   Tokugawa Museum, Nagoya.

the whole imagery of this delicate figure.   Sculptors endeavoured to match these pictures with corresponding sets of statues, but painting was the true medium for depicting such religious concepts.

Even more important than Buddhist painting is the development of *Yamato-e* ' Japanese painting ' as opposed to *Kara-e* or ' Chinese painting.'   The first recorded use of the word *Yamato-e* occurs in 999, but the distinction between the Japanese and Chinese styles must go back still farther—perhaps as much as a century.   *Yamato-e* denoted paintings dealing with essentially Japanese topics and inspired by Japanese sentiments.   The style originated in the highly coloured paintings of the T'ang dynasty but by this time it was completely Japanized.   According to the Japanese, the subjects of Yamato-e fall into four main groups—landscape scenes depicting the four seasons, views of famous beauty spots, paintings illustrating the tasks of the twelve months of the year, and finally and most important of all, the *monogatari-e* or ' story paintings ' inspired by contemporary literature. The *monogatari-e* are the most interesting.

By far the most famous examples of the fully-developed *Yamato-e* are the fragments of scrolls illustrating incidents from the *Tale of Genji*, of which Figure 62 shows a detail.   The basic technique of scroll painting in which the spectator unrolls section by section of a continuous narrative was, of course, a Chinese invention which the Japanese had known for centuries. As early as the Nara period, such illustrated texts as the E-Ingakyō (see Fig. 42, p. 48) had been a familiar type. The form was now taken up and a style was developed which became an exclusively Japanese art of major importance.

This new secular painting, using material from popular stories, has an intimacy of expression very rarely found in early Chinese painting. The surviving sections of the Genji scrolls are attributed (though by no means with certainty) to a mid-12th century painter, at least a century after Lady Murasaki's death. There are two sets of fragments—one of fifteen sections in the Tokugawa collection and one of four sections in the Masuda collection. They are obviously by different hands and the Tokugawa set is the more interesting.

The arrangement of the scenes, in which a view is given of the interior of rooms by the simple expedient of omitting the roof, is brilliant. Skilfully the eye is led on from one episode to the next by a crowd of people or a sloping rail. In later scrolls when the text with which the Genji scroll is interspersed disappeared, these devices were greatly developed. Mood and tempo are cunningly modulated. The faces, almost hidden by the billowing robes, are so simply drawn as to appear almost characterless but they reflect faithfully the etiquette-bound life of the time. The technique of 'one dash for the eye and one hook for the nose' may well be derived from Chinese models and it is often claimed that it is merely a painter's convention. In fact it may have been a very realistic representation. Etiquette of the time demanded that ladies should wear a thick mask of powder which left little else showing than the slits of heavily pencilled eyes and a small scarlet mouth. Fashions were more important than faces and passions were concealed behind a richly brocaded sleeve. The lack of facial expression in no way detracts from the drama.

Alexander Soper, who has made a close study of these Tokugawa fragments,[1] sees in the compositions a deliberate effort by the artist to express the underlying mood of the scenes by the manner in which he uses his lines. The scene in Figure 62 illustrates the Kashiwagi chapter of the Genji story in which Kashiwagi has fallen in love with Genji's neglected consort Nyōsan. He dies from the hopelessness of his suit. The clashing lines and colours of this section seem to express the confusion in the household caused by Kashiwagi's illness and the calling in of a holy man to exorcise the causes of the sickness. The whole picture conveys an impression of restlessness and agitation while attention is directed towards the monk, the central figure of the scene, by the way the other figures are turned towards him. In other scenes where a calmer mood prevails the lines are quietly ordered into restful horizontals.

The Genji scroll is from every point of view a remarkable and original work. It inspired, directly or indirectly, the large production of e-makimono in the following Kamakura period.

In the crafts a nation's genius often seems to express itself preferably through one material rather than another. Thus, jade is perhaps the material most characteristic of Chinese culture while lacquer seems to suit the taste of the Japanese most naturally. It was in the Fujiwara period that the Japanese craftsmen finally made its technique and expression completely their own.

Prior to the Fujiwara period craftsmen used three methods to decorate lacquer: either they mixed gold and silver dusts with glue and painted them on the lacquer or they mixed

[1] *The Art Bulletin.* Vol. XXXVII, 3. September, 1955.

the dusts with lacquer and similarly applied them. A third technique, called *makie* (pronounced maki-é), was invented by the Japanese. In this they painted the designs in lacquer, sprinkled the metal dusts on it while it was still wet and then smoothed down the whole surface. This is, of course, a method which is related to the earlier techniques but it gave the craftsman greater flexibility in his designs and made his products far more durable. From this period onwards the *maki-e* technique, very skilfully developed, achieved a degree of perfection which no other nation could hope to equal. As a result, the Japanese product became highly esteemed abroad and was much sought after in Korea and even in China.

The finest example of Fujiwara lacquer is generally acknowledged to be a cosmetic box (Fig. 63) which combines the faultless technique and refined taste of the period. The design is composed of segments of wheels rising out of water and may have been inspired by the custom of immersing them in a stream to prevent their drying and splitting. It is worked in *makie* and mother-of-pearl. Two shades of gold were used—plain gold and gold mixed with silver. These alternate on the waves, wheels, and spokes to produce a subtle but lively variety. Some of the wheels are of mother-of-pearl which blends with the precious metals and yet sets them off and holds the design together. The composition, though giving the impression of great freedom, is nevertheless most carefully contrived. In this it is characteristic of the art of the period. For all the elements of Fujiwara taste are here brought together in an harmonious unity—a simple realism unspoiled by over-attention to detail, an easy rhythm and movement, a close relation of form and design and, most important of all, a boldness in execution which refused to be bound by conventionality and tradition. In this earliest of all Japanese cosmetic lacquer boxes, very simple elements are cleverly grouped and varied to produce a design of great clarity, refinement, and vigour.

It is strange that the ceramics of the Fujiwara period did not reflect the distinctive, native Japanese taste as clearly as the other arts. The formal break with China, from which

63. Cosmetic Box.
Gold and mother-of-pearl
on lacquer.
Late Heian period.
9 by 13 by 6½ inches.
Cultural Properties
Protection Commission.

64. *Keman* (detail).
Late Heian period.
11¼ by 12⅞ inches.
Chūson-ji.

the Japanese potters had always received their inspiration, was here felt most seriously and it seems to have left them without direction. A trickle of fine Sung wares still reached Japan but only the aristocratic classes could afford them while poorer households used Japanese made wares. What has been discovered is of little distinction in shape, glaze, or decoration. The craftsmen seem even to have forgotten the technique of the potter's wheel and it seems that they returned for a time to the primitive method of making pots by coiling strands of clay. The products of the time are accordingly heavy and rough. The neglect of ceramics may partly be due to the tremendous development in the quality and output of lacquer-ware which came to take the place of pottery in well-to-do households. Lacquer products were lighter, more brilliant and more durable than any ceramics and as a result, fine pottery or porcelain became less necessary.

The nationalization of styles in the crafts is particularly evident in the metal-work of the Fujiwara period. Silver and gold was more frequently employed for objects produced for the aristocratic families. The pierced work commissioned by the temples matched the

65. Mirror back.
Bronze.
Diameter 9⅝ inches.

elaborate grace of the new architecture and became more and more delicate. Designers paid greater attention to detail in such decorative elements as figures and flowers. Figure 64 shows part of a *keman*, a hanging ornament used in temples. The cord pattern in the centre shows how these *keman* were developed from bunches of real flowers which were later replaced by hide, wool or metal substitutes. The piercing and embossing of these copper plates produces a much more sculptural effect than the work of earlier times. The whole design with its graceful curling flowers and delicately poised figures is of a superb elegance.

The backs of metal mirrors (Fig. 65) show the Japanese sense of design even more clearly. Whereas Chinese style decorations on mirror backs tend to be regular and repetitive, the Japanese tend to be pictorial, treating the whole area as a single unit. In order to achieve a unified effect even the divisions created by the casting, such as the inner circle, were ignored. Graceful autumn plants, bent over in the wind, cross with unconcern under it and onto the border.[1] The cranes move freely and realistically; one carries a twig of pine in its beak, another seems to be standing in water. Technically the casting is of the highest quality and the design full of interest, sensitive and without the monotony and the traces of careless repetition which often spoil later mirror backs. During the Fujiwara years the Japanese became as confident in metal casting as in the manufacture of lacquer and in both the newly discovered native decorative genuis went hand-in-hand with technical mastery.

[1] This distinctively Japanese tendency to ignore borders and frames is a feature of later art.

CHAPTER VI

THE KAMAKURA PERIOD

1185–1392

*

IT says much for the political adroitness of the Fujiwara that they were able to maintain their position long after the effective power had passed from their hands and into those of the big provincial landowners. Some of these almost independent chieftains, the *Daimyō* or ' Great Names,' were themselves off-shoots either of the Fujiwara clan or of the Royal Family for whom no room could be found in the capital or its immediate vicinity. During the Heian period the two greatest rural families were the rival Taira and Minamoto clans. The Fujiwara were only able to hold the balance by offering rewards for good behaviour—generally in the form of tax-free lands—to the more powerful of the warlike local lords. This expedient naturally hastened their own downfall. They had also the church to contend with. For it was an age of power politics, when the great monasteries followed the example of the landowners and built up their own private armies. The Fujiwara could only resist them by appeals for help to either the Minamoto or the Taira, and this in turn weakened their authority still further.

One Emperor tried to over-ride the power of the Fujiwara and to re-establish direct government, but his efforts were short-lived, and he lacked the backing necessary to enforce his reforms. A peculiar feature of the age was the number of abdicated emperors who ran their own courts and administrations sometimes from the monasteries to which they had retired. Their orders often carried more authority than those of the actual emperor. It was only because the local lords were to all effects independent and self-governing and the central authority little more than a charming façade, that the Kyoto regime was, for a time, allowed to continue.

Nevertheless this delicate balance was bound to be disturbed as soon as the final battle for power between the Taira and the Minamoto was joined and decided. At first the Taira were successful, but the Minamoto, under a great leader, Yoritomo, managed to regroup their forces and, after years of civil war which devasted the country, they finally overcame the Taira.

It was the age of the worship of the sword. As a symbol of man's honour, it has been respected down to the present day. In Japan ancient swords are still preserved and the Westerner may admire their unsurpassed technical perfection, their hardness and edge. They are acknowledged to be the finest swords ever made. But he often finds it difficult to share or even understand the emotions with which a Japanese connoisseur will unsheath a polished blade, not even letting his breath fall on it for fear of contamination. Centuries of Japanese history are reflected in its surface and the craftsmen who forged it shaped also the destiny of Japan.

By 1185 the Minamoto had achieved a position of undisputed dominance in the country. The Kamakura regime which they established gave political form to a conviction which had been steadily gaining strength throughout the Fujiwara centuries: that no military ruler was safe in Kyoto. The warring barons respected, and perhaps even secretly envied, the traditions and elegance which surrounded the court and the Royal Family, but they could not afford to allow the weakening effects of court life to sap the vitality of their warriors. This was a lesson which any provincial lord with a practical appreciation of history would have learned. Power in medieval Japan, as in medieval Europe, demanded constant vigiliance. Therefore, when the Minamoto emerged supreme they established a well-disciplined, military headquarters in eastern Japan at Kamakura, some three hundred miles from Kyoto. Kyoto remained the show-place, a capital only in name and inhabited by an impotent court while the effective power emanated from the soldiers in Kamakura.

This was the first time that the centre of government had left the Kyoto-Nara area and the move was significant in so far as it implied a determination, if not to make a conscious break with the past, at least not to allow outworn traditions to prevent necessary changes. Minamoto-no-Yoritomo thought in economical and military rather than in political terms. His main ambition was at first merely to preserve the efficiency of his fighting men and through them to increase his control over the large feudal estates. It is doubtful if he relished the responsibilities which the direction of national affairs entailed. For his primary purpose Kamakura was ideally situated. He considered himself initially only as a *primum inter pares*—as a steady fulcrum in a delicate balance of power. In his need to control men as ruthless as himself, the institution and person of the Emperor were not only useful but indispensable. Steadily, however, the commitments and responsibilities of the *Shōgun*, ' The Great Barbarian-Subduing General ' as his title was, grew. Many able men, seeking opportunities which the privilege-ridden Kyoto court denied them, joined the *baku-fu* or ' military headquarters ' where the new rulers welcomed their administrative talents and learning. Not only did they prove useful in mundane administrative affairs of which a fighting man would grow impatient, but they added those seemingly harmless touches of refinement which often attract even the most warlike regime. They helped to clothe the naked power of the Kamakura rulers with a mantle of respectability and learning. That men like Yoritomo felt a need to do this shows how deeply Chinese traditions had taken root.

The Minamoto, and the Hōjō family who succeeded them, gradually expanded their control over the feudal domains, and organized an efficient administration with a strict legal code to enforce it. It is an interesting sidelight on the complicated nature of the Japanese hierarchy at this time that the Hōjō regents, acting for the military dictators who followed Yoritomo, were themselves descended from the Taira clan defeated by the Minamoto in their fight for supremacy. For one hundred years they were the effective power in the land. It has been said that Japan in the 13th century presented " the astonishing spectacle of a state at the head of which stood a titular emperor whose vestigal functions had been usurped by an abdicated emperor, and whose real power was nominally delegated to an hereditary military dictator but was actually wielded by an hereditary adviser of that dictator."[1]

[1] Sansom, op. cit. p. 300.

It was not long, of course, before the attractions and pleasures of court life at Kyoto began to undermine the simplicity of Kamakura life; yet for a period the dictators remained rough, able, and, on the whole, fair administrators.

The arts responded to the outlook of the new regime in Kamakura. The sophistication of Kyoto life reflected in its decorative elegance was now regarded as effiminate and weak.

From such a radical break one might have been expected a completely new style to emerge. Instead, what can be called a renaissance of Nara styles took place. The revival of interest in Nara sculptures was stimulated by the fact that the civil wars from 1180 onwards had caused great damage, especially by fire, to the temples in the old capital and to their sculptural treasures. The Hall of the Great Buddha in the Tōdai-ji, was burned down by Taira troops in 1180, and the Great Buddha itself remained exposed to the elements for fifteen years until the hall was rebuilt in 1195 (this was again burned down in 1567 and only rebuilt in 1709, see p. 49). The restoration of Buddhist sculptures of the Nara period provided work and experience for a large number of artists. How great an influence this kind of work exerted is clear from the great popularity enjoyed by skilful contemporary reproductions of classical masterpieces, a number of which have survived.

However, there was a very real difference between the spirit which animated the Nara sculptors and those of Kamakura. The Nara workers, while retaining the human character-istics of the bodies inhabited by their gods, had idealized and spiritualized them. The Kamakura artists, by their use of a wider vocabulary and above all by the perfection of their modelling with its love of natural forms, emphasized the human and personal qualities of their models. If the Japanese craftsmen neglected the idealization of the Nara masterpieces, in returning to the human modelling of the Nara period, they were at least picking up the threads of their most fruitful tradition. Under the influence of the past they produced, from the late 12th to the 13th centuries, some remarkable sculptural works. With them Buddhist sculpture turned full circle—and expired. After this brilliant renaissance the art stagnated in fixed forms which steadily deteriorated over the centuries into insensitive repetitions. It is tempting to draw a parallel with the early sculpture of the Renaissance in Europe and the later armies of marble figures which fill so many galleries in our stately country homes.

Sculptures by eminent craftsmen known by name are more numerous in the Kamakura period. A number of guilds of sculptors, or *bussho*, grew up on the pattern of the *Shichijō Bussho* which Jōchō had established in the 11th century. This same *Shichijō Bussho* under its master Kōkei, a direct descendant of Jōchō, produced many of the finest surviving works of the period. This school had its headquarters in Nara, while most of the others, which had been formed during the Fujiwara period, had their workshops in Kyoto. Schools and artists strove to outdo each other in skill and artistry. The atmosphere in Japan, with each temple competing for the services of famous sculptors like Unkei, must have resembled that in Italy during the High Renaissance. Unfortunately fewer records have been preserved from the 13th century in Japan than from the 16th century in Italy. However, as in Europe, the emergence of the individual meant more freedom for the artist in so far as it enabled him to impose his own concepts. He became, to a degree, free from the stifling restrictions of iconography. But independence brings its own obligations: he now had to satisfy a public and attract patronage.

At the same time artistic imagination continued to find its most productive field in portrait sculpture which was unhampered by religious dogmas. The Chinese continued to regard sculpture, as opposed to painting, as a relatively lowly craft, and important individual artists never emerged from the ranks of craftsmen.   In Japan, the unmistakable imprint of a single artist's personality revitalized the art of the age.

The conservatism of the artists of the Shichijō School at Nara accounted for their comparative lack of popularity during the Fujiwara and at the beginning of the Kamakura periods. Kōkei's work in the Kōfuku-ji Temple, while not yet showing the fully developed characteristics of the Kamakura style, give evidence that the Shichijō Guild was not content simply to supply graceful works corresponding to Fujiwara ideals. But it is with the work of Kōkei's son, Unkei, that this school began to dominate the artistic scene.

Despite his fame and output, Unkei's exact dates are not known. His works, however, show that he was active from *ca.* 1175 to 1218, a period of over forty years, during which he held an unrivalled position. For him sculpture was the expression through realism of solemnity, dignity, and monumentality. Already in the *Dainichi* statue in the Enjō-ji

66. *Dainichi Nyōrai* by Unkei.
Wood. Kamakura period.
Height 39¾ inches.
Enjō-ji, Nara.

67. *Mūchaku and Seshin* by Unkei.
Wood.   Kamakura period.   Heights 6 feet 2 inches and 6 feet 2½ inches.   Kōfuku-ji, Nara.

Temple at Nara (Fig. 66), done in 1175–6 before he was thirty and at the very end of the Fujiwara period, although elements of esotericism remain in the gesture of the hand, it is possible to recognize the beginnings of a return to the calm, compassionate expression which characterizes the Nara masterpieces. The simple halo behind the figure, in its uncompromising plainness, is itself an indication of the artist's aim. The crystal inset eyes—a feature of Kamakura work—heighten the human effect. The draped knees are powerfully modelled and provide a firm base for the stern set of the body, arms, and head. The whole composition is conceived as a regular triangle centred on the hands and the sculptor has subordinated everything to this basic concept.

This *Dainichi Nyōrai* shows also influences from the sculpture of Sung China in the soft, fleshy feeling of the body, the beauty of the face and the tall coiffure. The Japanese had re-established official contact with China at the end of the Fujiwara period and scholars have noted a certain similarity between Chinese paintings and Japanese sculpture of this time.

We see the fully developed style of Unkei and his school in two of Japan's finest works of realistic sculpture—those of the priests *Mūchaku and Seshin* (Figs. 67 and 68) who occupy positions as attendants to the *Maitreya*, the main object of worship in the North Octagonal Hall of the Kōfuku-ji Temple. These large, over life-size figures (each over 6 ft. tall) are imaginary portraits of the Indian priests and brothers Asanga and Vasubandhu, who, according to tradition, lived a thousand years after the *nirvana* of the Buddha and formulated the teachings of the Hossō sect to which the Kōfuku-ji belongs. There were originally nine statues in the group. The project was started in 1208 under the superintendence of Unkei and with the co-operation of his six sons and two pupils. It represents the perfection of Japanese classicist portrait sculpture. The figures are carved completely in the round and the bodies give the impression of regal power. The drapery is modelled with complete naturalism and splendid variety. The heavy folds swing across the bodies from left to right in a weighty rhythm and fall with natural ease into long sleeves. The heaviness of the robes acts as a perfect foil to the intense faces—particularly that of the *Mūchaku* figure with its emaciated features and piercing eyes. The bones and muscles of breast and neck stand out powerfully, and the heads are poised in attitudes of compassion. The variations in the deep-set eyes, sensitive brows, strong lips, and large noses give each of these figures an appealing individuality. No muscular exertion is expressed in either but they convey a deep latent strength by the tenseness of the neck and hands, the slight assymmetry of the shoulders and the way they hold their heads. Through both of them runs a vitality which, unlike that in other works of this period, is implicit rather than, explicit.

Let us compare these figures with the earlier seated statue of *Priest Ganjin* (Fig. 36) which was made in the Nara period. The three statues belong to different ages but the same desire to portray inner compassion has inspired them. All three express pain as well as triumph but where the earlier statue sits calmly locked in contemplation, eyes turned inwards to the soul, the two later works look outwards towards suffering humanity. The one having risen above the human condition is sublime, the others having conquered the world remain human. The latter share the troubles of the world, preaching their doctrine of salvation to their fellow men. The trials of the Fujiwara wars are mirrored in their powerful, almost pugnacious faces. It is easy to imagine them being called to arms and wielding the sword when the occasion demanded. If the Nara statues represent the triumph of the spiritual over the material, those of Kamakura show the victory of humanity over the gods. They illustrate the differing outlook of Buddhism in their respective periods and at the same time the fundamental change in techniques. In the later figures, the carvers are greatly interested in a faithful reproduction of physical details whereas in the *Ganjin* figure they are hardly concerned with them. The drapery above all gives the clue to Kamakura work. It is no longer simply a necessary covering glossed over in a graceful but perfunctory manner and hardly distinguishable from the body. Here the folds are those of real clothes with a surface quite distinct from that of the bodies over which they are draped and rendered with a delight for their own sake. One is almost tempted to reach out and touch the cloth from which they are cut.

The sculptor has varied the two figures by lifting their opposite shoulders and by advancing their opposite feet. A slight twist of the hand, a different sway of the robe and above all a contrasting nobility of feature and expression reveal the subtlety of their maker. The hands perform a gesture of benediction almost as eloquent in expression as the faces. Here is no complicated iconography to appeal only to the initiated; in its place an almost overpowering sincerity sweeps the spectator into a world where the force of individual personalities is used to express spiritual values. Such figures would cause no surprise in the sanctuary of an austere Christian order. They rank among the world's most noble and appealing works and epitomize the Japanese sculptor's gifts for portraiture. Nothing comparable has survived from Chinese art.

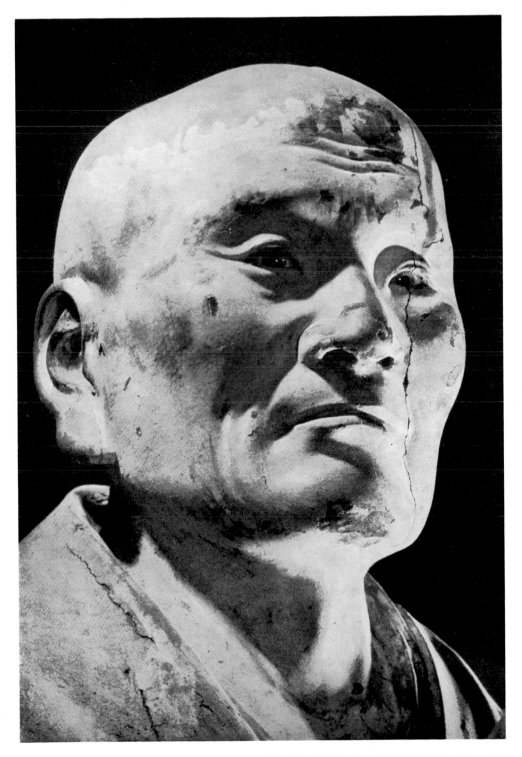

68. Detail of the head of *Mūchaku* in Figure 67.

A short walk through the streets and parks of Nara from the Kōfuku-ji to the Tōdai-ji
Temple is hardly enough to prepare the visitor for the different, almost shocking impact of
another pair of statues also by Unkei, Kaikei, and others of his school.   It hardly seems
possible that the hands which carved the calm *Mūchaku* and *Seshin* could also create the
two huge writhing *Kongō Rikishi*, ' the *Vajra* Bearers,' (*vajra* is a weapon symbolizing a
thunderbolt to strike down the evil doer) (Fig. 69).   These remarkable creations, nearly
27 ft. high, are the largest of all the wooden sculptures in Japan.   According to the temple
records, they were fashioned and assembled in the incredibly short period of less than three
months and finished in 1203, five years before the two priests.   Exposure to the elements
in the portals of the main gate of the temple where they stand has resulted in considerable
damage to their surfaces but, considering the 750 years which have passed since their
creation and the material of which they are made, they are remarkably well-preserved.
The figure on the east has its lips closely shut expressing thereby its inhaling power or
latent might and the other with its mouth wide open symbolizes its exhaled power.   These
two figures in their violent movement invite comparison with some of the earlier divine
protectors of Buddhism such as the clay *Vajrapani* in the same temple.   The two later
Kongō Rikishi embody the Kamakura predilection for violent, exaggerated action.   Here
every plane is conceived in terms of restlessness and movement and in this they differ
basically from the earlier *Vajrapani*.   The modelling of the torsos is so rich that the eye is
never allowed to rest.   They are intended to terrify and this they do by the ferocity of their
facial expressions, by the muscularity of their bodies and above all by a tense, poised swiftness
which is conveyed by their poses and by the swirl of draperies round the shoulders.   These
draperies, as well as heightening the effect of movement, serve also to lighten the bulk of
the huge figures.   Originally the statues were brightly painted, the heads in brown, the
ribbons in white, and the exposed parts of the bodies in red.   The clubs or *vajra* retain part
of their gold leaf and some of the 13th century decoration can still be seen on the skirts.
Both have been extensively repaired but much of the originals remains and the powerful
hands, in which the tension is consummated, are untouched.   It is as if Unkei and his colla-
borators were determined to carry *à outrance* the realistic tendencies of the times.   But
for all their size and exaggerated energy, towering above the mortals who must pass them
to enter the temple, they are extremely well-balanced.   Spiritual and physical power are
admirably combined.   When the temple ordered such figures, it naturally demanded that
they should equal the Great Buddha in size and impressiveness.   Unkei has tried to match
the monumental feeling of the 8th century bronze casters with his fierce expressions and
bunched muscles.   No doubt he took equal pride in the complex detail which taxed and
displayed his sculptural virtuosity.   He was also consciously responding to the spirit of the
Kamakura period in which a direct appeal to the worshipper was more effective than an
intellectual or spiritual approach, a simple warning better understood than an indirect
exhortation.   In expressing active rather than latent power, Unkei produced figures which
rough men in an age of violence could appreciate.   It is true that the Japanese love of
exaggeration has often run away with them.   Yet some degree of exaggeration is indispensable to a vivid representation of movement, and some of the most powerful and original
works of Japanese art owe much of their effect to it.
   The Tōdai-ji was at this time being rebuilt and about to enter the second great period
of its history.   Emperor Shōmu had founded it in A.D. 743 " for the protection of the
country and the welfare of the nation," and throughout the centuries the great sanctuary

69. *Kongō Rikishi* by Unkei, Kaikei and pupils.
Wood. Kamakura period. Height 26 feet 7 inches. Tōdai-ji, Nara.

had always been what might be called a 'National Temple.' From the time of its foundations in the 8th century, when it was placed at the head of the provincial temples and nunneries, it always closely reflected the national temper. It had always responded to the styles and influences of China and, when in the previous period communications with China were interrupted, the Tōdai-ji seems to have remained for a time static—as if in a vast backwater. In its second great period, now approaching, the huge Buddha damaged by fire was under repair and Unkei, inspired by the ancient works of the Nara period all around him, was producing his masterpieces in the old capital.

To look at the wooden sculptures of Unkei is to understand what Langdon Warner meant when he said of Japanese wood carving, " Stubborn, insisting on its own run of grain, sudden with knots, in the hands of a man who respects it, wood helps the carver to unexpected beauties of line. Although Japanese modellers of the eighth century have left us statues as glorious as any the world has produced in those other mediums, wood was perhaps, after all, what fitted the genius of the race. We see it persisting through the ages, shifting its shapes with the changes of fashion, flourishing, atrophying, decaying and then, of a sudden, alive with new purpose and fresh form under the knives of another generation. Down from the aloof Korean beauty of the Chūgūji and the Yumedono Kannons, through the flowering of Nara times, lapsing for a century, over-delicate for nearly three, we find statues in wood to charm us till Unkei, in the thirteenth century brings up the line with trumpets."[1]

The restoration of the Tōdai-ji was carried out under the determined leadership of a great monk, Chōgen, then just returned from his third visit to China. The opening of China once more stimulated religious thought and new dogmas swept Japan, completely revolutionizing Buddhist theory. The Fujiwara *Shingon* and *Tendai* beliefs, which promised salvation to a limited number of initiates, had already begun to lose favour and the process was accelerated during the Kamakura years. Henceforth Buddhism was to become an essentially popular religion. The most important of the new sects was the *Jōdo* or ' Pure Land ' sect whose introduction was noted in the previous chapter. Members of the Royal Family, the court, other sects and even hard-bitten *samurai* at Kamakura accepted the teachings of the *Jōdo* from its great exponent Hōnen (1133–1212). The commoners were particularly enthusiastic—especially those among them who were by now sufficiently educated to read Buddhist literature. The popularization of the Japanese phonetic script opened a world of learning to those who could not master the infinitely more complicated Chinese characters. But Hōnen's teachings struck at the root of the privileges enjoyed by the older clergy and they attacked and persecuted him. They argued that the easy means of salvation offered by this reformer led to the corruption of morals among those who followed the letter and not the spirit of the teaching. But the *Jōdo* offered a solution which was too attractive and spread too rapidly to be restrained by the jealous clergy of the entrenched sects, especially when their own immorality was often so blatantly conspicuous. Shinran (1173–1262) the founder of the *Jōdo Shin* sect even opposed the celibacy of monks and simplified still further the ' Pure Land ' theories.

Dangerous opponents of the ' Pure Land ' were the followers of the Lotus Sect, the *Hokkeshū*, founded by Nichiren (1222–82), who had been a *Shingon* priest. He rejected and attacked the ' Pure Land ' sect and its teachings as vehemently as all other interpretations. For him the way to salvation lay exclusively in the words of the Lotus Sutra, which, he claimed, embodied in purest distillation all the Buddha's teachings. Through this scripture any man or woman could identify himself with the Bhuddahood. This dogma was in a sense a return to the old *Tendai*, although now coloured by popular Buddhism. Again the only action required of the believer was a simple repetition; he need simply repeat the title of the Sutra. The vigour and invective of Nichiren's sermons appealed to the fighting men of Kamakura and his prophecies concerning the Mongol invasion brought him an easy fame. Women also flocked to hear him, for he alone offered salvation to women on an equal footing with men. Exile and threats of death failed to shake his faith and he finally returned in triumph to Kamakura. The universal appeal of these teachings encouraged the sculptors to produce statues which would appeal to believers from even the humblest walks of life.

These new sects, however, had to contend with yet another and more significant new Buddhist dogma directly introduced from China—the *Zen*. The foundations of the sect were already very ancient. In A.D. 520, a great Indian Buddhist missionary Bodhidharma, whose name means ' Law of Enlightenment ' brought the teaching from India to China where it is known as *Ch'an*. It is a highly mystical concept which gained great popularity in China incorporating there much of the popular esoteric beliefs of *Taoism*. Known in Japan as early as the Nara period, it gained its main following from 1200 onwards and

[1] Langdon Warner, *The Enduring Art of Japan.* Harvard, 1952.

particularly at Kamakura itself. The word *Ch'an* comes from the Chinese transliteration of the Sanscrit work *dhyana* which can be translated, although with only partial accuracy, as 'meditation.' Its teachings as formulated in China are most concisely summed up in words attributed to Bodhidharma himself as "A special transmission outside the scriptures; No dependence upon words and letters; Pointing directly to the heart (or intuitive mind) of man; Seeing into one's own nature and the attainment of Buddhahood." The third sentence is perhaps the most important one. Only by introspection and sudden enlightenment could man achieve the truth; explanations, scriptures, ceremonies, priestly introduction, worship—all were useless. The stern discipline it demanded of its adherents appealed to the *samurai*, and the saint-like frugality it encouraged was peculiarly fitted to the rigourous standards of early Kamakura life.

The philosophers of *Zen* have written surprisingly lengthy works to explain that *Zen* cannot be transmitted by words. This irrefutable position has naturally enough always infuriated its more vulnerable opponents. But for all its incommunicability by words, the teachings of this sect had the most profound influence on the art of both China and Japan. Its introspective, intuitive methods could be applied directly to art resulting in a mystical, highly imaginative approach which could not fail to enrich the artists' vision. The influence of *Zen* on art was particularly strong on painting (see p. 117). Since the followers of the *Zen* sect did not believe in the value of icons, religious imagery in sculpture declined in popularity. But a number of portrait sculptures produced at this period are of exceptional interest. The first is the portrait statue of the priest *Chōgen* (Figs. 71 and 72), mentioned above as the driving force in the restoration of the Tōdai-ji Temple at Nara. Originally he had been a *Shingon* priest but he left this sect to join Hōnen and help in the spreading of *Jōdo* principles. He was already 61 when the Emperor put him in charge of the restorations and he died in 1206 at the age of 86 after completing the great work. His portrait is a work in the best tradition of priestly portraits of which we have already illustrated a number. The artist's name is not known but he probably belonged to the Shichijō school of Unkei, Kaikei, Jōkei, Kōben, and others active at Nara. The statue was probably made at the beginning of the 13th century shortly before the priest's death. It is a most powerful uncompromising likeness, the portrait of a grimly-determined old man driven by the strength of an indomitable will to achieve a revival of the faith. The emaciated face with one eye half-closed is that of the bigot; the pugnacious attitude with head thrust forward, that of the zealot. The violent spiritual energy in the cadaverous face is so powerful that the spectator almost shrinks before it. The rosary seems almost out of place in his hands, but just as it was the centre of his faith in life, so it also forms the calm pivot for this image of restless, undiminished energy.

The contrast between the soft lines of the robe, the tender hands, and the hard outlines of the face emphasizes the tortured intensity of the work. No more lucid demonstration could be given of the extent to which the Japanese sculptors were prepared to go in their search for truthful likeness. The chisel has been used almost to a degree of cruelty. The portrait has an air of finality about it beyond which it is difficult to imagine any further development.

The British Museum has recently acquired a sculpture from about the end of the 13th century[1] which is in the best tradition of these Kamakura priest portraits (Fig. 72). It is rare

---

[1] Said by some Japanese scholars to be later. Cf. W. Watson "A Buddhist Patron of the Refectory," *Oriental Art*, Vol. III, No. 1.

70. *Priest Chōgen.*
Wood.
Kamakura period.
Height
2 feet 6½ inches.
Tōdai-ji, Nara.

that they were allowed to leave Japan. The gesso and lacquer which originally covered it have now disappeared and parts have been restored, the chest somewhat clumsily. The robes are most skilfully worked and the face has a fine tranquillity of expression. However, something of the intensity and austerity of the earlier statues is lost and the face is somewhat idealized, almost romanticized. It almost looks as if the head and robes were carved by different sculptors. Yet it is a most impressive ensemble which shows Japanese religious wood sculpture in its last great moment.

To the Kaikei-Unkei style also belongs the colossal bronze *Amida Buddha* at Kamakura itself (Fig. 73). It was begun in 1252 and completed by 1255 but strangely enough, nothing is known for certain of its creator. Including the pedestal, it is 42 ft. 6 inches high and is modelled on the *Great Buddha* of the Tōdai-ji, Nara. The handsome face radiates a compassionate calmness. Although technically perfect, it has been criticized on purely academic grounds for a certain lack of proportion; the Japanese say that the legs are too 'flat.' The proportions may owe something to the fact that it was originally housed, and therefore intended to be seen, in a large wooden hall. This suffered badly from earthquakes and tidal waves until it was finally swept away in 1495. Since then the Buddha has remained exposed to the elements, and as Kamakura is by the sea, these have been fairly damaging. Over the centuries the huge statue has acquired an attractive patina. Unfortunately, in the years succeeding the last war, a modern snack-bar and similar tourist

71. Detail of Figure 70.

72. *Buddhist Priest*. Wood (originally lacquered). Kamakura period. Height 32 inches. British Museum.

attractions were placed almost at its feet completely destroying the atmosphere of the precincts. One hopes that these monstrosities will be removed.

When the Japanese re-established relations with the mainland at the beginning of the Kamakura era, it was possible for priests like Chōgen to visit China frequently. But the China from which Japan was now to draw inspiration differed considerably from that of earlier times. The glories of the T'ang dynasty (618–906) were long past. After the mid-T'ang period, moral and political weaknesses destroyed the grandeur of that virile age. After a half-century of civil war the country was reunified under the Sung dynasty (960–1279). The Sung emperors ruled over the whole of China for only a comparatively short time. Under pressure from the warlike Tartar tribes in the north, they were forced back south of the Yangtze River where they established the Southern Sung dynasty, expending the energies and wealth of the country in fruitless efforts to recover the lost northern half of their kingdom. Eventually the Sung dynasty was completely crushed by the Mongols who overran China and established the Yüan dynasty (1280–1368).

In spite of their later military and political failures, the Sung centuries produced what many historians consider to be the finest artistic achievements of the Chinese race. It was an age in which Confucianism was re-interpreted and revitalized. Through the invention of printing, Confucianism and all literary achievements found a broader public. Daring reforms were attempted to put the country on a sound economic footing. Learning and the arts flourished. During the Sung centuries the temper of the Chinese people was fundamentally calm and philosophical. The search for spiritual values behind material phenomena engrossed all men of artistic inclination. Thus a poet and painter like Su Tung-p'o could say " . . . the inner law of things can be comprehended only by the highest human spirits " and dwell at length on the need for an artist to satisfy the soul of man by identifying himself with nature. But the Sung ideals—elegance, perfect proportions, and a sensual, relaxed dreaminess—were incompatible with the vigorous art demanded by a more violent age such as the Kamakura. The coming of the Mongols destroyed the Sung introspective mood for ever.

The Kamakura period spans the second half of the Sung and the whole of the Mongol or Yüan dynasty. Both left a deep impression on Japanese art, though in very different ways.

Sung painting and its influence on Japan will be discussed later. Sung influence on sculpture is well represented by the flying angels in the Kōfuku-ji. It is interesting to compare a typical Chinese Sung period *Kuanyin* (Jap. *Kannon*) in Figure 74 with one of the Kōfuku-ji *Angels* (Fig. 75), which shows the same relaxed pose, fleshy face, and appreciation of body surfaces. The similarities are equally apparent in larger-scale figures such as the *Shō Kannon* in the Kuramadera Temple (Fig. 76) or in the 14th century *Suigetsu Kannon* in the Tokei-ji. But the Japanese, though accepting the sensuous curves and mellifluous drapery of the Sung carvers, never feminized their works quite as much as the Chinese. Discipline in Japan at that time was perhaps too severe to allow a complete relaxation and the statues, for all their beauty, preserve a strong, dignified core. The *Zen* influence on Japanese sculpture is seen at its best in the portraiture of the Kamakura period. The practice of making images of gods was not in harmony with the spirit of Buddhism as interpreted by *Zen* adepts but they saw no objection to recording in wood the likenesses of great teachers. A most powerful statue of this type is the *Basu Sennin* (Sanscrit: *Vasu Bandhu*) in the Sanjū-Sangen-dō, Kyoto (Fig. 78). This is one of the twenty-eight

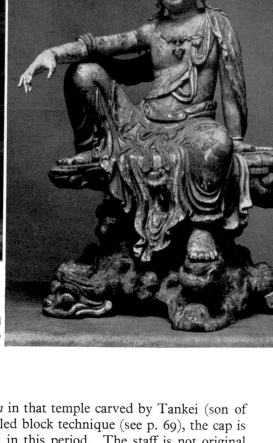

73. *Amida Buddha.* Bronze.
Kamakura period. Height 42 feet 6 inches.
Kōtoku-in, Kanagawa (near Kamakura).

74. (Right). *Kuanyin* (Jap. Kannon). Wood. Sung period
(A.D. 960–1268). Victoria and Albert Museum, London.

protecting spirits of the *Thousand-armed Kannon* in that temple carved by Tankei (son of Unkei) in 1254. It is constructed in the assembled block technique (see p. 69), the cap is separate and the eyes are crystal insets as usual in this period. The staff is not original but probably a faithful restoration. The emaciated face consists of little more than skin stretched over a skull. A few rags encircle the loins and the legs seem hardly able to bear the weight of the emaciated body. But the inlaid eyes shine as if with brilliant religious fervour. Here, too, spiritual energy is contrasted with physical decay though less painfully than in the *Chōgen.* The position of the body as it leans forward aided by the staff looks at first surprisingly simple but is, in fact, most complex. The balance is skilfully planned to create the impression of halting movement and insistence. How far the sculptors had travelled from the smooth softness of the Fujiwara ideals!

Another example of this realistic mid-13th century spirit is the extraordinary figure of *Kūya* by Kōshō (the fourth son of Unkei) (Fig. 77). Kūya was one of the most powerful priests of the *Jōdo* sect whose principal means of salvation, it will be remembered, was to

75.   *Angel.*
Wood.   Kamakura period.
Kōfuku-ji, Nara.

76.   *Shō Kannon* by Jōkei dated 1229.
Wood.   Height 5 feet 8½ inches.
Kuramadera.

77. *Kūya* by Kōshō.
Wood.
Kamakura period.
Height 3 feet 10 inches.
Rokuharamitsu-ji, Kyoto.

call endlessly on the name of Amida Buddha. He is shown as a typical travelling monk carrying a gong to call attention to his arrival. A string of little Amida Buddha figures is shown emerging from his mouth, as a way of representing the essentials of his teaching in plastic form. The modelling of this statue foreshadows the thousands of well-carved, small wood statues of priests and peasants which can still be found wherever oriental art works of a lesser order are sold.

The trend towards portrait-likeness and away from religious sculpture was encouraged by the vanities of important men in secular life. If priests could be honoured by a portrait why not they as well—especially when, as so often, they provided the finance for the temple? The seated figure in Figure 79 is of *Uesugi Shigefusa*, founder of the Uesugi clan, one of the families appointed as advisors to the *Shōgun* in Kamakura. The dictator gave this family lands in the Kyoto-Nara area and it thus became one of the strong-points of his influence in both the old and new capital areas. The Meigetsuin, Kamakura, where the statue is housed, is a monastery belonging to a *Zen* temple supported by the Uesugi family. The statue, which dates from the second half of the 14th century, contrasts strongly with the usual religious figures of the time. The ceremonial dress and head-gear of a *samurai*

78. *Basu Sennin*. Wood. Kamakura period. Height 5 feet 9 inches. Sanjū-Sangen-dō, Kyoto.

79. Portrait of *Uesugi Shigefusa*.
Wood. Kamakura period.
Height 2 feet 3 inches.
Meigetsu-in, Kanagawa.

are purely Japanese and owe nothing to Continental example. Such a worldly type of portrait sculpture is uniquely Japanese. The smooth but incisive lines of the stiff, inflated formal dress so carefully arranged direct the attention to the stern hard features of the successful warrior. The back is ram-rod straight, the eyes are calculating; he could equally well be wearing armour. With its ample proportions, broad shoulders and balloon-shaped trousers, the Uesugi figure is the most compelling of a group of such secular figures which have survived. The type appears frequently in paintings of the period, (Cf. Fig. 83) but the sculptural interpretation has an amplitude which no painting could reproduce.

To the second half of the 13th century also belongs the remarkable figure of a goddess *Benzaiten* (Sanscript: Sarasvati) a female divinity of speech and learning, generally depicted as a beautiful woman (Fig. 80). She was normally shown dressed in splendid robes with a stringed instrument in her hands. As a nude figure, however, she represents the climax of the Kamakura tendency to bestow worldly qualities on its gods. Seldom has the study of the female form, to which we in the west are so accustomed, been carried further. The female Japanese body with its smooth lines and almost childlike softness is most faithfully represented. It is impossible not to recognize a certain element of eroticism in it. This frank sensuality is so unusual in earlier Japanese art that it is difficult to trace its antecedents. In one step we are transported from the world of religion to that of man, from reminders of the corruptibility of the flesh to visions of its desirability. One is reminded of the gay yet innocent seductiveness of the *devas* in the paradise paintings of the Heian period (see Fig. 61) which the sculptor has here, with a different emphasis, transposed into wood. He surely modelled the face on some beauty of the day; it cannot be simply an idealization. The attention to detail also suggests a new interest in anatomy; the studies of muscular contortions in some other works of the period such as the huge *Kongō Rikishi* are further examples of this tendency.

The Fujiwara and Kamakura periods saw the full expression of the native Japanese character in sculpture. After the Kamakura period the art of religious sculpture declined rapidly. So much so that Japanese histories of sculpture generally ignore what was produced. How can one explain this decline?

The return to Nara ideals, allied with greater technical skill in realistic modelling produced many great works but its seems in the end to have had a fossilizing effect. The sculptors looked back instead of forwards to a possible new enrichment of Japanese art. The desire for realism degenerated into a search by lesser crafstmen for sensational detail in which the Japanese love of exaggeration found limitless possibilities for expression.

Mannerism is the word which springs immediately to the mind in considering later works of Japanese (and Chinese) sculpture. Kenneth Clark, in his recent work on ' The Nude ' says " what we call mannerism has its origin in the expressive distortions of Michelangelo to which, in the female nude, must be added the elegance of Parmigiano." It is interesting to draw a parallel in Japanese art where we can substitute Unkei for Michelangelo and the anonymous carvers of the *Benzaiten* figures for Parmigiano. In the East, as

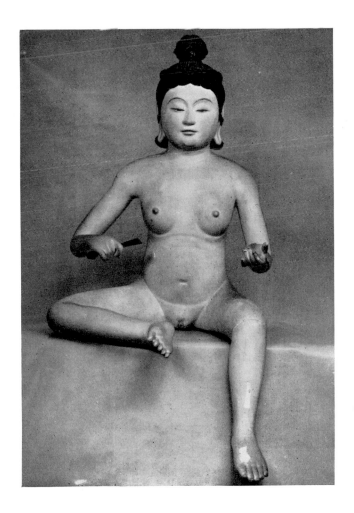

80. *Benzaiten.*
Wood.
Kamakura period.

in the West, mannerism in the female form expressed itself in countless graceful figures (notably *Kannons*).

Religious sculptures, of course, were made in later centuries, but few can compare with the earlier works either in workmanship or inspiration. The mass-production of traditional religious types deprived the artists of the incentives to seek new forms in Buddhist images. If some new inspiration had arrived from China, Japanese sculpture might have risen to fresh heights but the centuries of the Yüan and Ming dynasties made no great contribution to the art. After the Sung dynasty, Chinese sculpture languished and died; the Japanese crafstmen turned to other materials and sought inspiration outside the religious world which had hitherto absorbed them.

The pictures of the Buddhist painters equally expressed the teachings of the new sects. As the 'Pure Land' sect with its belief in the all-powerful mercy of the Amida Buddha spread throughout Japan, a new interest arose for painting scenes called in Japanese *Raigō* in which the Buddha is shown descending in all his radiant glory to meet the believer. In the Kamakura interpretations of these scenes there is a new sense of closeness to paradise; the divinity seems to be directly encouraging the efforts of the believer to achieve

81. Section of the handscroll *A Handbook on Hungry Ghosts*. Ink and colour on paper. Kamakura period. Height 10⅞ inches. Commission for the Protection of Cultural Properties, Tokyo.

82. Section of a
handscroll *A Handbook
on Illnesses*.
Ink and colour on paper.
Kamakura period.
Height 10¼ inches.
Sekidō Collection,
Aichi Prefecture.

salvation. It should be noted that the gods descending to meet the faithful often shed their light over a purely Japanese landscape.

While expressing the hopes of the new Buddhism, painting was employed also to depict its fears—the deterrents to sin, the hells awaiting the wicked. But these fears were represented in a new way. In the previous age a grim *Fudō* or a menacing guardian stood ready to strike down the offender. These avenging spirits were far removed from the world of man. But with the rise of the 'Pure Land' sect, even these darker gods were humanized. The belief in the transmigration of souls provided more scope for the horrific side of the Eastern artistic imagination than even the hell of Christianity did for the West. The Amidist, for instance, envisaged various postmortem conditions for the soul of man— infernal hell, the hell of hungry ghosts, that of the animals, the human world, and finally the world of the divinities. A *Handbook on Hungry Ghosts* (Fig. 81) in the Tokyo National Museum in places outdoes the imagination of a Dante or a Bosch. The *Handbook on Illnesses* (Fig. 82) illustrates man suffering from the various diseases of the flesh. The example reproduced here show a man suffering from loose teeth. The picture, a masterly combination of mockery and pathos, is full of a rather brutal humour.

With what emotional resonance the figures are contrasted and how expressive is the brushwork which depicts them! The woman, a sturdy peasant swift to mock the misfortunes of others, kneels in relaxed amusement. She points an admonitory finger at the sufferer who sits in agony clutching his stomach, his legs drawn up in convulsions, to suggest that his teeth have poisoned his whole system. The man's eyes seem to be trying to follow his fingers down his own throat. For all its jovial sadism, this is no secular plaisanterie; rather is it the portrait of a sinner—of a glutton with his heavily-loaded plates hardly touched before him. The artist has managed to convey something of the man's pique at not being able to touch his tempting meal. The chopsticks point tantalizingly at him. At any moment one feels the woman will take them up herself.

The drama is the simple, eternal one of the unexpected and its effect is produced by a remarkable economy of means. With what apparent relief the artist has turned away from the mask-like figures of the Fujiwara time as seen in the Genji scroll to the much more intriguing animated faces of the Kamakura man-in-the-street! There is nothing in Chinese art to compare with this intimate vignette which comes surprisingly close to Western ideas. It is an astute comment on plebian life of Kamakura times by a Japanese painter with the common touch of a Breughel.

The portraits of the period are quite different. They, too, are essentially Japanese and, like the portrait sculptures, show how the nobles, although lay figures, have come to share

83. *Portrait of
Minamoto Yoritomo,*
by Fujiwara Takanobu.
Colour on silk.
Kamakura period.
4 ft. 7 in. by 3 ft. 8 in.
Jingo-ji, Kyoto.

84. *Fan*, Ink and colour on paper. Kamakura period. Height 10 inches. Tokyo National Museum.

the stage with the divinities. The portrait of Minamoto Yoritomo (Fig. 83) the founder of the new regime, is a typical product. The paintings of the hells are anonymous and probably the work of some gifted artisan priest; but the name of the painter of Yoritomo is known. He was a certain Fujiwara Takanobu (1142–1205) famous at that time for the truth of his likenesses. The conception of this masterpiece is in keeping with the severe character of the sitter. His dress is austere and dark, the face white and almost luminous against the sombre background. Looking sideways out of the picture, the eyes of this warrior remind us of an *Aka Fudō* and, as if to dispel all doubt about the man's fundamental character, a sword-hilt peers obtrusively from beneath his voluminous ceremonial dress. The dramatic rigidness of the lines is peculiarly effective in characterizing his determination. The emphasis falls on the three main features, the hard face, the ready sword and the sceptre of office, and the eye is brought to bear on them in that order. This is Yoritomo the dictator seen through the perceptive eyes of a great portrait painter. Like *Uesugi Shigefusa* (Fig. 79) he is almost godlike, the incarnation of the sword which brought Japan together in the 12th century. The portrait is the epitome of the stern, impassive dignity which the Japanese consider to be the proper outward expression of a powerful personality. There is nothing of the elegance of Kyoto in the portrait.

The alliance of court sophistication with popular Buddhism was continued in a series of Buddhist sutras written on fans in the second half of the 12th century (Fig. 84). The rich, decorated paper has genre scenes of noble or plebian life in *Yamato-e* style with religious texts written over them. Beneath the colouring, traces of block-printing can be distinguished which antedate the perfection of the wood-block print by some 500 years.

Wood-block printing for holy texts and pictures was used in China during the T'ang dynasty though never to depict such secular subjects. The charming genre scenes, almost obscured by the holy writings, are a new departure. This combination of secular and religious motives is perhaps the most revealing indication of a changed mood in Buddhist art.

During the Kamakura period the range of paintings was suddenly and greatly enriched. Popular Buddhism accounts for part of this expansion. As Buddhism became more easily understandable, so the need arose for a type of painting with secular subjects or references which would appeal to the ordinary man. In addition, popular literature, steadily growing since the *Tale of Genji*, kept pace with the spread of literacy. It provided a rich fund of interesting material suitable for painting—fairy tales, biographies, battles, histories of temples, and travel stories. The many artists who took advantage of this wider range could choose one of their own, by now highly developed, native styles or seek inspiration from freshly introduced Chinese modes.

Although handscrolls are preoccupied with the human being, they sometimes include landscapes as backgrounds. Where Japanese scenes are depicted, the artist tended to choose a Japanese rather than a Chinese style. The Japanese must have had examples of Sung Chinese landscapes before them, but the painters of the time seem to have preferred their own *Yamato-e* styles. These are quite different from the Sung monochrome work which became so popular in later times. As previously mentioned they are closer to what we believe to be the T'ang style. The Japanese landscape elements in these scrolls are generally brightly coloured; gold and silver is often used to increase the decorative brilliance; above all they are extremely formalized. Whereas the Chinese painter was fascinated by the grandeur of inaccessible mountains in all their moods, the Japanese used broad sweeps of colour washes sometimes without outlines, to show his gentler native landscape. His brush was softer and calmer, expressing a lyricism which the Japanese attribute to their milder climate. The Chinese painter was awed by the overwhelming grandeur of nature and hinted at the delights that the human soul will find by seeking identity with it; the Japanese approached his landscape in a more friendly mood and beckoned the spectator to share in its simple enjoyments. The spirit which in China results from a deep mystical strain and produces the recluse has in Japan produced the flower-viewing parties which appeal to the native sense of form and colour. The instinct which led the Chinese artist respectfully to observe in a long landscape scroll the *Thousand Miles of the Yangtze River* expresses itself at the hands of a Japanese painter in a more intimate view of the soft regular slopes of rolling hills. There is a direct link between the *Inga-kyō* of the Asuka period, these handscrolls, and the Japanese decorative manner so adroitly exploited by the masters of the Tosa school in later times.

The *Yamato-e* or Japanese Painting style emerged in a time of violence and, appropriately enough, its genius is not so much landscape as for depicting dynamic action. The vivid sense of movement seen in the hand-scrolls undoubtedly owes something to the vigorous Chinese use of line but the subjects of Chinese painting are seldom dramatic. They are generally contemplative. The continuous narrative and powerful action displayed in Japanese scrolls are an entirely native invention. The Chinese emphasis is on nature; the Japanese shifted it to man which remained thereafter their chief interest. Genre works are found in Chinese painting but the acute observation of man in all his activities and conditions is a salient characteristic of Japanese painting. Mankind alone provided the

85. *The Nachi Waterfall*
Colour on silk.
Probably late 13th century.
5 feet 3 inches by 1 foot 10¾ inches.
Nezu Museum, Tokyo.

fullest opportunity for the Japanese artist to combine his predilections for the dramatic and sentimental, the sensational and grotesque which, it has been suggested in earlier passages, often dominate his art. In this respect, the *e-makimono* in *Yamato-e* style, which have no counterparts in China or the West, are the purest expression of Japanese art.

Yet one splendid hanging scroll of landscape has survived which is more than a simple landscape. The *Nachi Waterfall* in the Nezu Museum, Tokyo (Fig. 85) is to the Japanese an object of deep religious significance. The follower of *Shintō* believes that all natural phenomena contain spirits; and this landscape is intended to depict the spirit of the

86. Section of the handscroll *The History of Mount Shigi*. Ink and colour on paper. Kamakura period. Height 12½ inches. Chōgoson-ji, Kyoto.

waterfall. At the time when the painting was done Buddhism and Shintōism had to a degree been reconciled in a system called 'Dual Shintō' (*Ryōbu*) in which the *Shintō* gods were accepted as manifestations of the Buddha. This is a typical example of the way in which Buddhism was able to adopt itself to native beliefs without giving offence and the *Nachi Waterfall* represents a combination of Buddhist inspiration and native religious thought. Unfortunately it is too darkened by age to make reproduction easy. The follower of Dual Shintō would see in the sun in the top left-hand corner a suggestion of the Dai-Nichi Buddha, the Buddha of All-Pervading Light. His eyes would follow the dominating line of the heavy waterfall with its *Shintō* spirit, Hiryū Gongen, down to the misty secluded shrines at the bottom where the god was worshipped. The Kumano district in which this waterfall is situated was a popular centre of Dual Shintō beliefs and the painting was probably made in the last years of the 13th century. This Nachi landscape is a monumental work. It has a dramatic quality which is often found in Japanese paintings, and occurs even more strongly in the colour-prints of waterfalls made in the 19th century. A solid sheet of water falls heavily to the shadowy precincts below cutting the landscape into two equal parts. The stillness of the rocks and trees contrast with the urgent, almost audible, speed of the water. Japanese forests do indeed inspire the sense of mystery which this ancient painting so admirably evokes and it is easy to appreciate how it became an object of veneration to be worshipped in a shrine. The area is too holy to be spoiled by the intrusion of man—even by the tiny respectful figure which in a Chinese landscape would be found regarding the universe around him.

A number of *e-makimono* have been preserved, but unfortunately they are difficult to reproduce satisfactorily. However, something of their vitality appears even in the details which are all it is possible to show. Even if the sweep of the composition and the mounting tension created by successive scenes is lost, they at least give some idea of the urgency and concentration of the whole and of the compositional skill of their creators.

The *Genji* scroll was discussed earlier under the Fujiwara period, since it is a unique work which belongs there and nowhere else. However, two other famous scrolls actually made at the end of the Fujiwara have far closer affinities with the great Kamakura *e-makimono*. So to these we must for a monent return. The first, made in three parts, depicts the *History of Mount Shigi* (Fig. 86). It recounts most graphically a simple and amusing story with a Buddhist moral.

A Priest called Myōren, the founder of the Chōgoson-ji Temple on Mount Shigi, outside Kyoto, had been accustomed to receive alms from a wealthy man. By his miraculous power, the priest would make his alms bowl fly to the granary of his patron who was expected to fill it. It would then return to the priest by the same magical means. One day the rich man was too busy or too impatient to pay attention to the persistent bowl which he left neglected in the corner. The angry priest then made the alms bowl rise in the air and carry the entire building with all its contents to the priest's cottage on Mount Shigi. The rich man and his friends, thrown into consternation, followed its flight to the mountain where they found both priest and granary. Myōren declined any interest in the grain but said that he needed the building for his own storage needs. Then, using the bowl once more, he flew the sacks back to their original home where they were joyfully received by their owner.

The artist of this scroll is unknown. He was probably a professional Buddhist painter of the first half of the 12th century. The technique for joining the various scenes of the story, as seen already in a well advanced stage in other scrolls has here been skilfully developed into a much more natural continuous method. The style is also different. The stiffness of line, the immobile composition and the heavy colour of the *Genji* scroll have been replaced by a free flowing line, a black and white technique with soft colour washes, and a greater continuity. Only a few objects are emphasized by bright colours such as the bowl itself and the tassels on the horses. The draughtsmanship is infinitely more skilful. The figures leap about and gesticulate in genuine consternation when they see the granary leaving the ground, jumping up, as if to try to hold it down. Every figure is a precise and individual study in movement and emotion. Each scene is alive with its

87. Section of the *Animal Scrolls* attributed to Toba Sōjō (1053–1140). Ink on paper. Height 12¼ inches. Kōzan-ji, Kyoto.

own humour and character. Even the few landscape elements have a distinctive freedom. Nothing in the earlier scrolls leads us to expect these witty, unaffected stories in pictorial form which enliven the late Fujiwara period with their vivid glimpses into the lives of ordinary people. Here, if anywhere, are the forerunners of the intimate studies which fill so many of the colour prints of some 500 years later. No sterile conventions stifle their expression, no mannerisms reduce them to pure decoration. It is difficult to imagine more vitality of brush or spirit.

The second set of these scrolls (Fig. 87) in the Kōzan-ji Temple is even more surprising. They are in black and white only and two of the four scrolls appear to be somewhat later. The earlier two are commonly attributed to Toba Sōjō (1053–1140), an eminent Buddhist priest—though this attribution has been challenged. The deeper meaning of these paintings has not been determined but on the surface they seem to satirize man in the guise of animals. It has been suggested that a priest painted these figures as a protest against the squabbles and unpriestly behaviour of his fellow monks. Some of the scenes—especially in the finest scroll which shows animals and frogs in human activities—are singularly irreverent. The Buddha is depicted as a frog and the clerics fight among themselves (as indeed the quarrelsome monks of that time may often have done). The sprightliness of the strokes is uncannily effective. Chinese line drawings of divinities may have provided the priest with models for this kind of black and white draughtsmanship but they are here transformed by the Japanese artists into something quite unique. It is hardly likely that the painter of this scroll intended it as anything more than a private joke. Certainly it could not have served as an object of worship.

88.   Section of a handscroll *The Life of an Artist*.   Ink and colour on paper.   Kamakura period.
Height 11⅞ inches.   Imperial Household Collection.

89. Section of a handscroll *The Story of the Battle of Heiji*. Ink and colour on paper. Kamakura period. Height 16½ inches. Museum of Fine Arts, Boston.

The *Shigisan Engi* and the *Animal Scrolls* show that, however effete late Fujiwara court life may have been, there was no lack of invention and vitality in these priest-artists who could turn with such complete mastery of technique and pungent wit to the commoners and the animals for their subjects. And how refreshing it is to escape from the monotonous idealism of many Buddhist paintings of the Fujiwara period to the humour and imagination of these spontaneous creations!

By the 13th century three main styles had emerged in scroll painting—the *Genji* type which relied mainly on colour, the *Mount Shigi* type in which line is most important and colour used only sparingly, and finally the black and white type which we see at its best in the *Animal Scrolls*. The Kamakura period produced a flood of scrolls. Some follow one style, some another, and some aimed at combining two or more. Their titles give the best clue to their subjects: The *History of Kokawa Temple*, *The Story of Subduing the East* (the account of the Chinese priest Ganjin's mission to Japan), *The Illustrated Biography of Priest Hōnen*, *The Story of the Great Minister Kibi in China*, *The Handbook on Long-nosed Goblins*, *The Story of the Battle of Heiji*, *The Story of the Mongol Invasion*, *The Life of an Artist* (Fig. 88), etc.

Two of these superb 13th century scrolls are worthy of special study. *The Story of the Battle of Heiji* is one of the few paintings of this type which the Japanese have allowed to leave their country. One of its three scrolls is in the Museum of Fine Arts, Boston. During the First Year of the Heiji period two court nobles fought each other for supremacy. In the course of this war, the Sanjō Palace was set on fire. The Boston scroll, of which a section is shown here (Fig. 89), gives a magnificent battle scene with the actual burning of the palace most graphically depicted. The artists of these scrolls already had long experience in painting crowd scenes, but the unknown artist of the *Heiji* scroll was particularly skilled in portraying the high excitement and panic of the event.

The set of scrolls illustrating *The Story of the Mongol Attack* (Fig. 90) portrays one of Japan's greatest historical moments and the outstanding event of the Kamakura period. In 1263 Khubilai, Khan of the Mongols, made himself Emperor of China and founded the Yüan dynasty. The Mongols, 'the Golden Horde' were merciless fighters who swept through China, across Asia and into Europe, pillaging and destroying wherever they went, establishing and controlling by an iron discipline, the largest empire the world had hitherto known. Their arms were irresistible. The peoples who stood in the way of their early

90.   Section of a handscroll *The Story of the Mongol Attack*.   Ink on paper.   Dated 1293.
Imperial Collection.   Height 15¾ inches.

campaigns had only two alternatives—surrender or annihilation. They often suffered both. In 1268, the Mongol Emperor, by now secure in China and confident of his power, made his first approach to Japan suggesting that relations should be established.   This meant simply that the Japanese should completely surrender their independence and the Mongol hinted at the dire consequences of a failure to comply.   The Kamakura warriors, though aware of the significance of these threats, refused to be intimidated.   Such a refusal was the equivalent of a declaration of war.   The Mongols spent a year in preparing an armada estimated at 450 ships, 15,000 Mongol fighting men and 15,000 Korean auxiliaries.   They confidently landed on the west coast of the southern island where the local chieftains and their retainers opposed them with tremendous courage.   Honours seem to have been even in the first day's encounter of Japanese sword against Mongol arrow and artillery.   The Mongols returned to their ships and that same night a storm blew up, scattering and destroying their fleet.   This disastrous campaign cost the invaders, unaccustomed to such reverses, 13,500 men, to say nothing of their loss of prestige.

By 1280 Kublai was ready to return to the attack.   He was determined to revenge the two groups of envoys who had paid with their lives for the journey to Kamakura to demand submission from the Japanese.   This time both sides had more time to prepare.   The Mongol force, now numbering about 150,000 men, landed in June 1281.   The battle lasted for fifty days before another storm destroyed their fleet and, in a strange analogy to the fate of the Spanish Armada, drove what remained, perhaps as little as one fifth, back to the mainland in complete rout.   Although the threat of invasion lasted for another twenty years, the enemy never made another attempt and the Japanese could thus claim to be the only people successfully to have resisted the Mongols at the height of their power.

This valiant defence and the providential storms provided the Japanese with the corner-stone of a belief in their divinely-aided invincibility which lasted into our own times. A Japanese artist recorded his nation's most heroic moment in this scroll. It gives an authentic eye-witness account of actual battle scenes, the first incidentally in which cannon are represented.

In the minor arts, the all-pervading influence in this period was that of the Chinese Sung dynasty. Chinese ceramics, with a thousand years of development behind them, were the finest both technically and aesthetically that the world has produced. It is not surprising that the Japanese, although in the other arts capable of rapidly learning from and even surpassing their teachers, could not equal the perfection of Sung wares.

Nevertheless, the Japanese claim that their ceramic art was established during the Kamakura period by a man named Toshiro who is known as the ' Father of Japanese Pottery.' He went to China with a Buddhist priest and studied the craft during his stay there. When he returned to Japan (about 1229), he settled in the area now called Seto and for the more wealthy families began producing pottery in which he used Chinese techniques. Hundreds of kiln sites dating back to this period exist around Seto and it is still possible to find fragments of fine glazed brown and black pottery from this time. One can therefore claim that high-fired wares originated in these centuries. Seto has remained the largest pottery-producing area in Japan—so much so that the word *Setomono* (lit: Seto things) is still the accepted term for pottery.

The wares produced at Seto, and at a few other sites such as Tokoname, Shigaraki, Tamba, Bizen, and Echizen,[1] were far more primitive than the Chinese wares. In fact the

[1] These are called the ' Six Old Kilns of Japan.'

91. *Vase.*
Black glaze over grey body.
Kamakura period.
Height 9½ inches.
Tokyo National Museum.

112

92. Detail of *Cosmetic Box*
Lacquer with Mother-of-pearl
and inlay of precious metals.
Kamakura period.
N. Matsudaira Collection,
Kanagawa Prefecture.

Japanese have always admired a certain powerful roughness—especially for their tea-ceremony wares. But at this time taste did not come into it. It is more likely that they just could not match the Chinese workmanship. Tradition, skill, and spirit were lacking in Kamakura Japan, and of these the most vital failing was the lack of spiritual atmosphere. Sung ceramics were the result of a long tradition going back to the Han dynasty with which Japan could not compete, and they reflected a world of sensibility unknown to the Japanese, particularly at this time.

The vase shown in Figure 91 is a typical Japanese product of the period. Strangely enough, some potters continued for a short period to use the earliest Japanese pottery-making technique revived during the Fujiwara time, that of coiled clay, as seen in the neolithic *jōmon* pottery. The basic form was shaped by this primitive method and then both outside and inside were finished on a wheel. The pots were sometimes made in parts and then assembled. This clumsy technique can produce only very heavy wares. It is surprising that the Japanese potters by these crude means were able to produce such comparatively fine shapes. The black glaze of our example is uneven and not too skilfully controlled. What beauty the vase contains lies in its powerful shape allied to vigorous free-hand decoration which successfully covers the whole surface. The vase recalls some of the Sung *Tz'u Chou* wares. Although its place of manufacture is not known, it is the kind of ware produced at Seto. Green and yellow glazes also were made by adding kiln ash which reacted with the iron in the body. The black and yellow glazes were produced by putting iron directly into the ash-glaze, probably in imitation of the Chinese *Chien-yao*, popularly known in Japan as *Temmoku*.

Styles of lacquer ware and textiles were perhaps the slowest to react to the austere atmosphere of the Kamakura court. Kyoto always remained the arbiter of fashion in these two crafts and neither would have welcomed a move away from the elegance of the Fujiwara towards the sobriety of Kamakura taste. The new trends in lacquer are first noticeable in more solid and severe shapes.   The decorative designs increasingly reflect the more spontaneous and individual *yamato-e* styles and tend to take their inspiration from nature.   The broad sweeps and soft curves of the new type of landscape paintings were admirably suited to lacquer-work.   But even so the influences of the gentle Fujiwara court taste persisted in what was essentially a luxury art.   Techniques in lacquer application developed rapidly.   Where previously gold and silver powders had been combined to enrich the surfaces, now gold or mother-of-pearl alone were sometimes favoured.   The result was greatly to increase the impression of luxury and solidity.

Variety in the manner of applying the gold in different grades ranging from fine dust to flakes and even squares distinguishes the products.   When gold dust alone was used the textures were often mixed in a technique called *nashi-ji* which was frequently employed for backgrounds.   In earlier periods the *maki-e* had been a comparatively simple method in which the metal dust was sprinkled on the wet lacquer of the design and the whole surface then polished down with charcoal (see p. 76).   Now the *maki-e* was used in two important new techniques which served to emphasize the designs by raising them in relief.   In the *hira* or ' flat relief ' *maki-e* the decoration is applied in the usual manner but, wherever it is intended to raise the design slightly, it is overpainted with lacquer.   In the *taka* or ' high relief ' *maki-e*, the decoration itself is made up of a number of layers of lacquer in relief and then finished in the same way as ordinary *maki-e*.

93.   Top of *Incense Box*
with a design of peonies.
Carved lacquer.
Kamakura period.
Diameter 13 inches.
Nanzen-ji, Kyoto.

The detail of a cosmetic box in Figure 92 illustrates the Kamakura spirit in decoration. *Maki-e*, mother-of-pearl and sheet design are all used. The butterflies in sheet silver were further enhanced by skilfully incised lines filled with gold dust. Other parts of the decoration are in burnished gold and *nashi-ji*. The total effect is saved from confusion only by the liveliness of the design. Here the Japanese love of nature is happily fused with the equally strong native passion for pleasing decorative effects. Butterflies and insects were favourite themes for Kamakura decorators and their very lightness serves sometimes to offset the heaviness of the new techniques.

Lacquer became a very popular means of decorating armour and saddles and some fine specimens of the latter with rich mother-of-pearl inlay have been preserved. Yet fundamentally the very elegance and luxury of lacquer work seems somewhat out of harmony with the austerity of the Kamakura period—at least in its earlier decades. For a type of lacquer-work more in keeping with the spirit of this age we must look to a new kind which was made in Kamakura itself. This *Kamakura-bori* (Fig. 93) was directly inspired by a type of lacquer said to have been made for the first time during the T'ang dynasty in China. Although no early examples have survived, its Ming and Ch'ing equivalents are thoroughly familiar to the collector. In this technique, layer upon layer of lacquer are applied to build up a solid body of the material which is then carved very much like wood. Sometimes red and green layers alternate so that by a cameo-like technique of carving both colours could be used together; thus in a floral design, for example, leaves were left green and flowers red. The method was suitable for architectural decoration in temples and it is known that eminent sculptors, even descendants of the great Unkei, worked in this medium. The craft has survived in the city of its origin and has lately been enjoying a revival. Good examples in old and modern styles can be found there.

Kamakura textiles, like those of the Heian period, have not survived the centuries in any numbers. But paintings provide evidence of styles and decoration. Generally speaking, the 12th and 13th centuries contributed little of importance. It is easy to understand that the austere atmosphere which the new war-lords encouraged did not stimulate the creation of opulent styles of the use of rich materials and it seems that even the silk produced during the period was of poor quality. In dress design the general trend seems to have been towards simplification and sobriety (see the Yoritomo portrait, Figure 83). Dresses hitherto reserved for the plebian classes became popular among the nobility. Men who lived by the sword needed freedom of movement in their clothing. The *kosode* or 'short-sleeves' which had been the innermost—and the simplest—of numerous robes now worked its way to the surface as one after another of the inconvenient outer garments were shed. Sometimes it was used with *hakama*, the long, loose trousers which are still worn on ceremonial occasions. Both garments had larger, bolder designs and these were often laid down by regulation; *paulownia* leaves or bamboo and phoenixes for the Emperor, a modification of the same design for retired emperors, and so on down the scale. The crests or *mon* of the great families became popular motifs for the robes of the nobility. Tie-dyeing was revived, but now the rough outlines of the design resulting from the process were sharpened by painting the material after the dyeing. This so-called *tsuji-ga-hana* technique later produced some beautiful fabrics but most of the materials which have survived from the Kamakura period have a dry, archaistic appearance and are singularly dull compared with those of other times.

CHAPTER VII

THE ASHIKAGA OR MUROMACHI PERIOD

1338–1573

YORITOMO'S fear that the luxuries of court life would sap the strength of his warriors was well-founded. All the legislation which the Hōjō regents enacted to prevent over-indulgence in the enervating, expensive refinements of life proved useless. The plottings in Kyoto, the constant fighting between the clergy, the insubordination of unruly clansmen and finally their efforts to repel the Mongols, all weakened the internal strength of the regime. By the beginning of the 14th century the *Bakufu* had lost its authority. The regents could no longer claim the allegiance even of their own vassals and the struggle for power between the great landowners entered a new phase. The succession to the Emperor's throne in Kyoto which had been controlled by Kamakura was no longer undisputed but had to be decided between the regents and other discontented war-lords. In the ensuing struggle, the Kamakura faction lost their power, and in 1336 the Ashikaga family led by Ashikaga Takauji established Emperor Kōmyō on the throne in Kyoto. Japan seemed to be on the verge of a new and more auspicious age. The country was weary of the interminable rivalries between the great lords which the late Kamakura regime had been unable to control, and looked back with nostalgia to the great days of Nara when the local lords paid allegiance to and were ruled by the Emperor at the capital. The Emperor had then seemed an effective sovereign, his authority unquestioned and the nation prosperous. Throughout their history the Japanese have been deluded by the conviction that an escape from their troubles could only be found by a restoration of Imperial power.

Unfortunately, in this period too, their hopes were rapidly disappointed and Japan entered one of her most unhappy periods. The first fifty-six years (1336–92) are called the Namboku-chō, the period of the 'Northern and Southern Courts.' It took its name from a prolonged rivalry between the Emperor Kōmyō in Kyoto and a pretender who fled south to establish his court in Yoshino. Both had powerful supporters. Fundamentally the struggle, which lasted throughout the whole period, was still between the great feudatories to decide who should exercise the actual power behind the Imperial throne. Very soon the Emperor was again stripped of all but the dignity attached to his position and at times there remained little even of that.

The problem which remained unsolved during these two hundred years was how to bring the great lords into a system which guaranteed national stability. The discipline to which they had submitted during the early Kamakura period had disappeared. The ambitions of the landowners in this new phase of their history were now directed towards complete independence. The Kyoto nobility, which over the centuries had progressively lost control of whatever lands it once possessed, became a colourful but pathetic ana-chronism. It was swept away by economic forces. Thus, trends initiated by the Kamakura dictatorship were brought to a logical conclusion. Those court nobles who could salvage some of their lost position by merging with the new *Shōgun* class in Kyoto did so. But for all its promising start the Ashikaga power was at all times more apparent than real. Like that of the Fujiwara it survived because no single lord was strong enough to take over the undisputed control of the capital. The Ashikaga seem to have exhausted themselves in the battles of the Northern- and Southern-Courts period which left them no reserves to consolidate their power. And the blandishments of Kyoto were ever at work upon their character, refining, sensitizing—weakening.

However, by 1392 the problems of Imperial succession were settled and the Ashikaga family under Yoshimitsu (1368–1408) brought a welcome, if insecure, peace to the weary country. But the new overlords, different in temperament from their single-minded predecessors of the early Kamakura times, were never able to restore the authority of a man like Yoritomo. Under Yoshimasa (1449–1490), whatever authority the Ashikaga had ever had, was whittled away and the feudal lords again held the ultimate power in their own hands. The new rulers in Kyoto, willing victims to its enchantments, desired luxury rather than authority. Luxury, however, requires money and, since the pillage of neigh-bours provided only a limited and decreasing scope for enrichment, they sought new methods. Trade with China became one of the principal sources of income. Under the guise of embassies, a very considerable trade grew up in which the Japanese exchanged swords and lacquer-ware for bullion, iron, textiles, pictures, books, and drugs. The feudatories were quick to share in this commercial activity and the Ashikaga were not able to turn the proceeds to their exclusive benefit. The proportions of the trade and the drain of currency from the Chinese treasury alarmed the Ming court no less than the unruly behaviour of the ' embassies ' under whose cloak this trade was carried on. Nevertheless, these commercial activities continued almost unchecked and were of considerable signific-ance for the development of the arts in Japan.

In this politically sterile period, a number of interesting social developments had an invigorating effect on Japanese life. The emergence of a virile merchant class was perhaps the most far-reaching. The peasants, who since the 6th century had suffered without respite, also began to make themselves heard through risings to which they were driven by the misery of their condition. The sharp barriers between the classes began to break down and, with the decline of feudal loyalties, the importance of the family as a unit in-creased. This, however, affected adversely the position of women. Hitherto they had enjoyed considerable rights on an equal footing with men but, when the unity of the family became of paramount importance, it proved impossible to allow women to inherit and so to split family holdings. From this time dates the subordinate legal position which Japanese women held for such a long time.

Warfare, too, became more complex and a new class of masterless and landless *samurai* came into being. They formed a body of mercenaries, of wandering fighting-men whose trade was the sword but who were less bound by the strict code of the old *samurai*. As in earlier times, their exploits and their loyalties to a now outmoded code provided material for a rich popular literature which is reflected in the arts, particularly in later times.

Throughout the social and political upheavals of these two centuries, the Emperor and the Ashikaga *Shōguns* survived because they were in effect powerless and because there was no person or institution ready to take their place. A parallel is often drawn between this period in Japan and the Quattrocento in Italy. The authority of the Emperor of Japan had disintegrated like that of the Emperor of the Roman Empire. The feudal lords resembled the Rimini, Borgia, Visconti, or Medici in their independence and ambition, in their mutual distrust and treachery, in their patronage and their exchanges of works of art. In Japan, as in Italy, the same importance was attached to the acquisition of a painting or the writing of a poem as to the winning of a battle.

History provides many examples of politically decadent times which have nevertheless been artistically most fruitful. Why was this true of Ashikaga Japan? First, the country craved the pleasures and luxuries of peace. Fine works of art were the rewards of success at a time when other benefits were mostly illusory. The feudal courts often considered themselves the equals of the *Shōgun's* court in Kyoto and, backed by ample financial resources, they strove to rival the opulence of the capital. Men of letters and artists were, therefore, always welcomed at these provincial centres and their untutored masters gave them considerable freedom in matters of taste and looked to them for guidance. Such men of culture often preferred the relative safety of court or temple protection to the rigours of life in the constant civil wars; they were safe and able to pursue their activities untroubled. We see here another stage in the development of the influence of individual artists whose emergence from the ranks of anonymous craftsmen was noted in the Fujiwara period.

Yoshimitsu, a man of taste and patron of the arts, built and decorated his palace in the Muromachi quarter of Kyoto whence the period takes one of its names. He erected other fine monuments such as the Kinkaku-ji or ' Golden Pavilion ' where, in 1394, he retired, ostensibly to live the life of a priest while in fact he still manipulated the government. Yoshimasa emulated Yoshimitsu by building the Ginkaku-ji or ' Silver Pavilion ' and surrounded himself with priests, poets, and actors but, unlike his predecessor, he completely neglected administrative affairs. He is perhaps best remembered for his vast collection of Chinese paintings which formed a splendid body of reference material for Japanese artists of the time. Both Yoshimitsu and Yoshimasa were enthusiastic admirers of *Zen*-inspired art, and of all Chinese artistic qualities in general.

The influence of *Zen* Buddhism on the life and art at this time can hardly be exaggerated. It was perhaps the dominating force of the period. The teaching of the sect under such outstanding leaders as Musō became the official religion of the court. However, it surrendered to Kyoto some of its earlier austerity. *Zen* priests developed a taste for fine buildings set in beautiful gardens which their predecessors in the Kamakura period would have frowned on. As teachers they directed the colleges and they even served as political advisors to the *shōguns*. In this role, they developed what Sansom calls " a useful type of practical wisdom " and Warner, "A sort of common sense along with the highest flights of metaphysics." The direct, intuitive approach of *Zen* appealed to the un-schooled military mind of the Ashikaga as it had to the rulers of Kamakura before them. The influence of the *Zen* priests was not, however, allowed to develop unchallenged, for the militant monks of the *Tendai* monasteries on Mount Hiei, just outside Kyoto, often descended on the city and forced the court to satisfy their demands. Other sects, too, followed the example of the times in taking to politics and the sword either for expansion or protection. Many monasteries were razed to the ground in the inter-sect and inter-family wars. However, the *Shintō* beliefs, like the position of the Emperor, seem by their very passivity to have survived the turmoil unscathed.

Art during the Ashikaga period became mainly concerned with paintings. *Zen* influence, first evident at Kamakura, increased but, like the priests of the sect, lost much of its austere quality. Chinese *Zen* priests visited Japan and Japanese priests entered monasteries in China where they were often highly respected. Paintings which set out to express the *Zen* ideal of union with the infinite became the fashion of the time. Unqualified admiration of China doubtlessly stimulated the popularity of Chinese-style ink monochrome painting. It appealed equally to a deep Japanese love of simplicity and nature which is reflected in all the products of the age from gardens to painting. The style of painting as seen in the *Genji* scroll, with all its *Yamato-e* traditions went for a time completely out of favour— a phenomenon which can only be explained by the flood of Chinese paintings which were imported in hundreds by Japanese monks or by agents sent by the *shōguns* to buy them.

The *Zen*-inspired painter seeks the ' truth ' of a landscape, like that of religion, in sudden enlightenment. This allows no time for careful detailed draughtsmanship. After long contemplation, he seizes inner-truth in a sword-like stroke of the brush. This ' essential-ism ' can be expressed equally well in a large landscape or in the branch of a tree, in the broadest panorama as well as in each of its minute components. The flights of imagination manifested by these artists in black and white are one of the great contributions of the East to the art of the world. In their efforts to discover the very essence of reality, the *Zen* artists turned away from the ' emotional superficiality ' of colour and the ' trivialities ' of accurate detail. To them all natural phenomena were mere illusion, not to be copied painstakingly. They developed a highly stylized, seemingly spontaneous, black and white style to depict the various moods of nature and its inner reality. Selectivity was carried to its highest degree and with the most economical means of black ink in all its nuances, the *suiboku* (' water ink ') painters achieved a landscape painting of remarkable imaginative depth. Unfortunately, sooner in Japan than in China, the means often became the end. The result was that mannerism and dexterity with the brush took the place of artistic vision, thereby destroying the very foundations of the art. In art as in religion it was too easy for the facile and quick-witted to exploit the thoughts and ideals of *Zen* Buddhism.

The *Zen* sect had been introduced to Japan in the 13th century but it is not until the early 14th century that eminent *suiboku* painters known by name emerged. The two out-standing artists in this early period were Moku-an who went to China in 1333 where he stayed until his death, and Kao (early 14th century). Figure 94 shows an imaginary portrait by Kao of a simple Chinese priest called in Japanese *Kanzan*, one of the favourite subjects of *Zen* painting. This seemingly stupid priest who is said to have lived in the T'ang dynasty, but is probably a mythical figure, idealizes a *Zen* way of life—that of the poor, eccentric beggar-priest who scorns the intellectual attitudes of other sects. Having attained enlightenment, such followers of *Zen* were content to ignore all worldly considera-tions. He is often depicted in company of his fellow priest Jittoku. Pairs of paintings showing them both are frequent and many stories are told of their apparent simple-mindedness. They were popular subjects with such Chinese artists as Liang K'ai (active about 1200) and Yin-t'o-lo (13th century) both of whom were highly esteemed in Japan. The subject belongs to a group of paintings called in Japanese *dōshaku* which illustrate the deeds of great *Zen* priests or depict objects likely to stimulate a believer to achieve sudden enlightenment.

94. *Kanzan* by Kaō (14th century).
Ink on paper.
Height 3 feet 2½ inches, width 1 foot 1½ inches
Nagao Museum, Kanagawa.

The brushwork of the Kanzan portrait is masterly in its powerful economy and the strong outline contrasts effectively with the softer washes used for his apron and the tree above. The change in content is no less striking. The artist has lost interest in scenes of paradise and in representations of the Buddha. The intention is no longer, as with the handscrolls, to illustrate literature. The penetration of *Zen* ideals into his consciousness is complete. It is difficult to imagine a more revolutionary concept. The formalized super-human figure of iconographic tradition has descended to the lowest human plane. The half-witted priest is the final development of the tradition of dignified Buddhist figures of past centuries. To appreciate its spiritual message demands knowledge of *Zen* ideals. There is, as well, a great deal of humour which the Japanese enjoy in this as in many *Zen* inspired contradicitions. The painting attempts to give an easily comprehensible lesson in salvation administered in the form of a shock. It is so contrived as to disturb the aspirant to spiritual truth whose mind was fettered by traditional thought and religious practices. The posture of the monk, stomach thrust out, hands behind back, head craning forward, is the epitome of the idiot. Even his flat-footed stance and his gaze towards the largest blank space in the composition, contribute to the impression of vacuity. His face, like that of some cheerful gaper at a spectacle, is crowned with a shock of unkempt hair. The contours of the figure are set off by the tree; its trunk repeats the strong backward line of the left arm and the branch echoes the silhouette of the out-thrust stomach.

It was not long before the Japanese *suiboku* artists, like their Chinese fore-runners found the best outlet for their talents and ideas in landscape painting. Minchō, sometimes called Chō Densu, (1352–1431) is representative of the late 14th–early 15th century landscape masters. *The Hermitage by the Mountain Brook* (Fig. 95), dated 1413, is attributed to him. The scene is an imaginary Chinese landscape and a number of poems are written above it. It belongs to the class of paintings called *shiga-jiku* or 'hanging scrolls with poems and paintings.' The lonely cottage over the stream is intended to suggest the ideal solitary retreat of the *Zen* priest where, in peaceful communion with nature, he will achieve enlightenment. The composition is typical of Sung-Yüan painting in the manner in which it divides the picture plane into foreground and background with the eye skilfully led from one to the other by a bank of mist from which a few trees emerge. The ink-tones are subtle and the brushwork of the rocks, the trees, and the hut is most determined. There are, however, certain elements in the work which suggest that, in addition to his study of Sung-Yüan paintings, the artist had also seen early 15th century Ming paintings. This is revealed in the brushwork of the leaves, in the closeness of the spectator to the scene and, perhaps above all, in the absence of an indefinable quality of mystery and awe which abounds in the earlier works.

The priest-painter Shūbun (active in the first half of the 15th century) was put in charge of the first Ashikaga 'Court Painting Bureau' and through him *suiboku* painting became the official style. Many important works are attributed to him, but these attributions raise a number of problems since there were three artists with the same name. Nevertheless, the style which the most famous of the three Shūbuns used is quite clearly distinguishable. The smaller pieces attributed to him tend more towards the Sung ideals of the 'Northern' School of Ma Yüan and Hsia Kuei but his larger landscapes (Fig. 96) are typical Yüan-inspired work, recalling such eminent Chinese painters as Huang Kung-wang (one of the Four Great Yüan Masters). In the work of Shūbun, signs can already be seen of the virtuosity which was to endanger the sincerity of later works. The mysterious aspect of

95. (Left). *Hermitage by a Mountain Brook.* Attributed to Minchō (1352–1431). Hanging scroll. Ink on paper. 39½ by 13¾ inches.

96. (Right). *Landscape* attributed to Shūbun. Dated 1445. Hanging scroll. Ink on paper. 42½ by 20½ (approx.) inches.

Chinese landscapes, the life-spirit of this style, as formed by the Chinese is completely dispelled; foreground and background become flat and dead and the whole painting is artificially dramatized. The brushwork is strong but seen here in the first stages of formalization. This is particularly noticeable in the towering cliffs and in the gnarled roots of the pine trees; and the hut is consciously over-emphasized. The theme is familiar from Chinese examples though not less charming for its familiarity. Trees surround a scholar's hut deep in the country where alone with his books he seeks enlightenment. But the eye is tempted to explore the brushwork more than the landscape, to admire the technique rather than to respond to the spirit behind it. The painting does not inspire the viewer to contemplate its deeper meaning but only to share its nostalgia and to delight in its skilled draughtsmanship.

In Chinese and Japanese ink-painting the brushwork is a vital consideration. The ability to use the brush oneself is doubtlessly a great help in appreciating it but, contrary to the expressions of some critics, it is certainly not indispensable. The Far Eastern brush, conical in shape and narrowing down to the finest point, is a most sensitive instrument. It is very absorbent and flexible. The slightest difference in pressure varies the thickness of the stroke much more than with a Western brush. The speed with which the artist makes his strokes imparts to them the life and vitality and considered as all-important. The angle at which it is held is also significant. Held upright, the brush produces a hard, strong and incisive line. When held at a slant the line tends to become softer and weaker—in other words, the tip of the brush produces a powerful stroke and the side or 'belly' of the brush, a more diffused, softer line. In practice most brush-strokes share both qualities in various degrees. A brush-stroke can also indicate a degree of shading and this too depends upon the angle at which the brush is held. Hence it is possible to depict a spherical object with a single outline stroke. Generations of Japanese painters were made to practise the painting of a round jewel for as much as two years before being allowed to graduate to more advanced studies. Understandably enough, the weaker brethren did not survive the discipline! An experienced judge of brushwork can tell with what part of the brush a stroke was made, the angle, speed, and direction of the stroke and even how the brush was held in the fingers, the angle of the wrist, and the height and position of the arm which made it. Thus, to quote the Japanese, "the line is the man himself." In Far Eastern painting the brush reveals more of the painter's personality than in any other painting in the world.

Throughout the 15th century, the assimilation of Chinese styles went hand in hand with the development of Japanese style. The stage following that of Shūbun can be seen in the works of the 'Three Amis'—Nō-ami (1397–1471), his son, Gei-ami (1431–1485), and his grandson Sō-ami (1472–1525). *The Waterfall* by Gei-ami (Fig. 97) shows an increasing preoccupation with brushwork for its own sake and an advanced degree of stylization. The subject is a familiar one from centuries of Chinese painting and already somewhat hackneyed. A priest or scholar with his boy attendant approaches the simple hermit's hut in the peaceful depths of the countryside. The viewer, entangled in the multifold cares of the world, is expected to respond to the relief that this vision offers. But it takes a great artist to revitalize such a well-worn theme and in this painting everything is artificial and contrived. In his efforts to achieve a dramatic effect, Gei-ami has sacrificed the subtle union of reality and mystery which inspires the greatest Chinese landscape painting. The artist reveals, it is true, one of the great gifts of Japanese painters—the ability to see a rhythmical design in nature and to work it out boldly. The framework of the composition lies in the lines which repeat the basic curve at the top of the cavern sheltering the hut. These curves are taken up again and again. But brushwork outstrips his vision. The waterfall, from its source in the lake at the very top of the picture to where it disappears bubbling at the bottom, is reduced to lifeless, formalized lines.

Gei-ami knew nothing of Western perspective; nevertheless he has successfully solved the problem of what the Chinese call 'the far and the near.' In this he has been helped by the Ming painters who possibly were the first to overcome the difficulties of rendering the middle distance. But the outlines of the rocks are hard and dry in a manner alien to Chinese practice. The landscape completely lacks any relation to reality—an impression never created by Chinese landscape painting at its best. Gei-ami's affected rusticity and too elaborately balanced composition do injury to nature. The humbleness of Chinese masters before the grandeur of landscape is replaced by over-confidence and artificiality.

It remained for Sesshū (1420–1506) to raise *suiboku* painting to its highest level. He stands head and shoulders above his contemporaries and many critics, both Japanese and foreign, consider him to be the greatest landscapist of Japan. Sesshū was a *Zen* priest. He spent the years 1468–9 in China where, it is recorded, so great was his reputation that

97. *The Waterfall* by Gei-ami
(1431–1485)
Hanging scroll.
Ink and slight colour on paper.
Dated 1481.
Nezu Museum, Tokyo.

the Chinese even offered him the headship of a great monastery. Close familiarity with Chinese painting in the country of its origin and knowledge of the Chinese landscape which had inspired it gave him an advantage over many of his fellow painters and his works thereby gained authority and conviction. Unlike many other *suiboku* artists, Sesshū did not slavishly follow the styles and compositions of Sung-Yüan artists and their Ming dynasty followers. Influences of Chinese artists such as Li Ts'ai are noticeable in his work but it would be difficult to find any Ming painter from whom he could have derived his unique style.

In China at this period the painters and critics, tired of repetitions, were voicing the need for a return to nature. A little later Mo Shih-lung formulated this dissatisfaction in the words, " Painters of the past took the old masters as their models, but it is better to take Heaven and Earth as one's teacher." Sesshū learned this lesson better even than

98. *Winter Landscape* by Sesshū (1420–1506).   Hanging scroll.
Ink on paper.   18¼ by 11½ inches.   Tokyo National Museum.

99. *View of Ama-no-Hashidate.*
Hanging scroll. Ink on paper. 35 by 66½ inches. T. Yamanouchi Collection, Tokyo.

most Chinese painters of that time for whom dry copying was the rule rather than the exception.

Seeshū left notes of his stay in China in which he complains of the poor quality and lack of originality in Ming painting of his day. He was anxious to find something new from which he could learn, but did not find it in China. It was highly significant for the history of Japanese landscape painting that he was able to convince Japanese *suiboku* artists that their own landscape, which through some peculiar intellectual snobbery they seem to have considered unworthy of serious attention, provided in fact ample scope for their talents and that, by freeing themselves from dependence on Chinese models, they could immeasurably enrich their art.

Winter Landscape (Fig. 98) is typical of the style which made Sesshū famous. Snow, created merely by leaving parts of the paper blank, lies heavily over the countryside giving the mountains in the background the appearance of white sheets, and capping the rocks and trees with white. The roofs are covered with a heavy mantle. A traveller, bent with the cold, hurries towards a distant township huddled beneath the wing-like eaves of a great temple.

The scene is Chinese but the brushwork is unique to Sesshū. His work offers the supreme example of the nervous intensity which characterizes the Japanese brush. The thick, black ink has a sheen which makes it appear almost wet. He allows no Sung vagueness or softness, no hint of over-refinement. There is never an indeterminate or superfluous line: every jagged brushstroke has its reason and its life. Sesshū always understood just how much of his unusually powerful brush a picture could stand and he resisted the temptation to overdo it. What the Chinese call the ' bone structure ' of the composition is emphasized so as to be almost a bare skeleton.

100. *Spring and Summer*.   One of a pair of screens painted to represent The Four Seasons by Sesshū. Ink and colour on paper.   Courtesy of the Smithsonian Institution, Freer Gallery of Art, Washington, D.C.

This is more than just virtuosity. It is the work of an original artistic personality completely transforming into a valid Japanese interpretation the traditions of Chinese ink-painting as they had developed from Sung to Ming times. He has produced a synthesis of four centuries of Chinese painting. In his own way Sesshū succeeded in reinvigorating styles which in Ming China itself were rapidly degenerating into mannerism.

The *View of Ama-no-Hashidate* (Fig. 99) attributed to Sesshū shows the artist in a more gentle mood dealing with the landscapes of his native land. The place, situated on the picturesque Japan Sea, is one of the 'Three Scenic Beauty Spots of Japan.' A sand-bar extends tenuously towards an island; in the centre is a Buddhist temple and on the right a *Shintō* shrine, both with their names written over them to facilitate identification. The painting has a Chinese grandeur of conception but, in keeping with Japanese landscape, it is more intimately visualized. The softer and warmer ink-tones capture the steamy atmosphere of a Japanese summer—the mists enveloping the hills, the hot calm of the sea, the whiteness of the sand, and the luxuriant foliage in which temples and houses are almost lost. Sesshū is painting directly from nature and curbing his fantasy in order to do so. The minute details he wished to include have restricted his love of powerful abbreviated brushstrokes. The high viewpoint, which comes from Chinese painting, adds a bird's-eye dimension.

The composition is masterly. Three horizontal planes are skilfully connected. The foreground is almost neglected in order to draw the eye to the sand-bar and the town beyond. To give interest to the top register, the artist leads one up a winding path to a cluster of dwellings in the crown of the mountain. Its mass balances the heaviness of the island on the left, and breaks the monotony of the three horizontal planes. A Chinese painter would have been preoccupied with spiritual values and the mysteries of nature. Sesshū is engrossed in portraying its warmth and in exploring its intimate beauty—he created a direct and intensely personal approach which became one of the main distinguishing characteristics of all Japanese landscape painting.

Yet a third style used by Sesshū is seen in a pair of screens recently acquired by the Freer Gallery of Art, Washington D.C. These depict the four seasons—always popular subjects for Far Eastern artists. Figure 100 shows the screen which combines *Spring and Summer* executed in a more decorative style than he used for other works. The influence of the Chinese painter Lü Chi is clear. Colour is employed sparingly and the brushwork is incisive but restrained. The decorative effect at which he aimed is superbly achieved but he seems to be working within a smaller compass which gave little room for the exercise of his particular gifts. In spite of the clarity of the brushwork and the admirable organization of the various elements, there is less to stir the imagination in this work.

No account of Sesshū's art, however brief, would be complete without mention of his two great landscape scrolls. Figure 101 is taken from his *Larger Landscape Scroll* dated 1468 when he was 67. Nearly 60 ft. long by $15\frac{3}{4}$ inches high it is a most remarkable feat of sustained imagination which compares well with any landscape scroll produced in China. Sesshū takes the spectator on a friendly journey through the Chinese countryside. Hills and valleys, streams and rivers flow by; a path leads up jagged, beetling rocks under shady trees. A fishing village huddles amidst the reeds, its boats lie becalmed in mid-stream; a pagoda rises above the misty roofs of a township. Two travellers stop to pass the time of day on the way up to some mountain retreat, a crowd gathers at a rest house in a rocky glen. The owners of a fine walled estate sit calmly in a high room enjoying the view. Through the whole length of the scroll the interest never flags, the brush never weakens. This microcosm of China is strongly influenced by the style of Hsia Kuei and his successors but the incisive brushwork is again unmistakably that of Sesshū. It is without doubt the masterpiece of his mature old age.

Sesshū was the greatest and most individual Japanese master in the Chinese-inspired *suiboku* style. His work stands comparison with anything produced in China at his time. His successors continued the Japanization of these Chinese modes. In the process they removed the *Zen* Buddhist inspiration and tended to replace it with the over-powerful native sense of decoration. This began in the work of Kanō Masanobu (*ca.* 1434–*ca.* 1530) a contemporary of Sesshū, but was firmly established by his son Kanō Motonobu. The school of painting which the Kanō family created was to dominate the following two periods

101. Section from the *Larger Landscape Scroll* by Sesshū. Ink and slight colour on paper. Height $15\frac{3}{4}$ inches. M. Mōri Collection, Yamaguchi.

102. (Left). *The Sage Chou Mao-shu in a Lotus Pond*
by Kanō Masanobu (*ca.* 1434–*ca.* 1530).
Ink and colour on paper. 33¼ by 13 inches.
T. Nakamura Collection, Tokyo.

103. (Below). Detail of *Landscape with Flowers and Birds*
by Kanō Motonobu. (1476–1559).
Ink and slight colour on paper. Originally painted on a
sliding screen; now mounted as a hanging scroll.
70 by 46½ inches.
Reiun-in, Kyoto.

and lasted down to the end of the 19th century. It produced generation after generation of famous painters (either genuine or adopted members of the family) many of whom occupied important official positions in the service of the various rulers of the country. In the Tokugawa period the Kanō was recognized as the ' official ' school.

Masanobu, the first of this long line, was not a *Zen* priest. This, in itself, shows a break with the *suiboku* tradition. Although he inherited the style of Shūbun, he obviously felt himself free from any restrictions imposed by Buddhist thought. Only two authenticated works by him have survived. Figure 102 shows his painting of the Chinese sage *Chou Mao-shu* (1017–1073). Chou Mao-shu is considered second only to the great Sung philosopher Chu Hsi whose interpretations dominated Confucian philosophy for nearly seven centuries. He is venerated as an ideal Confucian scholar-official and is a popular subject for didactic Chinese and Japanese paintings. His famed love of lotus flowers provided painters with an ideal setting.

Japanese scholars see in this painting a great difference from that of Gei-ami, illustrated in Plate oo. But, apart from the fact that the subject, Chou Mao-shu, had nothing to do with Buddhism, there seems no great diversity between the approach of the two painters. If anything, Masanobu's work shows a finer appreciation of the true Chinese Sung feeling for landscape. However, the somewhat dry, formalized brushwork and the tendency to an uninspired neatness in this essay in the Chinese style, as seen particularly in details like the large lotus-flowers, unmistakably reveals the Japanese hand. The typical Kanō quality of this painting is visible in the clear-cut lines and still atmosphere. Masanobu's other surviving painting is of a *Zen* subject, the *Priest Pu Tai*. This in itself is an added indication that, although not a member of the priesthood, he sometimes painted very much in the manner of the *Zen suiboku* masters. It is tempting to conclude that the Chinese style was more a social convention inherited from the Ashikaga *Shōguns'* veneration of Chinese work than a genuine native predilection.

The true Kanō style is seen more clearly in the work of his son Motonobu (1476–1559). The detail in Figure 103 was originally painted on a *fusuma* in the Reiun-in, a temple in Kyoto where most of his works are still preserved. These *fusuma* are light sliding partitions made of reinforced wooden frames covered on both sides with paper that are used to divide Japanese rooms. They provide ideal surfaces for large-scale decorations, but are extremely delicate and easily damaged—as anybody who has lived in a Japanese house knows to his cost. This painting is one of forty-nine *Landscapes with Flowers and Birds* which Motonobu did to decorate the temple and which have now been mounted as hanging scrolls in order to preserve them.

The artist's aim here was simply to decorate a room in Chinese style and the painting has no greater pretensions. Judged by these standards the work has many good qualities—confident brushwork and strong ink tones are used in a striking composition. The elegant birds contrast effectively with the gnarled pine branch. It is conceived in two sharply differentiated planes—the background of the hills being only sketchily indicated—and it shows a decorative interpretation of Sung styles inherited from such eminent landscape masters as Hsia Kuei. But there the relationship ends. Although of excellent draughtsmanship, it has neither the humility nor the depth of feeling of the Sung masters. Motonobu's aim was a satisfying decoration expressed in terms of generally accepted brushwork, and everything is sacrificed to these two requirements. The standards by which we judge Kanō works must therefore be different from those applied to Chinese ink painting. They inhabit a less exalted world. Nevertheless they enjoyed a great vogue and Motonobu's paintings were the forerunners of a vast school of decorative art which will be discussed later (see p. 167).

The Kanō paintings were made under Chinese influence. But what became of the native Japanese style of painting which flourished so vigorously in the early Kamakura period?

During the 15th century another great painting family made its appearance—that of the Tosa. In this school the traditions of *Yamato-e* were preserved for later generations ot develop. The *Yamato-e* style of painting had perhaps been the greatest achievement of the Kamakura period. By the end of the Ashikaga period it had been somewhat overwhelmed by the impact of Chinese styles but it never died out completely. Some of the painters of this time seem to have worked in both the Kanō and Tosa styles so that it is not always easy to say whether an artist belonged exclusively to one or the other school. A further indication of the friendly mixture of schools and the happy eclecticism of Japanese painters can be inferred from Kanō Motonobu's marriage to the daughter of Tosa Mitsunobu (1434–1525) who is generally considered to have established the Tosa school. Kanō Motonobu occasionally worked in the Tosa style, although whether this was for family reasons is not recorded.

Only few good *Yamato-e* scrolls were produced towards the end of the Kamakura period. In 1414, however, a number of artists of different schools co-operated to paint a scroll entitled the *Yuzu Nembutsu Engi* or 'History of the Yūzū Nembutsu Sect of Buddhism.' Among them were a certain Tosa Yukihiro and his son Tosa Yukihide, the two painters who are credited with founding the Tosa school proper. Tosa Mitsunobu who, as mentioned above, firmly established the school was the grandson of Yukihide. In 1469 he was put in charge of the *E-dokoro* or 'Bureau of Painting,' thus receiving official recognition and patronage from the Ashikaga *Shōgun*. This was against the general run of Tosa school fortunes for mostly the Kanō school effaced the Tosa and, after Mitsunobu, few great Tosa names appear until the Tokugawa period. Mitsunobu's grandson was even forced to leave Kyoto, the centre of artistic life; he was probably driven to seek employment in less fashionable areas.

The eclipse of the Tosa by the Kanō is an indication of the weakness of the native traditions in the face of foreign art styles even when the latter were pressed into a usage for which they were unsuited. Considered purely as decoration, however, the stylized compositions and rich colours of the Tosa were far better media than the inflated Kanō works with their formality and dry ink. It is fortunate for the Japanese decorative arts that the *Yamato-e* traditions did not entirely vanish. A small number of screens painted at the end of the Ashikaga period give a foretaste of the decorative splendours of the next period. The survival of the *Yamato-e* interest in genre and crowd scenes of contemporary life can be seen in the screen by Kanō Hideyori, a son of Motonobu. This *Maple Viewing at Takao* (a famous beauty spot outside Kyoto), of which a detail is shown in Figure 104 is a remarkable essay in the style of the *Handbooks* (see pp. 100–1) applied to large decorative surfaces. In the treatment of the figures it recalls the *Man with Loose Teeth* (Fig. 82). There is, of course, no didacticism in this work. Very real human figures are arranged in a highly decorative landscape. Strangely enough, the combination does not disturb the eye, perhaps because there are no pretensions. The colours are rich and effectively matched. Everything is subordinated to the demands of gaiety and pure decoration in which the Japanese are here seen in their element. Its very colourfulness gives it a particularly unaffected charm.

104. *Maple Viewing at Takao*
(detail)
by Kanō Hideyori.
Part of a six panel screen.
Ink and colour on paper.
Tokyo National Museum.

' Detachment without lifelessness ' is the quality which the Japanese admire in this work. After some of the stiff, self-conscious Kanō products, it comes as a warm breath of gay spontaneity in which the Japanese spirit shows itself without reserve.

Just as Chinese styles dominated Ashikaga painting in general so, too, its ceramics were inspired by the products of the great Chinese kilns. Japanese records list large numbers of Chinese Sung and Yüan period wares imported into Japan at that time and Korean inlaid celadons were very popular. The Ashikaga period was, above all, the age of the Seto kilns and the large production from them is an indication of the demand for good ceramics.

Wares with a high-fired celadon-type glaze had been introduced into Japan from China as early as the 9th century and the Japanese first made them at the Owari kilns near Seto which previously had produced the finest Sue type pottery. In the 12th century, the centre for the manufacture of celadon type wares moved to Seto itself where the potters further perfected the techniques necessary for their production, and made their finest examples in the 14th and 15th centuries. The British Museum has recently acquired a fine example of these 14th century Seto wares (Fig. 105), a pot with strong shoulders and a crackled glaze which runs in streaks to the base. The design is a fairly regularly arranged series of inter-locking commas which infuse it with a lively rhythm and give distinction to the shape. The neck and glaze, in particular, are typical of these wares. Broadly speaking, one can say that the Ashikaga period saw the real beginning of Japanese ceramics.

These Seto kilns produced their celadon-glazed wares in a large variety of shapes. The most popular colours were yellow and amber and occasionally both were applied to produce a two-coloured ware. Though heavy, the shapes of these wheel-made wares are much more graceful than in the Kamakura period and the clay is more refined. The decoration, frequently of peonies, became more stylized and is often carefully arranged in wide bands round the bodies. The British Museum specimen is unusual in its all-over design. Sometimes pairs of fish were incised in imitation of Chinese celadon plates. At the same time, the shapes and often the designs of the wares begin to show indications of Japanese taste, especially in objects which were then beginning to be used for the ceremony of tea drinking.

One of the most popular Chinese wares of this period was the *chien* type, a deep brown or black iron-glazed ware, probably first made in the Chien-ning district of Fukien in the 10th century. The Japanese call this type of ware *temmoku* which is the Japanese reading of T'ien-mu, the name of a mountain in Chekiang. Several famous Buddhist temples situated on this mountain popularized the *temmoku* pottery which the priests used in tea-drinking ceremonies. The deep, lustrous glazes of this ware appealed to the eye and especially to the touch of the connoisseurs of tea. The conical shapes are simple but most perfect in their union of strength and elegance. The glaze, subdued and lustrous, is allowed to form a pool at the bottom of the cup and run into large globules where outside it comes down to the foot-rim. The ware was copied at Seto.

The cult of tea-drinking ceremonies originated in China where it was popular among the *Ch'an* (Jap. *Zen*) monks and it was introduced into Japan with the *Zen* sect. There it was taken up, at first in a dilettante manner, by Ashikaga Yoshimasa (1435–1490) and aristocratic circles around him. Under the most famous tea master, Sen-no-Rikyū (1520–1591), it was refined and developed into a cult which had great influence on pottery design and on other arts such as architecture and painting.

Reduced to its essentials, the ceremony gave an opportunity for active men to retire from the busy world for an hour or so, to a small hut carefully designed and landscaped in their own gardens. There they could enjoy, in the most beautiful surroundings, a bowl of tea prepared and served by their host with quiet grace and gentility according to a prescribed ceremony. It is a peculiarly Eastern concept whose aim is to induce men to contemplate the more refined and eternal aspects of life. To conform to the basic requirement of strict equality, the *samurai* was required to leave his sword outside the hut. In China a recluse, perhaps with a few friends, would drink his tea before some broad landscape and contemplate a famed panorama; in Japan everything was reduced in scale and the grandeur of nature was simulated by the most cunning landscape gardening. Peace, respect, rustic serenity, and solitude were the aims of the ceremony in its purest form. Under Ashikaga Yoshimasa its general lines were formulated. The great age of the ceremony was short and later under the Tokugawa *shōguns* it was stripped of all its sincere, spiritual values and vulgarized.

Sen-no-Rikyū is an important figure in the history of the ceremony. Through the financial support of a wealthy father, he was able to devote himself completely to the study of the arts. His concept of the tea ceremony became extremely popular, especially with the more bucolic *samurai* who came to Kyoto in search of political fortune. For them, his classes acted as an easy finishing school in manners, putting them at their ease in the refined society in which they found themselves. (The ceremony still fulfills this function for aspirants to the social graces.) Conversation on art and politics flowed freely in these

105. *Vase*, Seto ware.
14th century.
Height 10 inches.
British Museum.

salons and it has been suggested that, had they continued in the course set out for them by Sen-no-Rikyū, they might have fulfilled the same function as the *sociétés de pensée* of 18th century France in the diffusion of liberal thought and democratic ideas.

Unfortunately, Sen-no-Rikyū was put to death by Hideyoshi, the dictator of the next regime. The reasons for this are not clear, but there is evidence to suggest that the tea master, a man of very high moral standards, did not approve of Hideyoshi's exploitation of the ceremony for political purposes.[1]

For the arts, the most important result of the tea ceremony was the cult of the rustic which it created. This coloured the whole artistic outlook of Japan in succeeding centuries. Elegant Chinese Sung and Ming wares were greatly appreciated for use in the tea ceremonies but, since it was the aim to approach nature as closely as possible, many of the rougher, less sophisticated native wares seem to have been even more popular. The old Bizen and Shigaraki kilns were at the time producing strong but crude wares for everyday use which now became very fashionable—both for their vigour and because they served to offset the elegant Chinese products. Often these Japanese wares contained flaws— dents, faults of shape, places where the glaze did not cover the body, and volcanic-looking irregularities. These were so much admired that later potters consciously, though not altogether successfully, imitated them. Sometimes these later craftsmen in the rustic style created outstanding works. At others they produced objects as senseless as the more exaggerated niceties of the tea ceremony itself. At their best the rough tea wares have

[1] E. Herbert Norman. *Andō Shōeki and the Anatomy of Japanese Feudalism.* Tokyo, 1949.

an organic, monumental quality which can only be discussed in sculptural terms; often they are only as ' genuinely rustic ' as the seats and pergolas in an English garden suburb.

Jean-Pierre Hauchecorne, a Frenchman who has lived in Japan for the last twenty-five years and has reached deeply into the Japanese way of life wrote about the true *Zen* influence which permeates all aspects of Japanese life. His remarks have a bearing on the basic concepts which animated the early tea-ceremony masters. Referring to the spirit of *Zen* as one of ' clear poverty ' he says " The lesson of *Zen* . . . has taken me toward human beings, and it has shown me the beauty which is expressed in the least movement, in the most humble type of work: those of the peasant, as he attends carefully to his earth, as he plants his rice stem by stem, as he decorates the very ridge of his humble straw roof, as he also beautifies the entrance of his farm with a few rocks and a twisted plum tree; those of the craftsman, as he turns his pot and, with a few strokes of the brush, throws on it a design, the sheen of which will never be known until it comes out of the wood-fed kiln; those of the most ordinary way of packing, where wood, straw or a twig of vine will wrap up in a living warmth the inanimate object inside."[1]

The aesthetic approach inspired by *Zen* leads to the perception of beauty in the most lowly object and to the appreciation of even its most insignificant variation. This is by no means a small contribution to art appreciation and to the formation of a sensitive taste. The tea-ceremony provided the stage for the display of this refined rusticity, this conscious play of opposites.

The finest metal-work of the Ashikaga period is found in two kinds of objects which throw light on two conflicting sides of the Japanese character—the brutal and the sensitive. Each of them, taken separately, shows this same contradiction of spirit. They are sword fittings and iron kettles for the tea-ceremony. The aim of the decorators of the sword fittings was, especially in later times, to make them as elegant and sophisticated as possible. The casters of the kettles tried to give them a virility of shape and design which seems, at first sight, almost out of keeping with the gentle spirit of the ceremony.

Sword guards or *tsuba* were first used as early as the Nara period but few of these have survived, and not until much later was so much artistry applied to their manufacture that they rank as works of art. Large collections of these guards exist outside Japan. Their technical and decorative variety is inexhaustible—piercing, chiselling, punching, inlays of all kinds create an unending variety of highly original decorations. Among the thousands which poured from the workshops to satisfy the cult of the sword the collector seldom finds two which are identical, even in the products of the same workshop.

Many of these *tsuba* are signed by their makers and works of acknowledged masters were much treasured—and consequently forged in later times. These craftsmen took as much pride in the perpetuation of their families and schools as did the painters. When a line was in danger of dying out, they often adopted a suitable apprentice to continue the family name. Thus Gotō Yūjō worked during the reign of Yoshimasa (1435–1490) and the family continued for seventeen generations of craftsmen down to the end of the 19th century when the carrying of swords was forbidden by law.

In the Ashikaga period the craftsmen began, though still only very tentatively, to explore the possibilities of decorating the surfaces of these *tsuba*. At first, simple designs based on figures or simple motifs taken from nature were made in relief or incised on the flat surfaces. The small area and circumscribed shape presented a challenge which constantly tested the

[1] *This is Japan*, 1956. Tokyo, 1956.

Japanese genius for decorative invention. It always seems to thrive under such restrictions, and the solutions which the *tsuba* makers discovered are inexhaustible.

Two *tsuba* in the Hosokawa collections by two of the most famous masters of the time are representative of the late 15th century styles. The guard in Figure 106a is fist-shaped with a figure of Bishamonten[1] on the right balanced by a tree on the left. The decoration is in relief with touches of gold and silver set into the figure. The maker was the famous Kaniei. The other by Nobuie (Fig. 106b) is of a more graceful quatre-foil shape and, to offset this, very simply decorated with an incised branch simply but effectively arranged to curl round three-quarters of the circumference. It is placed in such a way as to follow the line of the fist. Such simple guards, however, are only just beginning to move away from the purely functional. They hardly give a suggestion of the technical masterpieces of the following centuries when the designers replaced their practical vigour by decorative fantasy.

Cast-iron kettles as objects of art developed from the every-day kitchen pots of earlier times. The tea-ceremony lifted them out of the kitchen into the cultivated atmosphere of the tea-hut and transformed them to serve the Japanese cult of the rustic. The humbler an object, the more the Japanese delighted in exploring its potentialities. But popularity is the greatest enemy of the craftsman. It is remarkable that, even when the rustic taste became an affectation, enough skill and tradition remained to produce simple works which come up to the highest standards. The example in Figure 107 was made about 1500 and

[1] The equivalent of Kuvera, the Hindu god of riches. He is shown in full armour with a fierce expression, carrying a small pagoda-shaped shrine in his right hand and a lance in his left. The latter accounts for his being confused with the gods of war.

A

B

106. (a. and b.). *Two sword Guards* by Kaniei and Nobuie. Iron. Muromachi period.
About half size. M. Hosokawa Collection, Tokyo.

107. (Below). *Kettle for the Tea Ceremony.* Ashiya type. Iron. Muromachi period.
Height 7½ inches. Tokyo National Museum.

is typical of one of the most famous makes of the period, the Ashiya type, so-called from its place of manufacture, a seaside village in Fukuoka. The beautiful proportions of the kettle reflect the assurance of centuries of experience in the craft. The well-fitting lid, slightly concave with a coiled animal handle, increases the firmness of the outline. The animal-mask handles lighten the impression of heaviness in the body. The design is carefully planned to set off the material, and attract the eye. Five energetic horses gallop round the sides against the faint outlines of hills on the shoulders of the kettle. This is very much in the style of Chinese Yüan-Ming horse painting and shows how such artistic knowledge had permeated down even to the village craftsmen. The successful adaptation of painting styles to cast iron is proof of a rare taste and ability. The designs and workmanship of European gold and silver work are admirable—how much more surprising is the loving care which the Japanese lavished on plain iron!

These iron kettles were, of course, intended to contribute to the atmosphere of simple country life sought by the adepts of the tea ceremony. They served also, by the roughness of their material, as a foil to the more delicate objects in the tea ensemble—to the pottery bowls or the bamboo ladle, to the small square of rich brocade which glittered all the more brilliantly against their dull black surface. Everything in the little room was carefully

108. *Box for an Ink-stone.*
Lacquer.
Muromachi period.
9 by 8¼ inches.
Nezu Museum, Tokyo.

planned to catch and reflect or to set off the qualities of the various components—smooth and rough, simple and intricate, rustic and sophisticated. The possibilities were infinite and they still exercise the Japanese mind.

As one might expect, the lacquer workers of the Ashikaga period rapidly adopted the contemporaneous painting styles and adjusted their products to the taste of the times. Thus boxes and tables reflect Chinese painting styles as interpreted by the Kanō masters. However, craftsmen also kept alive the *Yamato-e* traditions which seem to show more persistence in lacquer than in painting. The lacquerers had less need to adhere to any particular style and they indulged in greater eclecticism. Thus a typical Kanō element is sometimes quite happily combined with a *Yamato-e* background—a tree will come straight from a Kanō screen while above it hang the horizontal bands of mist used so effectively in the Japanese handscrolls.

The peculiar taste for combining elegance and rusticity pervades especially articles made in the Higashiyama period when Yoshimasa was in power. Techniques became more involved and strove to create richer effects, designs became less meticulous but heavier. *Taka-makie* was particularly popular as were also objects made in China from the familiar red lacquer. Accordingly *Kamakura-bori*, which had been inspired by it (see p. 113), found favour and there seems to have been a considerable interchange between Japan and China of their respective lacquer wares. It is of significance for the wedding of the arts and crafts that Michinaga, a lacquer master who served Yoshimasa, used the work of such famous painters as Nōami, Sōami, and Tosa Mitsunobu as prototypes for the designs on his wares.

The *makie* box in Figure 108, formerly owned by Yoshimasa, shows a typical and happy combination of Kanō and *Yamato-e* styles. It also illustrates a distinguishing feature of the lacquer of this period—a preference for simplified pictorial motifs boldly expressed. The designers of the preceding Kamakura period generally chose crowded surfaces, often filled with repetitive designs; Ashikaga work shows more restraint and feeling. The designers, at least in this period, resisted the temptation to surrender to the extremes of over-brilliance and sentimentality. The designs on these lacquer objects often carried strong literary over-tones. This box illustrates a poem about ' the falling of cherry blossoms in the spring at Shirakawa.' A clue to the source of inspiration is provided by the characters for Shirakawa on the tree trunk and the rock at its base. The possibilities in the decorative use of characters, so greatly developed in later periods, first occurred to the designers at this time.

An atmosphere of springtime pervades the design—in the mists and the falling petals which settle around the lonely figure. All unnecessary detail has been omitted to clarify and simplify the scene. The spectator is induced to identify himself with the wistfulness of a passing moment in an intimate, confidential way which is typically Japanese. This gift for the communication of intimate experiences is rarely found in Chinese craftwork. There the Westerner stands back and admires a product which is quite obviously perfect and just as obviously of a world entirely different from his own. The experiences communicated by Japanese art are more warm, passionate, and universal.

The writing table in Figure 109 shows how the *Zen* ideals of simplicity and 'emptiness' influenced the crafts. Here an oblong shape has been skilfully filled with a springy plum tree reaching out over a stream and dividing the surface into two triangles. A crescent moon forms the compositional counterpart for a rock in the water. The movement of the

109. *Writing Table*.   Lacquer.   Muromachi period.   14¼ by 24 inches.   Tokyo National Museum.

stream is shown by a few schematized waves which push in towards the bank. By opposing the direction of the plum branch, they provide balance and tension. Could anything better illustrate the Japanese instinct for design—the union of the natural and the artificial, the appeal to the eye and the sentiment? It is easy to understand why such objects, which seem to combine the skill of the craftsman and the sensibility of the painter, appealed to the Chinese. Their workmen had nothing comparable to offer.

Unlike the lacquerer's craft, that of the textile designer reached its nadir in the Ashikaga period. When the Kamakura regime destroyed the wealth and power of the Kyoto aristocracy, it removed the patrons of the expensive textile industry. The elaborate many-layered costumes which envelop and weigh down the figures in the *Genji* scroll belonged to a past age. Dress had become more simple and austere in the Kamakura period and this tendency, allied to the *Zen* ideals, continued in the Ashikaga period. In the civil wars and social disturbances of the 14th and 15th centuries many of the skilled techniques of textile manufacture were forgotten. Even good quality silk was no longer produced. Thus the Ashikaga period was the drab conclusion of a process of decline which had been gaining momentum since Fujiwara times.

In this period of eclipse, however, there begins a significant development which was to have major consequences in the next period. The garment called *ko-sode* or ' short hanging sleeves,' which replaced court dress, was the forerunner of the modern *kimono*. To decorate it, the Japanese returned to an earlier technique of tie-dyeing suitable for large, bold designs. This was quicker and cheaper than the old system of weaving and enlivened the dress of the poorer classes. The tastes of the richer sections of the population were satisfied largely by imports from abroad. Fine textiles of the Sung, Yüan, and Ming dynasties came from China. Indian cotton prints and fabrics from the South Seas, materials from the Near East and Europe also found their way to Japan—especially after the Portuguese opened their trading activities in the Far East. Fragments of the most costly of these were used as mountings for valuable paintings and for wrapping the precious objects used in the tea-ceremonies. They were highly treasured and, in their turn, they stimulated local factories to emulate them and thus to revive a dying craft. This is another example of the readiness of the Japanese to accept and assimilate foreign products which has enriched Japan from the earliest times. The effect on later craft-work provides many interesting sidelines to the general development of Japanese art.

It is interesting to observe how, when foreign example inspired the Chinese, their products usually lack the vitality and charm which we see in Japanese products made under similar influences. Perhaps the Chinese, lacking the adaptability of the Japanese, are temperamentally less suited to making the inventions of other lands their own.

The Ashikaga *shōguns* proved no more successful in solving the vital problem of disciplining the feudal lords of the provinces than the late Kamakura rulers before them. In the new fight for supreme power, which lasted a hundred years, old families disappeared, new ones took their place and their possessions. Slowly the lands and forces of many of the old *daimyōs* were absorbed until the struggle resolved itself into a contest between about half a dozen of the most virile competitors. From these one emerged supreme— Oda Nobunaga (1534–1582).

CHAPTER VIII

THE MOMOYAMA PERIOD

1568–1615

THE Momoyama period initiated by Nobunaga was short—it lasted only forty-seven years. Yet politically and artistically it was a most important half century in the history of Japan. It was a period of intense warfare, yet it laid the foundations of modern Japan, and of two hundred and fifty years of peace such as the country had not enjoyed since the 10th century. ' Modern ' Japanese art likewise stems from these fifty years, the most ebullient and colourful phase in the whole development of Japanese art.

Nobunga, though of an ancient clan, was a typical example of the way in which members of relatively obscure families could rise to power in the anarchical 16th century. He had steadily consolidated his strength at the expense of neighbours less virile than himself and, by the early 1560's, was numbered among the most formidable of the lords. His actual seizure of national power followed the pattern established by the rise of other great *shōguns* before him, for a helpless and threatened Emperor appealed to him to come to his aid. In 1567 he answered the call, marched on Kyoto and made himself the effective ruler. It is an indication of Japanese respect for traditions that he retained not only the Emperor but also a member of the Ashikaga line in their positions of empty dignity. The latter, no sooner secure, was rash enough to plot against Nobunaga who promptly disposed of him.

Nobunga spent the following years in ensuring his supremacy. This entailed defeating the most powerful of his fellow barons and putting an end to the threats of the militant monks. His general Toyotomi Hideyoshi and his ally Tokugawa Ieyasu, both of whom had risen from humble origins, served him well. Death or defeat removed some of his main rivals. He put down the warlike monks on Mt. Hiei, whose descents on the capital had been such a constant threat in previous centuries, and burned their monasteries. Other more impregnable temple-strongholds gave him greater trouble. The most powerful of these, at Osaka, fell in 1580 only after ten years of siege.

In 1582 Nobunaga was assassinated by one of his own men and it was left to Hideyoshi to revenge his master and to complete the work begun by him. By 1587 he controlled the southern island of Kyūshū; by 1590 the north was subdued and one third of the country was in his power. After this, other lords found it wise to come over to his side.

Hideyoshi, who is often compared with Napoleon, was the first plebian ever to rise to supreme power in Japan. He was more astute than many *shōguns* before him in his appreciation of the difficulty and danger of disbanding an army which in some of his campaigns

110. *Himeji Castle.*
Momoyama period.
Himeji.
Hyōgo Prefecture.

had numbered a quarter of a million men. Judging from the results of earlier pirate raids on the mainland, foreign conquest seemed a practical and profitable way of exploiting their energies and diverting their ambitions. He felt strong enough to contemplate attacking even China (then in the last weak decades of the Ming dynasty) but finally chose Korea. He invaded this country twice—in 1592 and 1597–8. The second campaign was cut short by the death of Hideyoshi in 1598 and Tokugawa Ieyasu was forced to spend the next seventeen years in a struggle for absolute control at home which he finally secured only in 1615. With this the short Momoyama period gave way to the long Tokugawa period which lasted until 1868.

The Momoyama or 'Peach Hill' period is named after a castle of that name built by Hideyoshi at Fushimi in 1593. The decorations which artists evolved for such castles set the pattern for the arts. Nobunaga had initiated the fashion with a splendid stronghold beautifully situated on the shores of Lake Biwa near Kyoto. This was destroyed in 1582 after his assassination. The largest of all these fortresses, erected by Hideyoshi at Osaka from 1583–85, also perished in 1615. But a number built by other feudal lords throughout Japan have survived. Himeji Castle, also known as the *Shirasagi* or 'White Heron Castle' (Fig. 110) is one of the finest. A fortress existed here in the 14th century but its shape is unknown. The present castle was built at the end of the 16th century and expanded in 1608–9. The large seven-storied tower built on granite walls is about 100 ft. high and around it cluster smaller four- or five-storied keeps forming one massive compound. This type of castle architecture is unique in its combination of elegance and strength, a bold union from which Momoyama art drew its authority and its momentum.

The new war-lords spared no expense to furnish their rooms in the richest styles that artists could devise. It was a truly baroque age of buoyancy and brilliance. Feudal lords vied with each other in the splendour of their castles. Lavishness of decoration and entertainment became a mania—precious metals and costly lacquer were squandered in efforts

111. *Garden of the Sambō-in.*
Completed in 1615.
Daigo-ji, Kyoto.

to produce ever more dazzling backgrounds against which the new masters of Japan could parade. Art was also made to serve politics, for the aim of Nobunaga and his successors was to secure obedience from possible rivals by every available means—by the display of material advantages as well as by threats of military sanctions. The works of the decorators who enriched the castle interiors are among the world's finest products of the baroque spirit in art.

In the short Momoyama period, the divisions between the various schools seemed to break down and styles were in the melting-pot. Colour was liberated from all restraint and artists welcomed the opportunities this freedom gave them. What were the causes of this sudden outburst? The new men in power were of a coarser grain than their predecessors and the refining influences of Kyoto had lost their centuries-old appeal. The desire of the dictators to impress only partly explains the phenomenon. There was also a practical reason: gold and silver backgrounds were needed to bring light into the otherwise gloomy interiors of these huge fortresses. But in fact Japan was growing tired of the austerity of the Kamakura and of the restrained good-taste of the Ashikaga periods; even the spirit of *Zen* simplicity was losing its attraction and vigour. At the same time, with peace came a prosperity hitherto unknown.

If the rulers set the fashion, it was joyfully followed by the rest of the country. The *recherché* Ashikaga atmosphere of tiny tea hut and rustic clay pot gave way to vast gardens lined with painted screens in which hundreds sat down to drink tea from golden vessels. The discreet alcove which offered but a few evocative brush strokes of black and white surrendered to vistas of florid colour in magnificent sweeps intended to overwhelm the senses. The simper of the late Ashikaga court went down before the swagger of men like Nobunaga. Everything gave way to the search for novelty.

The garden of the Sambō-in of the Daigo-ji Temple (Fig. 111), restored under the patronage of Hideyoshi and completed in 1615, gives an impression of the rich effects that were sought for even in temple settings.

In art, colour and movement took the place of monochrome and stillness. Through the centuries artists had been feeling their way towards techniques which could be used in exuberant ways—one sees glimpses of it in Tosa scrolls, in *Yamato-e* landscapes, in lacquer, and even in metal-work. The artists often seem to have restrained their native urge for vivid decoration with only the greatest difficulty. From now on all restraint is removed and even the oldest themes find new life and original interpretations. The general conception of Japanese art in the West is understandably, though not always fairly, based on this art of the ' modern ' period as the Japanese call it. The quieter but nobler products of earlier ages are often overlooked.

One of the few furnishings in Japanese rooms are folding screens which consist mainly of panels, and sliding doors covered with paper. Every possible space on these was now covered with bold paintings generally planned in pairs or series. One reads of commissions even for sets of a hundred such screens. These paintings on walls, doors, and screens (with the generic name of *sho-hei-ga*), are yet another typically Japanese development. Large painted screens, of course, were not an innovation. Early examples have been preserved in the Shōsō-in (see Fig. 39). Chinese paintings dating back to the 11th century show them although, curiously enough, none have survived on the mainland. In Japan, too, they were used in the Kamakura period or even earlier. Kanō Motonobu painted ink monochrome screens in the Ashikaga period, and *Yamato-e* styles, particularly suitable for decorating large spaces, had also been revived for decorating them. But the Momoyama artists now combined the two styles—giving the outlines the powerful brushwork of *suiboku* painting and filling the areas so defined with bright colours. To this they added the extravagance of gold which was lavishly used for the backgrounds. The large areas to be decorated naturally led to broad, sweeping brush-strokes, monumental designs, and large-scale motifs. In what seems an attempt to bring nature itself into the castles to serve the new rulers, trees, flowers, birds, and animals are often introduced, even in life-size.

At the head of the movement stands Kanō Eitoku (1543–1590), the grandson of Motonobu. Nobunaga commissioned him to decorate his castle at Azuchi. The castle was soon burned down, but we know that he, possibly aided by his pupils, furnished five of its seven stories with both Chinese and *Yamato-e* style paintings. It is likely that what now remains of his work does him less than justice. The six-panelled screen of *Chinese Lions* (*Kara-shishi*) in the Imperial Collection (Fig. 112) is one of the few that have survived. The animals, symbolical of peace and dignity, recall the fierce mythical beasts which decorated Chinese roofs from the Ming period onwards. The background is a rich sweep of gold applied in squares. The manes of the animals are in green and brown and their bodies are mottled. A few cliffs and rocks on the left are in green and brown. A small twig of a tree provides the only naturalistic element in the whole composition. After the restrained paintings of the Ashikaga period, such work comes as a shock. It is frankly gaudy and not very sensitive but it has a tremendous verve and ebullience. The composition is audacious—the dynamic figures seem hardly containable within their frames. The artist has abandoned himself completely to the demands of a lusty, unconventional age and one senses a joyous release from the restraints of the last centuries.

Other works by the same artist show that, like many Japanese painters from the 15th century onwards, he, too, was very eclectic in his sources. He could adapt the new rich style to imposing landscapes filled with realistic trees set against a decorative gold background. He painted also, if not at his most original, such familiar subjects as *Sages in Landscape* in the traditional Chinese ink styles. The combination of monochrome and polychrome painting is one of the features of Momoyama work. It must

112. *Chinese Lions* (*Kara-shishi*). by Kanō Eitoku (1543–1590).
Colour on gilt paper.   7 feet 4½ inches by 15 feet 1 inch.   Imperial Collection.

always be remembered that these men were decorators and, like good craftsmen the world over, they fitted their styles to their commissions. The records are very confusing and, since most of the screens are unsigned, many problems of authorship remain unsolved. A screen painter, Kaihō Yūshō (1533–1615), is mentioned in literary sources as having the skill of the Chinese painter Liang K'ai, yet a typical work by him of peonies and plum blossom against a golden background is the complete antithesis of a Chinese monochrome. It seems that the forces which swept away the Ashikaga destroyed for a short time also the snobbism which had insisted on painting rigidly in the Chinese fashion.

Hasegawa Tōhaku (1539–1610) was another painter who, like Kaihō Yūshō, was equally at home in both Chinese and Japanese styles. The detail in Figure 113 shows a most striking individuality of style in ink painting combined with a very Japanese lyrical feeling for landscape. This detail is taken from two screens of pine trees which are among the finest achievements of the Japanese talent based on Chinese technique and inspiration. The artist has used mist and light rain as a black and white lens through which to see the dark green of the trees. The soft Japanese ink, quietly modulated from black down to pale grey, creates an impression of hazy depth; the tops of the trees emerge from an eerie mist which evokes the stillness of the Japanese landscape in one of its mysterious moods. Thus the cool calm of the woods is brought into the house as if to provide a visual relief during the humid heat of summer. Tōhaku's work represents an attempt to revive *Zen suiboku* traditions and to give them meaning in a more modern context. He disliked the Kanō school—an attitude shared by his friend, the great tea-master Sen-no-Rikyū. He traced his origins back to the great ink paintings of Sesshū and styled himself ' Sesshū the Fifth.' It is an indication of the importance attached to such a claim that he had to fight a law-suit for the right to the lineage. How unfortunate it is that no verbatim records exist of what must have been a most interesting litigation! He lost his case but his work shows without any doubt that he belonged to the same lineage as Sesshū, which includes the Sung Chinese ink painter Mu Ch'i who has had a great influence on Japanese artists. Tohaku's art illustrates the persistent Japanese love of the dramatic in its simplest and purest form, but how closely it borders on sentimentality!

It is worth while digressing for a moment to discover, if possible, why the Kanō screens so often fail where Tōhaku brilliantly succeeds. Ink painting is only suitable for broad landscapes if the actual elements of the painting are on a comparatively diminutive scale—if the brush is small and delicately used. To use a term from another art, it is suitable for lieder and not for grand opera. To attempt in such media a full scale imitation of nature in huge spatial compositions destroys its most sensitive qualities. Only a few artists like Tōhaku were able to modify the Chinese method and to impose their own personalities on views of purely Japanese landscape. Even then, the nearer they came to the Chinese ideal, the more fruitful were their efforts. But the Japanese have always been able technicians; perhaps it was inevitable that they should have become absorbed with the pure mechanics of Chinese painting and, as a result, unable to resist the temptation to push them to extremes—destroying them in the process. Nevertheless the example of Tōhaku shows that some artists were impatient with the formalism and insensitivity of the Kanō school screens. If they could not all find a solution to the problem in painting screens they could, like Eitoku, reserve their Chinese style for smaller works which tended to be essays in the classical manner of Liang K'ai or Mu Ch'i.

A painter who successfully fused the Japanese vision with the Chinese manner was Miyamoto Musashi (1584–1645) (better known by his 'art-name' Niten), who spans

113. *Pine-trees* by Hasegawa Tōhaku
(1539–1610).
Two panels from one screen of a pair
of six panelled screens.
Ink on paper.
Height 5 feet 1½ inches.
Tokyo National Museum.

both the Momoyama and Tokugawa periods. He was a famous swordsman, and the adopted son of a *samurai*. With such a background one might expect him to reflect the tastes of the newly victorious generals. But, strangely enough, this is not so. His *Shrike* (Fig. 114) in the Nagao Museum (one of about ten surviving paintings attributed to him) is in the best Chinese tradition; yet its dramatic quality and its studied simplicity immediately show the Japanese hand. The picture plane is divided vertically by a single, impetuous sweep of the brush depicting a dead, dry branch. The Japanese like to compare this line to the stroke of the sword, a simile with which Niten no doubt was familiar. The comparison is not entirely inappropriate. The bird perches precariously at the top of a branch hardly strong enough to bear its weight. The interplay of forces in the painting is masterly. At the bottom of the picture the artist had started a thick bamboo branch but, no sooner started, than he left it to fade into the mist, lest it should detract from the bird on its branch and destroy the balance. Horizontal streaks of mist in the Japanese manner provide an illusion of depth and loneliness in the cold season. Throughout the painting the ink tones are skilfully modulated (much more so than in Ashikaga work), ranging from pure black to a luminous grey. Miyamoto's work shows influences not only of the classical Chinese masters like Liang K'ai but also of late Ming painters whose work he must have seen.

The fortunes of the Tosa school during this period declined as those of the Kanō rose. The snobbism attached to the Kanō name and the popularity of Chinese style painting in general reasserted itself. We have seen that many of the Kanō masters were well able to use *Yamato-e* elements when they wished and the very few pure *Yamato-e* paintings which have survived are most colourful and sprightly. The majority of the Tosa artists, however, were either driven out to the provinces where they had to earn their livings in less fashionable circles or, if they chose to stay in Kyoto, necessity sometimes forced them to provide rough drafts for their Kanō employers. A new genius was needed to fulfil the possibilities of *Yamato-e* style. He appeared in an early 17th century artist named Sōtatsu whose work will be discussed in the next chapter.

During the Momoyama period, Western influences first began to affect Japanese art. In 1543, a boat carrying four Portuguese landed by chance on the island of Tanegashima in the south of Japan. Only six years later, the Portuguese Roman Catholic missionary Francis Xavier, introduced Christianity to the islands where it met with considerable success. The Japanese appetite for novelty was greatly stimulated by the Portuguese. Before the end of the century it had become the fashion at the Shōgun's court to wear Portuguese clothes, even to carry rosaries, and to exchange a word or two in the Portuguese language.[1] The missionaries also brought 16th century European religious paintings which fascinated the Japanese and inspired many copies. Between 1590 and 1614 a number of screens were painted showing the ways of life and the adventures of the Portuguese in Japan. Some of these were brought to Europe in the Portuguese ships which had a monopoly of the trade at the time. Basil Gray says of this influence which extended to guns, architecture, and Western learning as well as art, " . . . it is not something to be thought of as imposed, but on the contrary the result of a sustained curiosity and of a readiness to learn or adapt which was strikingly different from Chinese self-sufficiency." This openness to foreign influences is a Japanese characteristic which we have seen in one form or another in most periods from the 6th century

[1] See Basil Gray, *Oriental Art*, New Series, Vol. II, No. 4.

114. *Shrike* by Niten (1584–1645).
Hanging scroll.   Ink on paper.
49½ by 21½ inches.
Nagao Museum, Kanagawa.

115. *Namban or ' Southern Barbarian' Screen.*
Detail showing the arrival of a Portuguese ship in Japan. Colour on paper.
Early 17th century. Lisbon Museum.

onwards. The detail in Figure 115 is from a typical *namban* or ' Southern Barbarian '
screen shown in the recent Royal Academy *Exhibition of Portuguese Art*. The wit and
acute perception, the variety and character study in this gay scene are a delight in
themselves. The chief merchant, cigar in mouth, sits on deck in oriental splendour;
his crew unload the boxes and chests to trade with the Japanese waiting on the shore.
Two villainous-looking sailors peer excitedly from the bows, a sad priestly figure, breviary in
hand, is almost obscured by the rigging. Three assistants stand ready to receive the in-
structions of their master, one points to the rolls of material behind them as if discussing
the prices, another looks slightly apprehensively over his shoulder, the third seems to have
had his cap knocked off by the sun-shade held over the master trader. All is bustle and
eagerness, nothing has been missed. The Japanese artist has obviously welcomed the
opportunity to exercise his talents for depicting personality offered by the strong, unusual
features of the Europeans; priests seem to have intrigued him particularly. Western
influences had free play only for a brief half century before all Westerners were excluded,
but from what was produced during this time, it is interesting to speculate on the possible
effect on Japanese art had the West been tolerated in Japan.

To turn from the arts to the crafts is to appreciate to the full the *éclat* of the Momoyama
period. The great age of Japanese ceramics began in these years. The Japanese had seen

and admired the ceramics of the Chinese Sung period, but they had never learnt its secrets. Until this period their products were comparatively crude wares, strong but of little finesse. From the 16th century, when modern ceramics may be said to have started, they took a very individual turn.

It is difficult for many Westerners—especially if they have a taste for Chinese ceramics—to appreciate the aesthetics of Japanese tea-ceremony wares. Compared with the highly accomplished Chinese products they appear at first sight, sometimes rightly, as rough, misshapen and even thoroughly ugly. A snobbery of the antique, found not only in Japan, has given false values to a number of pieces which have little artistic or technical merit. On the other hand, the tea-ceremony, and the large demand for pottery created by it, provided an incentive to study and experiment with form, a demand for originality and a deep knowledge of the organic qualities of clay. Generations of craftsmen-potters contributed to the development of an art form which is still very much alive in present-day Japan. It is one of the few old crafts that have successfully withstood the impact of the West and the mass-production methods of the 20th century. The genius of the Japanese potters and the value placed on their creations raised them to the status enjoyed only by the most successful painters in the West. A renowned potter put his work on exhibition recently and realized £4,000 in two weeks for his wares. Such is the continued appreciation and demand. The respect enjoyed by potters encouraged them to cultivate the bold expression of personality, a development quite unknown in China. As a result, Japanese pottery has perhaps had the greatest influence on modern potters throughout the world. What Chinese porcelain did for the European factories in the 18th and 19th centuries, Japanese pottery is now doing for the artist-potters of the West.

It is extremely difficult even for Japanese experts to distinguish some of the pottery produced by Japan—especially in its early period. A number of small kilns were established and they often imitated each other's wares in similar clay. It is not possible here to illustrate objects from each kiln or even the variety of wares from a single kiln; only the most important groups will be considered.

It is to the old kilns that we must look first. The Seto kilns in Gifu Prefecture had, by this time, a considerable experience of pottery making. They were the first to react to new tendencies in the craft. Strangely enough, Japan turned once again to one of her earliest sources of inspiration—Korea. The most fruitful result of Hideyoshi's otherwise barren campaigns in Korea was that his armies brought back with them, often as prisoners, Korean potters who instructed the Japanese in the manufacture of Korean-style wares. New ceramic centres in addition to the Seto kilns were set up in Karatsu and Arita in the south. Arita was soon making porcelain, hitherto known only in wares imported from China. It was not long before the Korean element was displaced by the Chinese enammelled wares of late Ming—early Ch'ing Chinese porcelains, but Korean influence resulted in some pottery of high technical and artistic skill.

The wares of the Korean Yi dynasty (1392–1910) which appealed particularly to the Japanese were celadons with inlaid decoration in white under the glaze and white glazed wares with underglaze decoration (Fig. 116). In the late 16th century the Seto kilns for a time moved to a nearby site in Mino province. The products of these kilns however, are still considered as Seto wares. The most outstanding of these 'Mino-Seto' wares are the Ki-Seto or 'Yellow Seto,' the Shino, and the Oribe. As the name suggests, the Ki-Seto has a yellow opaque glaze often covering an incised decoration which was coloured with a brown iron-oxide or copper-green glaze. Japanese experts see in these wares the influence of Ming ' three-coloured ' wares rather than that of Korean styles.

The Shino and Oribe wares made at Seto are more difficult to distinguish. The difference is mostly in time, for the Oribe were developed from the Shino. The Shino products usually have a thick, white glaze with brown iron-oxide decoration under the glaze. The drawing of the decoration is very free, recalling the Korean *egorai* wares or even the Chinese *Tz'u-chou* types. Sometimes the white paste is completely covered with a brown glaze and the decoration is cut *s'graffiato*-like to reveal the paste before the whole vessel is again covered with a white glaze. This produces what the Japanese call *Nezumi-Shino* or ' Grey Shino,' (Fig. 117). In both types of Shino ware the designs are notable for their free drawing and vitality.

Oribe pottery is said to have been named after Furuta Oribe, a famous late 16th century tea-master who, it is claimed, established their style. Although closely related to Shino, it has a very different character. The earlier types (Shino-Oribe) are a compromise in which Shino glaze was refined and the colours made brighter. The most famous of these Oribe wares are the Ao-Oribe, or Green Oribe, in which a green glaze predominates. The designs on this type (Fig. 118) tend to be geometric and very Japanese in their conscious unevenness. Sometimes they include Western, even Christian, elements such as crosses. But their manner of arrangement is peculiarly Japanese and they are the most colourful of the late 16th century wares.

The products of the Karatsu kilns, next in importance to the Seto, are technically much less advanced than the Seto wares and much closer to their Korean *mishima* inspiration. The painted Karatsu wares with designs in brown iron-oxide under the glaze resemble the painted Shino ware. These types will be discussed in the next chapter. Kyoto, the centre of the tea-ceremony, was not far behind the Seto kilns in producing pottery. One of the most characteristic and valued types was initiated by Chōjiro (1515–1592) under the artistic guidance of the tea master Sen-no-Rikyū. Chōjiro is credited with the invention of *raku* wares (Fig. 119), so called because Hideyoshi gave his son, Tōkei, a gold seal with the character *raku* which means ' pleasure.' This he stamped on each of his pieces. The character

116. *Ewer* Korean. *Egorai* type. White glaze with under glaze decoration. 15th–16th centuries. Tokyo National Museum.

117. Nezumi ('Grey')
Shino ware.
Momoyama period.

118. *Square Bowl*. Oribe ware.
Momoyama period.
Diameter 9 inches.
Nezu Museum, Tokyo.

119. *Tea Bowl* by Chōjirō, Black Raku ware.
Momoyama period.
Height 3¼, diameter (mouth) 4¼ inches.
Z. Kōnoike Collection, Osaka.

has been used as a mark in one form or another by 14 generations of the family down to the present day, a record surely unsurpassed anywhere in the world. The ware is low-fired and the glaze generally plain black, salmon-coloured, or white with a high, wax-like sheen and pitted surface. The shapes are rough and irregular but not fantastically so. The bases are generally small, the bodies wide and capacious, often turning in slightly at the lip to give the impression of a fruit shape. These bowls, the classical ideal of the tea-ceremony wares, are quite simple but very satisfying to the touch and their glaze exemplifies the sophisticated simplicity which was the aim of the tea-ceremony. In some respects one can call them a revival of Chinese *temmoku* along Japanese lines.

In all the crafts during these fifty colourful years styles were created which were to dominate the next three centuries. Textiles were particularly richly developed. The Asuka-Nara period had been the first great age of Japanese textiles based on the example of the Chinese T'ang dynasty craft. In this second great period the Japanese built on their own native traditions. The sumptuousness and variety of design is all the more surprising as this period followed on the Ashikaga period when the craft had reached its nadir.

Japanese design from this time bewilders by its inexhaustible variety. It has been said of European design that it should not seriously engage the mind or strike deep into the imagination but should be accepted without question, like an ancient code of behaviour. In consequence, it must make free use of clichés, of figures which, whatever their origin, have already been reduced to satisfactory hieroglyphic form. The Japanese have never been content to treat decoration in such an uninspiring manner and it is this which makes their decoration so unusual and ever fresh to the Western eye.

Just as the taste of Nobunaga and his successors in interior decoration was frankly extravagant, so they also demanded robes to match the brilliance of the screens against which they would be seen. And for the first time for centuries money was available to support factories which could produce them. No jaded court aesthetic hindered the free expression of a *nouveau-riche* taste. The products were only saved from vulgarity by the ingenuity of the designers and the skill of the textile workers.

Every possible technique new and old was tried—tie-dyeing, hand-painting, embroidery, weaving, gold-foil, gold-foil appliqué, and the previously mentioned *tsuji-ga-hana* method (see p. 114) in which the colour was tie-dyed and the outlines added in ink. A combination of embroidery and metal-foil appliqué provided a particularly brilliant type of decoration (*nui haku*). But the most original aspect of Momoyama textiles was the way in which materials made or decorated in different techniques were bodly combined in a manner which exploited to the maximum all possible contrasts of colour, material, and design. In some, the two, sides of a garment were made of contrasting material (*katami-gawari*) or the robe was divided horizontally; in others only the shoulders and wide hem were used for the contrast. Figure 120, a short-sleeved garment shows how the shoulders and the hem were made to stand out against a plain wide central band. The decorated surface is made of embroidery on gold foil. The robe was worn by an actor taking a child's part in a *Nō* play and it was intended to create a gay, youthful impression. The technique used in the embroidery suggests that it was ultimately inspired by Ming examples but that is all that remains of Chinese inspiration.

The astonishing vividness and variety of the design, the richness created by adding embroidery on gold and, perhaps above all, the treatment of the entire surface as a single decorative unit is characteristic of the Momoyama feeling for the decorative arts. What a brilliant impression the actor must have created as he turned on the stage in this scintillating gown—a masterly combination of the simple and the gorgeous.

Figure 121 shows a *Nō* costume which is even more dramatic in its design and use of colour. Tokugawa Ieyasu, whose circular crests or *mon* it bears, gave this striking man's gown to a group of *Nō* actors. The background is white and the shoulders purple. A thick yellow-green branch of bamboo sweeps up one side of the back in a powerful curve,

120. *Short-sleeved robe* (Kosode).
Momoyama period.
Height 51 inches.
Tokyo National Museum.

154

121. *Short-sleeved Robe* (Kosode).
Decorated with bamboo on a white and
purple background.
Momoyama period.
Height 4 feet 9 inches.
Daihiko Senshū Bijutsu Kenkyūjō,
Tokyo.

intersected by a more slender branch crossing from half-way down to the left shoulder.
A few sprays of pale-blue leaves in the *tsuji-ga-hana* technique curve gracefully from the
bamboo joints to complete the design. The most surprising feature is the unusual harmony
between geometric and natural forms which are subtly connected by the curve of the thinner
bamboo where it runs parallel with the zig-zag pattern on the shoulders. The few basic
elements, in unconventional lines and strong colours, are boldly and clearly used in a manner
more typical of painting than of textile design. The Japanese have successfully solved the
problem of combining elements and colours which are normally considered as alien to
each other. The results, though sometimes a little gaudy, are brilliantly original and full
of imagination.

The arts of the metal-worker contributed their share to the decorative splendour of
the Momoyama. In these, too, the Momoyama period provided the foundation on which
the craftsmen of the next 250 years were to build. The rich metal decorations, sometimes
in gold, which the *shōguns* used for the clasps and catches of their screens, have already
been mentioned and a commentator of the time even mentions gold catches on their
lavatories! But it was chiefly in sword fittings that Momoyama metal-work excelled. From
this time onwards the ingenuity of many hundreds of artisans in workshops throughout
Japan produced an unending stream of *tsuba* of astounding variety.

In the Ashikaga period the guards had been comparatively plain with rough designs
added as if by afterthought (Cf. Figs. 106 a. and b.). Subsequently a far wider variety of
techniques raised the craft of guard-making to a standard of artistry in the forefront of all

metal work. New metals such as silver, bronze, and pure copper were introduced. Three alloys peculiar to Japan were invented, *shakudō* (copper with a small amount of gold), *shibuichi* (copper and silver), and *sentoku* (a variety of brass). Even solid gold was used but in 1830 a law was passed prohibiting such extravagance. None of these gold *tsuba* have survived; one can only imagine how they would have appealed to Nobunaga, Hideyoshi, and Ieyasu. The various alloys were often submitted to a pickling process which gave variety and beauty to their surfaces—*shakudō* thus treated acquired a lustrous raven-black or violet-black hue, *shibuichi* took on a wide range of colours from deep olive-brown to a pale tint resembling oxidized silver, *sentoku* turned chrome yellow and copper itself gained a subdued, fox-red tone. Such processes were often closely guarded studio secrets which to this day have remained undivulged.

Many innovations were made in the physical treatment of the surfaces. In the popular *nanako* (lit. fish-roe) technique for example, by incredibly accurate punching, the whole surface is covered with tiny granules which at their best are perfectly regular and uniform. This technique was first introduced as early as the 15th or 16th centuries and many different schools subsequently used it, particularly for soft, dull backgrounds against which the polished decoration stood out even more boldly.

Piercing and openwork in a wide range of styles was also very popular. These range from simple geometric designs to the most complex patterns. Effects were created which resemble the finest relief or types of low intaglio. Engraving methods attempted to reproduce in metal the effects of painting. Incrustation and inlay were perhaps the most popular method of decorating the surfaces of the guards. When three or more metals are used, the type is called *iro-e* or 'colour picture.' The *nunome* (lit. cloth-texture) technique popular in the Momoyama period was another method involving the application of gold or silver foil. By this method it was possible to simulate the impression of colour-wash drawing and it opened up an inexhaustible mine of decorative possibilities. The metal-workers thus followed other craftsmen in their emulation of the painters.

The guard in Figure 122a is signed by Umetada Mioju (1588–1613). He was the 25th master of the Umetada school of swordsmiths which had flourished for centuries before him. His headquarters were in Kyoto but he travelled widely leaving his influence on many schools throughout the provinces. The guard is flatly modelled in the form of three wisteria sprays shaped like commas leaving three tapering perforations which spring from the *seppadai* or stand for the *seppa*, the two elliptical washers separating the front of the guard from the hilt and the back from the scabbard mouth. This is pierced by the *tang*-hole. The widest end of this was fitted with a plug to enable the guard to be used for a narrower blade than was originally intended. Originally the guard was probably adorned with gold *nunome*. Sir Arthur Church recorded in his catalogue that, when he acquired this specimen, the signature was invisible as were many of the details which had been obscured by rust. The decoration is simple and bold, although very sensitive in detail. The effect is energetic and rhythmical, and preserves a masculinity which the later guard makers were to lose.

Figure 122b is an unsigned work by a *tsuba* master as opposed to the armourers or swordsmiths who made the guards in the earlier periods. Specialization in *tsuba* manufacture is said to have begun about 1400 when the Ashikaga *Shōgun* Yoshinori (1394–1441) established private guard-makers at his court in Heian-jō (Kyoto) and employed artists to design guards with piercings (*sukashi*) of a more refined and decorative character than those

122. *a.* (Left). *Sword guard* by Umetada Miōju (1588–1613). Iron. Momoyama period.
        b. (Right). *Sword guard* by an unknown master. Iron. Momoyama period or slightly later.
        Slightly reduced. Museum of Eastern Art, Oxford.

produced by the earlier swordsmiths and armourers. This is a *Heianjō-sukashi* of the 17th century, possibly of the Momoyama period or slightly later. The piercing technique is fairly advanced and the design in positive silhouette. The border is formed of four brackets each joined by a bar either to the *seppadai* or the *riohitsu* (lit. ' pair of compartments ') intended to hold the *kozuka* ' knife ' and *kōgai* ' skewer ' which are housed in the scabbards of certain types of swords. By means of these separate holes, the smaller blades can be drawn without unsheathing the whole sword. The design, a typical Momoyama fusion of elegance and power, maintains a fine proportion between decoration and utility.

These two early 17th century guards, however, give little hint of the fantasy and refinement later lavished on *tsuba*. They preserve a stern quality and a workman-like technique in keeping with the practical use. Within a short time the *tsuba* become more like the work of jewellers, and their function ceremonial and decorative rather than practical. Many were never even intended for use.

The craft of the lacquer-maker, like those of the screen painter and the textile worker, was well suited to express the taste of the Momoyama period. Lacquer had always been a luxury product demanding a great deal of time and skill. Japanese lacquer had already established a high reputation and throughout the East (including China) kings were pleased to accept it as presents. Examples even reached Holland, but often foreigners who obtained examples of Japanese lacquer did not realize its value. T. Volker, who has made an extensive study of the Dutch trade with Japan, tells how some magnificent lacquer presented to Aurangzeb in 1662 was valued by the Indian court appraisers at nearly two-thirds less than it had cost in Japan itself![1] Officials of the Dutch East-India Company stationed in countries other than Japan showed how little they appreciated the difficulties involved in lacquer manufacture by thinking that rush orders for the objects they wanted could easily be met. They did not realize that in Japan itself there was always a ready-market for first-class lacquer work.

Momoyama lacquer work shows the same bewildering variety which gives all the works of the period their particular interest. But the design differed greatly from that in the Ashikaga period, when a complete picture, a landscape with figures, for example, was reproduced on a box so as to be contained within the area to be decorated. In the Momoyama period the designers no longer took a whole scene but rather a segment which was

[1] T. Volker. " Japanese Export Lacquer," *Oriental Art*, New Series, Vol. III, No. 2.

then emphasized or exaggerated and splashed gaily over the whole surface. If parts of the design fell outside the borders of the main surface, that offended nobody's sense of symmetry; on the contrary it added to the attraction. The Kanō screens served as inspiration. Just as one had to stand back to admire the screens, so also the designs on lacquer no longer required minute inspection. It was as if the lacquer workers eagerly responded to the manner in which the new rulers had taken liberties with the traditions. It was, indeed, an age of showiness but also one in which freedom from the old restraints enabled the craftsmen to indulge their fantasies.

The search for novelty, keynote of Momoyama art, coloured the following three centuries of Japanese art. New forms from other countries—Ming China, Korea, and even Europe —were quickly absorbed into the lacquer worker's repertoire and fitted to the Japanese taste. We have seen frequent examples of the way the Japanese adopted and adapted Chinese art. But since Chinese art itself is so foreign to the West the differences between the two are possibly not so easy for the Western observer to recognize. The container for the host, presumably made for a resident catholic missionary (Fig. 123), has the familiar Western Christian IHS on its top, but lively scrolls of grape-vine in *makie* decorate the sides. The grape-vine scroll is, of course, one of the oldest decorative motives in the East; by this time it had been used well over a thousand years. But here the craftsman has joyfully revitalized and re-interpreted it. Like much of Momoyama art it is a happy marriage of careful observation and conscious simplification. It bounds along the outside, overflowing its borders, the leaves and grapes overlapping in a most natural manner. It has a carnival quality. After centuries of formalization this new naturalism is intensely refreshing. The balance between design and detail is so well maintained that the eye never tires. Even in such a small object there is a bursting self-confidence, a new gaiety which shows the craftsman as the main arbiter of his own products.

The host box is inspired by the West. What of Japanese-style decoration? The Kōdai-ji Temple in Kyoto has a number of objects presented by Hideyoshi or his widow. The

123. Top of *Christian Host Box*.
Lacquer. Momoyama period.
Diameter 4¼ inches.
Tōkei-ji, Kanagawa.

124. *Reading-stand, 'Kōdai-ji' type.*
Lacquer. Momoyama period.
Height 22 inches, width 19 inches.
J. Tsushima collection.

generic name *Kōdai-ji* is given to the most characteristic type of Momoyama lacquer. The reading-stand in Figure 124 does not belong to the temple group itself but is similar in technique. It shows the fundamental approach of Momoyama craftsmen, their desire to treat decoration and object as inseparable aspects of a unity, and results in the same breadth of treatment which distinguishes the robes of the period (Figs. 120 and 121). The design of plants is in flat *makie*, the favourite technique of the period. Unlike in other periods, no attempt was made to obtain variety and richness by contrasting techniques. This they entrusted entirely to the sureness of the brushwork and to the effective contrast of black and gold, which emphasize simplicity of line and boldness of motif. In the painting of the autumn plants which cover the surfaces there is hardly a single straight line. This offsets the stiffness and angularity of the sober lines of the furniture itself. It typifies the extraordinary feeling for the charm of the exquisite which put a civilizing touch on the rough manners of the Momoyama warriors.

As in textiles, designs in contrasting halves were popular. In a new ' untouched sprinkle ' (*makie-hanashi*) method the gold dust was dropped on the lacquer but left in its natural state and not ground down or polished. This produced a rough glitter reflecting the taste of an age which worshipped both wealth and power. Aventurine (*nashi*), which had hitherto been used mostly for backgrounds, now formed elements of the design itself in a technique called *e-nashi-ji*.

We have here treated the many changes and innovations of the Momoyama in a separate chapter. This can be defended on grounds of convenience rather than validity. It was a very short era; many of its artists lived on into the next period, and many of its innovations were only then fully developed. For the full flowering of modern Japanese art we must turn to the Tokugawa period.

CHAPTER IX

THE TOKUGAWA OR EDO PERIOD

1615–1868

HIDEYOSHI died in 1598. But it was not until 1615 that Tokugawa Ieyasu, the third of the triumvirate and his logical successor, was able to establish undisputed control over the country. This he enjoyed for only one year since he died in 1616. Nevertheless, so complete was his domination by then that his family was able to maintain its position for the next two hundred and fifty years.

Ieyasu spent the seventeen years following the death of Hideyoshi in bringing the most powerful local *daimyōs* under control and in organizing an efficient system to keep them permanently submissive. Some of them had seen in Hideyoshi's death a last chance to put down the parvenu generals and restore their own independence. Ieyasu's victory over them at the Battle of Sekigahara, in 1600, destroyed their hopes and laid the foundation for his final supremacy. The last group of opponents who stood out in support of Hideyoshi's son was finally destroyed at the seige of Osaka in 1615. The Tokugawa period dates from this year.

The capital was moved from Kyoto to a little village called Edo then situated in the middle of a marsh. From such an unpromising beginning it has grown into the modern Tokyo or 'Eastern Capital.' The period is sometimes called the Edo Period from the name of this village.

Once, in earlier times, Kamakura had been made the capital but its bleak atmosphere could not compete with the attractions of Kyoto. Ieyasu determined to make Edo not only a military and administrative headquarters but also an economic and, above all, a cultural centre to outshine the old capital. Like his predecessors, he did not destroy the monarchy but he reduced it to landless impotence, weaker than the least of the feudal lords. Under Ieyasu, feudalism reached its highest integration and the institution of emperor, its lowest point. That in 1868, after two and a half centuries of ignomy, it could be revived and the emperor restored to the dignity and influence befitting his high office is an indication of the latent strength of the Japanese respect for their monarchy—a respect which seems to survive all humiliations.

The dictatorship of the Tokugawa *shōguns* was of a type which to-day would be called fascist. Supervisors or censors where placed among the feudal lords to watch their behaviour and to report to Ieyasu. The heads of families were obliged to attend court, in Edo or, when they left the capital to look after their lands, they were required to leave hostages. Communications were closely guarded and the building of local fortifications was rigidly controlled.

Two important developments, one in the field of foreign relations and one in the economic sphere, deeply influenced the cultured life of the period. The first was the complete isolation of Japan through the exclusion of foreigners and the prohibition of foreign travel. The second was the rise to power of an astute, active merchant class.

The closing of the country was intimately connected with the activities of Christian missionaries who had steadily gained influence since their arrival in the mid-16th century. The rulers of Japan shrewdly recognized in the Portuguese and Spanish missions the thinly-disguised forerunners of military conquest. They could observe the process close at hand in China and the Philippines. The quarrels between the Jesuits and Franciscans, each jealous of the other's influence, increased the *shoguns'* fears of foreign intervention. Unlike the Buddhist missions, their Christian counterparts were backed by foreign militaristic powers. Before the 1620's, Christianity had occasionally been attacked but never entirely suppressed. Had it not been for the foreign military threat, the Japanese would probably have granted the Catholics the same amount of religious tolerance as was enjoyed by the various Buddhist sects. But the *shoguns* could not run the risk of local *daimyōs* allying themselves with foreign powers. By 1626, after some harsh measures, Christianity seemed no longer dangerous, and the authorities began to relax the restrictions imposed on it. But in 1637 some thirty thousand peasants at Shimabara, apparently inspired by some vague Christian ideals, rose in rebellion. The *shogun's* forces put down the insurgents with great brutality, sparing only about one hundred and fifty of them. This rising convinced the Tokugawa rulers that they must ruthlessly eradicate Christianity and exclude all foreigners. They also found it convenient to divert the social unrest evidenced by the Shimabara rising into a campaign against foreigners. Only a closely-guarded handful of Chinese and a small settlement of the Dutch on an island near Nagasaki were allowed to remain. No sea-going ships could be built, vessels calling at Japanese ports were curtly turned away. Japan was hermetically sealed off from the rest of the world.

It was unfortunate for her that the following centuries were periods of great Western progress in all fields of knowledge and it is interesting to speculate what Japan, with her great ability to absorb foreign cultures, might have achieved had she been open to them. But it would be wrong to regard the period of isolation as one of sterility. Japanese culture may have been inbred but it was never emasculated. One sees in this period the vitality of the race working at a feverish pace. During the decline of feudalism in the West national energies were turned to the creation of parliamentary institutions; in Japan the same energies were spent in a pursuit of pleasure and extravagance which is most vividly reflected in the arts. It is a peculiar feature of Japanese life in this period that, for all its intellectual stagnation, the arts flourished.

The rise to power of the mercantile classes in Japan is particularly important for the study of Japanese art. It created, among much that was new, the art of the colour print—often called Japan's most individual contribution to the world's art. A distinct class of merchants had existed at least as early as the Ashikaga period, partly as a result of trade with China and partly to serve as commissariat to the armies of the large landowners. Priests and *daimyōs* shared in this earlier trade with China and the guilds of merchants had then been content to pay the monasteries and landowners for their protection. But merchants of Sakai, near Osaka, became so wealthy that they even acted as money-lenders to the Ashikaga *shoguns*, a development which should have served as a warning to the Tokugawa rulers. In fact, although the Tokugawa made it quite plain that they would not tolerate the power which the guilds had gained, they were unable to check the rapid growth of the merchant class in Edo. In the course of less than a century these tradesmen amassed large fortunes and took over the real economic power in the land. As in Ashikaga times, it was the peasant-farmer class which suffered. Although in good Confucian fashion lip-service was paid to the importance of the farming population in the economy of the country, the peasants were, in fact, crushed between the *samurai* and the merchants, exploited and cheated by both. A commentator of the time likened them to oil-seeds, " the harder you press, the more you squeeze out."

A poet of the time, Rai Kyōhei, described the life in the countryside as follows: "A village is like a palsied invalid, too weak to stand on his own feet. The people flee from the villages like leaves before the wind and it is impossible to stop them." Those who could find employment in the cities swelled the bustling urban population. Those of an independent turn of mind sought refuge in the remote districts of the north-east where for a few more generations they could enjoy their freedom.

The new, growing city of Edo itself created a large population of merchants and transport contractors to supply their own needs and those of the *samurai*. The complex city life stimulated the development of exchange by currency rather than by rice. This led to speculation which in turn increased the wealth of the merchants. By the end of the 17th century, the *samurai*, too, found themselves deeply in debt to the townspeople whom they professed to despise. The *shōguns* issued edicts aimed at depriving the merchants of the enjoyment of their wealth. On occasions, they even confiscated the fortunes of over-confident tradesmen—but they were overwhelmed by a modern, complicated economic process which they did not understand. They could neither control it nor exploit it for their own ends. The isolation of the country deprived them of the benefits of foreign trade which could have filled their purses. That they withstood the steadily mounting pressure for so long is only to their credit, and the country benefited greatly by the peace they preserved in the country. Histories often do the Tokugawa rulers less than justice.

By the time of the *Genroku* era (1688–1703), the hey-day of Tokugawa art, the so-called commoners (i.e., the townspeople rather than the farmers) had consolidated their position. They became the patrons and arbiters of taste in certain new arts which their needs created. Two distinct standards now became evident in the arts as well as in society. On the one hand there was the *samurai* with his dignity and the consciousness of high social standing who clung desperately to his privileges endeavouring to preserve his traditions while the *chōnin* (commoners), unfettered by a strict ethical and social code and with no prestige to uphold, could afford to be spontaneous and experimental. At this time, therefore, we find, two separate cultures, the old, which was a perpetuation of ' classical ' standards; the new, which was popular and unrestrained.

There are, of course, no watertight compartments in art or in society. Wealth, like poverty, is a great leveller. Distinctions between classes tended to become vague and, as wealth was more widely distributed, the new-rich often patronized artists who in former days would have catered only for the aristocracy. Sansom records how a *shōgun* confiscated the fortune of a rich Osaka rice merchant which included no less than fifty pairs of gold screens and three hundred and sixty carpets. A new and wider market was being created for the products of the artists and craftsmen.

All classes, for instance, seem to have appreciated the works of what is known as the Sōtatsu-Kōrin School. The founder of this very distinctive decorative style is generally

125. *Box for Writing Accessories by* Kōetsu.
Lacquer. Tokugawa period.
9½ by 9 by 3½ inches.
Tokyo National Museum.

acknowledged to be Honnami Kōetsu, a sword appraiser by profession but also a man of many parts—calligrapher, potter, and lacquer worker. He seems to have been the spiritual leader of a group of artists in Kyoto. Examples of all his types of work have survived and they show that he had a very original mind; he was perhaps the most representative artistic personality of his time. He seldom painted and his most striking achievements are in pottery and lacquer. Pottery tea-bowls ascribed to him are of the *raku* type with strong irregular shapes and thick glazes subtly enlivened with luminous under-tones. It is known that Kōetsu was an intimate friend of several tea-ceremony masters and these bowls show the influence of their taste. His lacquer pieces are far more sophisticated and refined. Without appreciating the conscious rusticity of the tea-ceremony wares, it is difficult to understand how they could come from the same hand. The most famous of his lacquer works is a box made to hold an ink-stone and writing equipment and decorated with the design of a pontoon bridge (Fig. 125). The bridge is represented by a wide band of lead which contrasts effectively with the golden background of boats and waves. A few characters in silver, taken from a poem about a bridge in Sano, East Japan, are scattered over the surface. Calligraphy as an integral part of design was not a new departure (Cf. Fig. 108), but the emphasis placed on it is characteristic of the works of the Sōtatsu-Kōrin school. Sōtatsu, his collaborator in many works, was particularly famous for his calligraphy and some authorities have suggested that this box, like so many other works, is a joint production of the two artists. Japanese critics say that the characters merge into the design. In fact they dominate it. But if Kōetsu stressed the calligraphic aspect, he also made the design broader and bolder in order to compensate. A few simplified elements are splashed with artful carelessness across the surface with no effort to contain them within their boundaries. All is movement and eye-arresting effect. Proportion is disregarded in such works—a fan looks as if it had by chance fallen on the surface and stuck there, a tablet with an inscription lies at a striking angle across a branch of plum blossom, a leaf of bamboo wanders off the edge of a tray onto its border. This uncontainable, irrepressible quality is the essence of modern Japanese decoration. Quirks in design sometimes come dangerously near to whimsy and occasionally the effects are a little too artful. Nevertheless, the compositions are brilliantly original. At their best they have a breath-taking audacity—the power to make even a small area appear like a broad canvas imaginatively and boldly decorated. Size was a challenge which the artists always welcomed as a test of their ingenuity.

Sōtatsu, the real founder of the school, died in 1643, and was related to Kōetsu; very little else is known about his life. Most of his works were probably done in the early years of the Edo period. A considerable number of these have survived which show him to be an extremely eclectic painter using and combining the styles which his predecessors had created. It was mainly the *yamato-e* tradition and the Tosa style which appealed to him but his products were Tosa with a difference. Although he, too, often took his subjects from Japanese literature, he allowed himself considerable artistic licence, and his interpretations are far from literal. There is a good deal of humour in his work—and his was an age which set great store by a sense of humour. In many of his works we find a combination of the powerful Kanō line and the Tosa sense of colour. He had studied the scrolls of the Kamakura period as well as the works of Kanō masters like Eitoku. But he subordinated everything to a decorative effect. Hills become broad, flat sweeps of colour, unnecessary detail is omitted, he often ignored perspective or even inverted if it suited his purpose. He paints in rich colours a still world of suspended animation. It was as if these

126. *Screen representing 'The Barrier Hut' (Sekiya)* by Sōtatsu.   Colour on paper. Early 17th century. 5 feet 2 inches by 8 feet 7½ inches. Seikadō Foundation, Tokyo.

127. *Screen of Irises* by Kōrin.
(1658–1715).
Colour on gilt paper.
5 by 8½ feet.
Nezu Museum, Tokyo.

artists regarded the whole world as a stage and their screens as huge back-drops to an eternal pageant.

Figure 126 reproduces a screen called *Sekiya*, its subject taken from the evergreen *Tale of Genji*. The composition is carefully balanced and highly dramatic in a peculiarly Japanese way which leaves the most pregnant moments as if suspended in motionless silence. To those familiar with the Genji story, the scene represents the highly sentimental climax to the tale of the Prince's affair with the Lady Utsusemi.

Quite early in the *Tale of Genji*, the Prince has a fruitless encounter with Utsusemi. Sometimes after this episode she married a provincial governor and went to live in a distant province. Genji had meanwhile been disgraced and banished from the capital but he had just been pardoned and was back in court. The incident shown in this screen took place when Utsusemi's husband was returning with her via the Barrier to Osaka and Genji happened to be on his way to attend a service at Ishiyama Temple in company of a vast procession. Genji's entourage was so numerous that Utsusemi's husband, in order to let him pass, had to halt and unharness his carriages at the Frontier Hill. Genji scanned the coaches and then quickly lowered his blind for he had recognized Utsusemi's brother of whom he had been very fond. He called him over and jested, " I hope your sister notices how attentive I am to her. It is not often I go all the way to the Barrier to meet her." These words, when reported to Utsusemi, brought back a flood of tender memories.[1]

The picture is dominated by the barrier hut surrounded by a few old tree-trunks to suggest the time of year, the frosty ninth month. Utsusemi's decorated ox-cart, unharnessed, occupies the top left-hand corner. Genji's cart surrounded by his followers has just arrived at the gate. We feel the clandestine atmosphere as Genji peeps from his curtain and then secretly sends Utsusemi a letter. Yet for all the literary and dramatic over-tones, the screen is a beautiful work in terms of pure decoration.

Sōtatsu shows so many styles that it is difficult to account for his art in any other way than as a continuous search for aesthetic alternatives. His conscious simplification is an attempt to escape from the trivial and the detailed. Even with such broad canvases to work on, these artists are unwilling to keep within the given framework. The impact of their huge areas of bold colours is overwhelming.

The school continued under a number of less-inspired painters until the appearance of Ogata Kōrin (1658-1716) who was related to Kōetsu through the latter's sister. Kōrin brought the decorative style to its climax. His work seems to synthesize the elegance and taste of the sumptuous *Genroku* period (1688-1703). He, too, had many styles at his command and he shows the same restless seeking for new subjects to enliven his paintings: portraits, *shintō* ceremonies, illustrations of stories, flowers, birds, and even a delightful imaginary portrait of the Lady Murasaki writing her novel flowed from his brush. His most famous and most characteristic works are perhaps the screens on which he painted dense clusters of *Irises* growing against a rich background of squares of gold (Fig. 127). Their leaves are painted in a naturalistic bright green, the flowers in two shades of blue. This contrast of realistic flowers in front of an artificial background faithfully reflects the Tokagawa attempt to combine art and nature. The balance between blank space and design shows a fresh effort to reinterpret in decorative terms, one of the basic Far Eastern pictorial concepts. In the hands of a lesser artist this mass of flowers would have created

[1] Arthur Waley, *Tale of Genji*. London. 1957.

only a confused effect. With only four strong colours Kōrin produces a brilliant design out of a superb natural phenomenon without in any way doing violence to nature.

Many rich merchants patronized Kōrin but his wealth and elegant way of life courted the disfavour of the *shōguns* as they tried in vain to curb the exhibitionism of the *nouveaux riches*. A delightful story is told of a picnic which he and his friends held. Kōrin had wrapped the food in bamboo leaves which, when opened, revealed delicate paintings in gold done by himself. After the meal his guests casually tossed these wrappers into the stream where they floated down to be retrieved by less fortunate aristocrats. Gold was prohibited to the lower classes and Kōrin was prosecuted. As a result, he is said to have moved from Kyoto to Edo. Although this story is probably apocryphal, it illustrates the bravado and the growing confidence of the merchant classes which found their outlets in the commoners' art of the period. Colour instead of outline, clipped compositions, daring angles, eye-catching disproportions, stimulating subjects, all appear in very original forms and combine into a highly sophisticated art-form.

Kōrin's younger brother Kenzan (1663–1743) was a man of milder temperament and quieter tastes. His *Flowers in Baskets* (Fig. 128) shows a close connexion between painting and poetry. It is the composition of a literary-minded man who had probably seen Chinese paintings of the early 18th century when individualistic painters and poets were doing similar things. Indeed, most of his work stands near to Chinese traditions. The poem above the painting can be translated,

> " Flowers, even wild flowers,
>   Are enticing,
>   Bewitched by their colour and fragrance
>   The mist of the fields emulates them."

This fusion of poetry, calligraphy, and painting, unfamiliar to Westerners, is common in the East. Each element is of equal importance in the whole. The poem sets the mood, adds another dimension to the enjoyment of the work and acts as an emotional bridge from artist to spectator. It also gives the artist an opportunity to show his skill in the basic exercise of brushwork, i.e., calligraphy. The few characters, which look casually scribbled in an empty space as if in afterthought, were generally as carefully planned as the painting itself. The danger, inherent in such Japanese work, is that the verses like the paintings, tend to substitute sentiment for profundity.

Kenzan's temperament fitted him more for the *Zen* approach to art and some of his best works are in pottery, which he took up at the age of thirty-seven. His brother Kōrin often did the designs for these as in the hexagonal dish in Figure 129. The subject, a favourite with ink painters, is Jurōjin, an old man who symbolizes for the Chinese and Japanese a much admired longevity. Kenzan has transferred his brother's subtle nuances of ink to the much less sensitive medium of pottery decoration with remarkable skill. The free-hand, brownish-red lines abound in vigour and the *raku*-type glaze adds the rustic component. Eclectic taste and complete technical mastery go hand-in-hand. In later generations the painters of this school did not reach the same heights but the decorative style is still alive and some contemporary artists—especially those of the Nihon Bijutsu-in, the Japanese Academy for the Fine Arts, are influenced by it. The pottery of Kenzan led us away from the painting but there were other prolific schools in the Tokugawa period which deserve considerable attention.

To the average observer in the 17th century it must have seemed that the Kanō dominated the world of painting. Members of the Kanō family were the official painters to the Tokugawa *Shōgunate* and such patronage meant a great deal financially and socially. They were given land, houses, and honours in return for their services. Their official position was unassailable but it was not long before lavish privilege removed all incentive for individual, creative work. They reduced their school works to a series of monotonous variations on wearied themes. Originality is seldom a feature of academy painting and the works of the Kanō were no exception.

The ramifications of the Kanō school would require volumes to explore. The main line of the school answered Ieyasu's summons to the capital at Edo where he counted on their help in establishing a new cultural centre to outshine Kyoto. Some Kanō painters remained in the old capital and continued the southern branch of the school, but the most ambitious and accomplished artists chose Edo where more tempting rewards were offered. The foremost of these was Tanyū (1602–1674) who became official court painter at the early age of seventeen and the owner of a splendid estate which went with the office. Various other members of the family established in Edo their own schools known by the

128. (Left). *Flowers in Baskets* by Kenzan (1663–1743). Colour on paper. 44 by 19½ inches. Mrs. H. Saigō Collection, Kanagawa.

129. (Below). *Dish* made by Kenzan and painted by Kōrin. Stoneware. Max. diameter 10½ inches.

130. *Lute, Chess, Reading, and Painting* by Kanō Tanyū (1602–1674).
Ink and colour on paper. 9 feet 8½ inches by 12 feet. Destroyed by bombing during World War II.

names of the quarters in which they lived. The principal four families held the monopoly of palace commissions and were called collectively ' The Palace Painters.' Other members of the family were not favoured with quite such eminent patronage. Some fifteen families of these were called ' Outside Painters.' Somewhat lower down the scale came the ' Town Painters ' who were members of the Kanō family or pupils allowed to use the name. All were blood relations or connected by the ties of master to pupil which are even more binding in the East than in the West.

It is remarkable that there was enough work to support all these Kanō painters. Fortunately for them the provincial lords, quick to follow the Tokugawa lead, provided a market for their huge output and the more affluent, society-conscious among the merchants and townspeople were eager to acquire Kanō paintings.

Tanyū, the founder of the Edo School, was a painter with a very definite consciousness of his aims. His Chinese style landscapes are full of the moralizing which the Tokugawa appreciated. ' *Lute, Chess, Reading, and Painting* ' (Fig. 130) on a wall of Nagoya Castle (destroyed during the bombing of the war) was a work of his early thirties and shows clean, accomplished brushwork applied to a hackneyed theme. The ' Four Liberal Accomplishments ' of the ideal Chinese gentleman may have meant something in Sung and even in early Ming China but in 17th century Japan they were little more than an anachronistic affectation. The landscape itself is composed of a series of painter's clichés—none of which cohere spontaneously. A waterfall comes from nowhere, froths around an impossible-looking rock and then, as if the artist did not know what to do with it, is allowed to fade out. A dramatically conceived tree without roots dominates the foreground. The whole left side of the painting is left blank in a manner which only reveals the artist's lack of imagination. The brushwork affects the power of Sesshū but is studied, smoothed out, and emasculated. A comparison with the Sesshū reproduced in Figure 124 provides perhaps the best lesson for a Westerner anxious to understand what is vital and what is shallow in

131.   One of a pair of Screens
Pine Trees under Snow by Ōkyo
(1733–1795).
Ink and colour on paper.
5 feet 1 inch by 11 feet 10½ inches.
T. Mitsui Collection, Tokyo.

the Eastern brush. Tanyū's work illustrates the fact that even the loftiest sentiments are no substitute for genuine artistic experience. Whereas Sesshū's work is a valid naturalization of Chinese forms, that of Tanyū is an impersonal façade created by technical virtuosity, without life or meaning.

While the Kanō style still dominated the art world of Edo, the old capital of Kyoto saw the rise of a new school under Maruyama Okyō (1733–1795). His style sprang from that of the Kanō but later he came under the influence of Western painting which reached Japan in the form of Dutch etchings brought into the small colony allowed to stay on in Nagasaki. Also at Nagasaki was a small group of Chinese painters which included Shên Nan-p'in, a realistic painter of the conservative Chinese tradition. The works of these Chinese artists, already influenced by the West, include botanical studies comparable in accuracy with any the world has produced. As works of art, however, they are dry and spiritless. The followers of the Maruyama school were particularly intrigued by Western style perspective and Okyō eventually perfected a realism which combined with the adroit Chinese brush and ink to produce a vision which was new in Japanese art. This acted as a healthy corrective to the technically perfect but empty brushwork of the Kanō masters and the over-formalized patterns of the successors to the Sōtatsu and Kōrin school. At its best Okyō's work has a natural atmosphere and an imposing grandeur. His famous screens *Pine Trees Under the Snow* (Fig. 131) painted in ink and slightly coloured have a freshness and a clean quality which are the outcome of a rare artistic purpose and integrity. The general concept owes much to the decorators and preserves strong traces of the idealism of Chinese ink painting but his finished works show a bold and original mind facing and solving problems of the synthesis of East and West which have defeated most of his successors.

The Kanō School took its inspiration from Chinese ink painting from five to seven hundred years earlier. Since then painting in China had developed along different lines and important changes had taken place. What were these and how did they influence Japanese art?

By far the most important was the rise of the *Wên-jên-hua*, transliterated into Japanese as *Bun-jin-ga*, or 'literary men's painting.' During the Ming dynasty the ability to paint became indispensable for every 'man of culture.' The use of brush and ink for writing was in itself a training for it. As the amateur steadily encroached on the art of painting, a tendency developed to denigrate the professionals as prostituting the art. The political atmosphere in Tokugawa Japan favoured such Chinese scholar-official ideals. Like the Chinese Manchu rulers, the Tokugawa saw in Confucian traditions the best way of governing the country. They also saw no political dangers in the pursuit of literature and art.

The style of painting popular among the literati of late Ming China was called 'Southern Painting.' This is a vague distinction created by contemporaneous Ming theorists whose writings were closely studied in Japan. According to them, the Southern style stood in opposition to the drier, more formal and studied styles of the so-called 'Northern Painting.' The distinction is a very confusing one and by no means water-tight. Were it not for the influence it has had on later generations of Eastern painters, it would be best ignored. Southern Painting or *Nan-ga* was said to have developed from Yüan-Ming painters who lived in the fertile and more atmospherical south of China along the Yangtze River. Southern-style painters were supposed to be more spontaneous and freer in their use of the brush. But this spontaneity and the individuality it was said to encourage had, by

132. *Visiting a Hermit on a Bamboo-covered Mountain* by Buson (1716–1783).
Ink and colour on silk.   46½ by 16 inches.   S. Ueno Collection, Osaka.

133. (Right).   *Landscape* by Taiga.   Ink and colour on paper.
49 by 10 inches.   British Museum.

山旬四面總玲瓏綠野青疇一望中從兒課農
農力盡何曾妨卻讀書

134. *The Convenience of Cultivating the Land*
by Taiga (1723–1776).
Album leaf. Ink and slight colour on paper.
7 by 7 inches.
Y. Kawabata Collection, Kanagawa.

the end of the Ming dynasty, begun to wither. A large number of pattern books were produced which provided the amateur painter with ready-made models for every aspect of nature he might care to represent. This spelt an end to the great tradition of Chinese ink painting. Japanese artists eagerly studied such pattern books and many followed their directions. However, looking through the creations of the Japanese *bun-jin* one is struck by the variety of styles and influences which they reflect. There can be little doubt that the Japanese with their happy eclecticism, modelled their styles upon any Chinese painting wherever it might have come from, provided only it pleased them.

The *bun-jin* movement in Japan started about 1700 but was not firmly established until half a century later. Its two greatest exponents are Yōsa Buson (1716–1783) and Ike-no-Taiga (1723–1776). In keeping with his Chinese literary counterparts Buson was equally famous as a poet. When he finally settled in Kyoto, he devoted his last years to the writing of poetry. He seems to have been self-taught and to have followed whichever master of the Ming and Ch'ing dynasties appealed to him.

Buson's *Visiting a Hermitage on a Bamboo-covered Mountain* (Fig. 132) echoes clearly a typical mid-17th century Chinese style. The landscape is very atmospheric with that sharp contrast between the black ink and the white paper which is a characteristic of Japanese painting in the Chinese style. A hermit is shown travelling to the mountains to visit a well known beauty spot or a famous temple. Visions of such idylls have exercised the artistic imagination of Chinese artists for almost a millenium and were often as conventional as the classical ruins which decorate the backgrounds of some European paintings. Buson's composition is well balanced and carefully thought out but not particularly original. By this time it was difficult to produce anything new within the framework of such threadbare ideas. For more original work we must look elsewhere.

Ike-no-Taiga had a smiliar training to that of Buson and his larger works on screens show the same reliance on Yüan-Ming masters. His grandiose sweeping landscapes with grotesque rocks and fanciful mountain formations (Cf. the hanging scrolls in Fig. 133) are sometimes little more than an excuse to outdo the Chinese in exaggeration. At times a fussiness creeps in which stiffens the brushwork and weakens the whole effect.

However, both Taiga and Buson painted also in another style which they seem to have reserved for smaller works. This is seen at its best in an album entitled *The Ten Conveniences and the Ten Enjoyments of Country Living*, of which, also in good Chinese fashion, each painted ten leaves. The *Conveniences* were painted by Taiga and the *Enjoyments* by Buson. These scenes are inspired by simple poems by Li Li-wêng, a Chinese poet of the Ch'ing dynasty. They are said to be replies to a visitor who commiserated with the poet on his uncomfortable living conditions at the foot of a mountain in the depths of the country. The 'Conveniences' listed by the poet were cultivating the land,

135. *Landscape inspired by Ni Tsan* by Tao Chi (1630–1714). Chinese. Ink on paper.

drawing water, washing, watering the garden, angling, reciting poems aloud, gardening, gathering fuel, safe and quiet nights, and beautiful scenery. The 'Enjoyments' painted by Buson were the views of the four seasons both at dawn and at night, and the landscape in wind and rain, in fine and in cloudy weather. Figure 134, the *Convenience of Cultivating the Land* in ink and water colours, is a delightful impressionistic study. The crops painted in various shades of green are pushing up young shoots. Around the open, thatched hut grow trees and bushes rendered in washes of pale blue. With all this to please him and good hard work to tire him out, why, indeed, says the poet, should he read books?

Poetry greatly influenced these painters. A particular type of short evocative poem called *haiku* was very popular. Typical are the following lines by Buson:

> Of scattered peonies,
> Two or three petals lie piled,
> In a little heap.

Many painters tried to express such sentiments in painting.

This painting is obviously different from the more familiar paintings inspired by Yüan-Ming models. Where does it come from?

The answer is again from China but from a very different artistic milieu. In China from 1600 to 1750 a group of painters, discontent with the copying of former masters, began to paint in a very individual manner. They stressed the need for a painter to express original ideas even though his training may have begun with a close study of the old masters. These Chinese painters are grouped together as 'Individualists' and their work is one of the most refreshing aspects of later Chinese art. One of them Tao Chi (1630–1714) is famous for his trenchant remark, "The beards and eyebrows of the old masters cannot grow on my face. The lungs and bowels (i.e., the thoughts and feelings) of the old masters cannot be transferred into my stomach (i.e., mind)."[1] His work (Fig. 135), like that of Hsü Wei (1521–1593) and Chu Ta (1626–?1705), must have reached Japan in the late 17th–early 18th centuries. Along with this there were new movements in China in the art of calligraphy. The calligraphers, who were also often the painters, sought new sources of inspiration in T'ang and pre-T'ang styles. There was doubtless a movement among the more individual painters to *épater le bourgeois*. The movement was involved with the opposition of the more independent (and generally unemployed) scholars to the foreign Manchu dynasty then ruling China. A literary or political protest would have been most dangerous and the artist-scholar could best show his opposition to the status quo by producing eccentric, very untraditional work. We have evidence that their work was highly considered in China and many of their paintings have been preserved in Japan.

The works of Taiga and Buson reflect the Japanese attempt to escape from conservative styles of painting. We do not know if they were fully aware of the political atmosphere which influenced the Chinese but it is possible that the stifling restrictions which the Tokugawa imposed on the country made them likewise insist on their artistic liberty. The freer brushwork and greater spontaneity of the new Chinese styles struck a responsive chord in the Japanese and helped to release them from slavish dependence on Chinese models. Henceforward landscape painting became more personal and less mannered.

---

[1] O. Sirén. *The Chinese on the Art of Painting.* China, 1956. p. 182 ff.

136. *Landscape 'Snow Falling from the Eastern Clouds'* by Gyokudō (1745–1820). Ink on paper.
57½ by 24 inches.
Y. Kawabata Collection, Kanagawa.

137. *The Octopus Fishermen* by Chikuden (1777–1835).
From an album *Sketches from a Boat Window*. Ink and slight colour on paper.
8¼ by 5¼ inches.
K. Tamura Collection, Osaka.

138. *Sunny Morning at Uji* by Mokubei (1767–1833).
Ink and colour on paper. 19½ by 24 inches. Commission for the Protection of Cultural Properties, Tokyo.

This new trend in painting is carried a stage further in the work of Uragami Gyokudō (1715–1820) and Tanomura Chikuden (1777–1835). Both in their earlier years were officials but, in mid-life, following an old Chinese ideal, they gave up their positions to devote themselves exclusively to the arts. In Kyoto they found an atmosphere congenial to their mood and, although this kind of artistic life was supposed to be conducted on a strictly amateur basis, there can be little doubt that, as in China, they found a ready and profitable market for their work.

Gyokudō had no teacher and formed his own original style. Like his Chinese counterparts, he spent much of his later years in travel as an itinerant musician seeking inspiration from the beauty-spots of his native land (Fig. 136).

Chikuden's work reflects the same demand for something new on the part of the educated public. In 1829, during a journey to Kyoto via the Inland Sea, he painted a typical Japanese *bun-jin* album in ink and faint colour to record his passing impressions. Figure 137 is one leaf from this album *Sketches from a Boat Window*. It depicts an incident at Tadami where he saw a boatman trying to sell an octopus. This simple scene is painted with great sympathy and humour and with the sure touch of a master. The daring angle of the boat and the rhythmic swirl of the water give added movement to the lively and spontaneous scene. An attactive genre quality, a feature of later *bun-jin* painting, shows the new zest with which artists of all classes were turning to the colourful world around them for inspiration. When they did so, the pertness and wit of the Japanese artistic spirit came to the surface with irrepressible force. In such unpretentious, often bizarre, sketches of every-day life, the tradition of Chinese painting remained alive until the middle of the 18th century in China and until the middle of the 19th century in Japan.

A third painter in the *bun-jin* style was Aoki Mokubei (1767–1833), a poet, calligrapher, and painter but perhaps even more esteemed for his pottery. As with Kōetsu and Kenzan before him, his wide interests show a catholicity and a protean talent in both the arts and crafts which was unknown in China and has occurred only recently in the West. Mokubei's most famous painting, *Sunny Morning at Uji* (Fig. 138), in colour on paper, is a highly personal impression of the beauty spot where the graceful Byōdō-in stands. The painting in its gentle atmosphere, recalls Sesshū's *Ama-no Hashidate* (Fig. 99) and the work of the Chinese individualist Tao Chi. It is more abbreviated, fuller of suggestion and intimate touches than Sesshū's work and closer to the whirling, swift freedom of Tao Chi (Fig. 135). The Chinese tradition perssits but the vision is purely Japanese. The boat in the centre of the River Uji is the focal point, the whole landscape seems to revolve around the lonely traveller who drinks in the still beauty of the early morning sunlight. The brushwork is varied and full of vigour, the colour tones are skilfully blended to create the impression of soft clear light. Centuries of Chinese painting are reflected in this landscape but it is essentially a Japanese synthesis of their own and Chinese art in the Tokugawa period. The friendly, human Japanese temperament strikes a happy compromise with a style alien to it. Like most good Japanese landscapes it is the result of a sharp rather than a profound eye and the product of a warm love of their own country rather than of a universal mysticism.

139. *Souvenir Sketch.*
Ink on paper.
10½ by 9½ inches.
Museum of Eastern Art,
Oxford.

Facility with the brush was an indispensable accomplishment of any man with pretensions to culture. ' Ink-plays ' became a feature of Japanese intellectual life which has
by no means entirely disappeared. Even to-day a host, though perhaps not one of the
younger generation, will sometimes produce a piece of gilt-edged paper about a foot
square, mix some ink and dash off a charming black and white sketch with the ease with
which a Westerner will sign an autograph (Fig. 139). During the last two centuries such
souvenir sketches were even more common and must have been produced in very great
numbers. Often amateur and professional artists would gather together in clubs to discuss
the arts. On special occasions, the various guests of these bohemian gatherings would
contribute to an album which would then be presented to a member of their group whom
they wished to honour. T. Volker has drawn our attention to some of these *libri amicorum*.[1]
The combination of sensitivity and skill in some of their pages entitles them to a high
place among the minor masterpieces.

Figure 140 is one leaf from such an album dated 1815. It is signed Isui but the identity
of this man is unknown. He probably had no pretensions to professional standing and
may well have been a poet or even an actor. The subject is *Fukurokujū*, the ' God of Good
Luck ' easily recognized by his elongated head which is sometimes made to appear even
longer than his body. The name is compiled of the three characters meaning ' wealth,'
' prosperity,' and ' long life.' He is always depicted as a friendly humorous figure much
beloved by children who are often shown clambering over him. Here the artist has given
him an unusually melancholy expression. The vitality of the brushwork derives from a
complete mastery of the brush and a dazzling speed and sureness of execution. These can
be appreciated even by somebody unfamiliar with Eastern painting. The grey ink-washes
express a wide range of shade and colour. The ink seems to dance over the paper, the
outlines leap and spin in perfect control. The Japanese hand reveals itself in a light-hearted
fluency of brushwork, in the rounded softness of touch, and above all in its warmth of
feeling. A 19th century Japanese amateur here echoes, with faultless ease, the style of a
Sung master. As in China, the stern incisive quality of early ink painting had long-since
disappeared and little originality can be claimed for this work. Nevertheless it is not
simply a pictorial catch-phrase; the vitality of the Japanese brush still flows generously
through its outlines. The painter is a worthy heir to a long tradition and his work compares
favourably with anything produced in China at the beginning of the 19th century.

All the works discussed above were done either by professional artists or by relatively
well-educated amateurs. The most surprising aspect of art in the Tokugawa period was
the immense creative urge which flowed through the artisan and craftsman classes. The
amazing variety of their output, which reached staggering proportions, makes originality
seem almost commonplace. Even the most humble craftsman seems to have had the eyes
and the skill to produce attractive works of art from the smallest details of the world around
him. Lafcadio Hearn, at the beginning of the century, was completely captivated by these
works of art on a minor scale. "Aesthetic taste," he said, "followed the line of least resist-
ance. Observation concentrated itself upon the interest of every-day life, upon incidents
which might be watched from a window, or studied in a garden, upon trees, flowers,
birds, fishes or reptiles, upon insects and the ways of them, upon all kinds of small details,
delicate trifles, amusing curiosities." Seldom in any other country or time has a whole
nation been so constantly on the alert for a scene or a moment which could be turned to

[1] *Oriental Art*, New Series, Vol. I, No. 3.

140. *Fukurokujū.*
'The God of Good Luck.'
Album leaf by Isui dated 1815.
Ink on paper.

artistic purpose. Each slight change, added emphasis or nuance, each adaption or novelty was noted and applauded by a wide and critical audience.

A village in the north of Kyoto called Otsu, for instance, became famous in the 18th and 19th centuries for a type of painting which at the time sold for only a few pence. These *Otsu-e*, which are lively, imaginative coloured sketches of local deities or illustrations to proverbs, are now highly prized by collectors. Unpretentious and generally anonymous, they are full of rustic good-humour and broad, sometimes bawdy, wit. They abound in the vitality which is a feature of peasant art throughout the world. The desire for originality and variety seems to have permeated the whole of society. They are folk art at its very best—the pure distillation in line and colour of the peasant imagination.

Figure 141 is taken from an early *Otsu-e* album and depicts a peasant. Comparison with the previous illustration is illuminating. Instead of the highly accomplished brushwork of a cultured scholar deeply versed in the arts of China, a peasant painter of acute perception here interprets his companions in a lively, intimate manner. The skill betrays a long tradition and the only possible comparison is with some of the figures on Tosa screens. The range is restricted but within it the artists were completely confident of their ability. The irrepressible native humour shows itself as readily in these paintings as in the masks of earlier times. This window on the village life of the Tokugawa period is as amusing and stimulating to the Westerner to-day as it was to the traveller through Otsu over a century ago.

Finally, in this survey of Tokugawa painting we come to the colour print. Snobbism and official disfavour in Japan resulted in the finest collections being formed in London, Boston, Chicago, and Paris. A pioneer in oriental art studies, Dr. Cohn, recalls how on his first tour of Japanese art collections in 1908 he was not shown a single colour print. Even the Kabuki theatre which inspired many prints was still not considered respectable and visits to it were perforce incognito. However, it is one of the few branches of Japanese art adequately represented in the West. From the second half of the last century when, about 1890, French painters like Pissaro, Cassatt, Bernard, Gauguin, Dégas, Van Gogh and, of course, Toulouse-Lautrec discovered that Japanese colour prints and book illustrations vindicated their theories of design and colour, they have enjoyed a tremendous vogue. Western writers have produced a flood of excellent studies of the colour-print which have made it the best-known and most deeply explored aspect of Far Eastern art. The originality and vitality of the prints, their beauty of design and perfection of technique and above all their infinite variety can be treated here only in the broadest outline. For all its interest, the colour-print is only one facet of the long history of Japanese art and should not be over-emphasized.

The printing of pictures from wood blocks did not originate with the Japanese in the 17th century. It had been used in T'ang China in a more rudimentary form and in Japan

141. *Peasant.* Leaf from an Otsu-e album.
Colour on paper. Early 18th century. 4½ by 3¾ inches.
Author's collection.

142. *Two Lovers* by Harunobu
(1725–1770).
Colour print. 9⅛ by 7⅝ inches.
British Museum.

during the Fujiwara period for the outlines of background paintings on which scriptures were then written (see p. 103). The Chinese had used the colour print technique for their pattern books such as *The Ten Bamboo Studio* and *The Mustard Seed Garden* published in 1622–43 and 1679 respectively. Van Gulik's excellent but unfortunately inaccessible book on the erotic colour prints of China shows that the Japanese owed much both in technique and content to the Chinese forerunners,[1] but it was left to the Japanese to develop the art and refine the technique to a twin perfection.

What gave the Japanese colour-print its unique character? Above all it was a cheap form of reproduction within the means of all, created in order to meet an insatiable demand among the plebeian classes of Edo, the people who could not aspire to the Kanō products even if they had appealed to them. In brief, it was art for the masses, but the most highly-developed and sophisticated the world has ever seen. The Chinese subjects and calm styles of the Kanō schools made no appeal to the citizens of the busy capital. This robust society, somewhat intoxicated by its growing power, earthy and quick-witted, colourful and chafing under the restraints which their rulers had put on their enjoyments, demanded a frank and sensational art form. The disfavour and censorship of the authorities gave the colour-print movement a clandestine flavour which added considerably to its zest. Nothing is more stimulating than the opportunity to flout ineffective regulations. This 'under-ground' aspect was due partly to the fact that a considerable proportion of the prints were what the Japanese call *shunga* or 'Spring Paintings'—a delicate Eastern euphemism for what is the world's most explicit erotic art. Figure 142 gives a very modest hint of what these artists could achieve in this direction. Others show how the commoners of Edo made bawdy fun of their superiors. In these gross confections they mostly ridiculed the *samurai* or even the *shōguns*, the nobleman being revealed a cuckold to his servant, the rulers inextricably entangled with tea-house courtesans. The *shōguns* made constant efforts to control or censor the prints but with little effect. Alack, even to-day in our free

[1] Van Gulik, *The Erotic Colour Prints of the Ming Period*. Japan, 1951.

country, none of the really outspoken *shunga*, for all their artistry, can be reproduced. This is sad for, apart from their art, they are an interesting social and political phenomenon. Certainly they make it extremely difficult for the scholar to produce a catalogue raisonné of almost any artist's work.

When the print designers turned away from the set manners of traditional painting to the genre scenes of every-day life around them what a rich, gay, colourful world they found! The limits of painting seemed to burst apart. Almost every print reflects the joy of some newly discovered beauty, some striking moment seen with fresh eyes. The *ukiyō-e* movement may have had no deeper aim than to render this ' Floating ' or ' Fleeting World ' but how much more alive and real it was than the countless repetitions of *Sages in a Bamboo Grove* or *Landscape in the Style of Such-and-such a Chinese Master*. The graceful beauties of the Yoshiwara, the great prostitute area of Tokyo, parade before us in all their finery; we look into the bath houses with their nude figures and into the theatre with its grimacing actors in their bright costumes; ladies with their attendants exhibit their charms and their dresses by the river, a thousand intimate scenes in the houses and streets are exquisitely recorded, the newly discovered beauties of the Japanese countryside are vividly captured. There is hardly any aspect of public and private life which has not been explored by the long line of colour-print masters from the last half of the 17th century to the middle of the 19th. Through them we share the excitement of the bustling, seething life of the time. Edo is brought to life, a city of " Brawling samurai, pleasure loving merchants, skilled craftsmen, its streets swarming with retainers, flunkeys, palanquin bearers, a swaggering and truculent horde." The life-blood of Japanese painting during the Tokugawa period ran in the *ukiyō-e*

The combination of talents which made possible the vast output of colour prints is one of the most remarkable features of the movement. The publisher who commissioned the print, if he were a man like Jūsaburō, would have been a guiding force, an impressario in his own right. The designer whose name is probably familiar to Western readers— Harunobu, Hokusai, Hiroshige, Utamaro, Sharaku—produced the model. Finally they all relied on the block-cutters and printers, the countless unnamed craftsmen whose deftness secured the perfection of the final product. To these must be added as a formative quality the taste of an eager and discriminating public which demanded the best of artist and craftsmen, whose fickle favour kept the designers constantly on their toes, but who faithfully supported the craft through nearly two centuries. An intense spirit of competition within society enlivened the whole atmosphere of the Tokugawa scene.

Until about 1740, only black-and-white prints appeared. These were subsequently often coloured by hand. Later, by increasing the number of blocks, true colour-printing was introduced, a technique which, once discovered, the printers rapidly developed, until in 1764 they perfected the full polychrome print. Sometimes, by using more than ten separate blocks they produced what the Japanese call *nishiki-e* or ' brocade paintings.' The accurate cutting and printing of so many blocks in perfect register, and the mixing of the dyes required the most exacting standards.

The first *ukiyō-e* artist is generally held to be Matabei (d. 1650) but there is little in his surviving work to support his claim as the founder of the movement. Historians have tended to attribute any very early painting in *ukiyō-e* style to ' Matabei.' Moronobu (1618–1694) was certainly the man who established the art. It was he who discovered that, by using the wood-block printing method, he could produce pictures cheaply to

143. *Street Scene* by Moronobu (1618–1694).
Unsigned, black and white print. 15 by 11 inches. Museum of Eastern Art, Oxford.

satisfy a wide market. He illustrated books, made albums, designed large single sheets and eventually hand coloured prints. These hand-coloured prints are called *tan-e—tan* being an orange-red colour. Sometimes the addition of yellow and grey areas produced three-coloured effect. The colours of these *tan-e*, originally very brilliant, have not lasted and their present discreet shades, although greatly admired, bear little resemblance to the originals. Moronobu's strong black line influenced not only his contemporaries but all later artists. He had been trained in the Kanō and Tosa styles and in adopting the Kanō line, he took over the one element of value which the Kanō style had to offer. The Tosa style provided the interest in people. Figure 143 is typical of much of his work.

He was the first to reveal the intimate, lively aspects of every-day Edo life—fishermen selling their wares, ladies viewing flowers, scenes of the Yoshiwara. Variety and interest abound but the figures, though individually pleasing, tend, as often in *ukiyō-e*, to be somewhat monotonous *en masse*. The faces show little variety and the compositions are often stiff and synthetic. However, he was one of the first Japanese artists to explore human relations and his successors owed much to this departure.

One of the most characteristic and colourful aspects of Edo city life was the *Kabuki* theatre. The theatre as a source of inspiration for artists is familiar in the West, so the form does not surprise us; only it is a different type of theatre. The fully developed *Kabuki* which means literally 'song-dance art,' was a product of the Tokugawa period, but had its roots in many traditional Japanese forms—in the old religious dances often performed with masks, in the *Nō* drama which developed from them, in the popular puppet plays which thrived then as now in Osaka. The *Kabuki* theatre as still performed to-day provides one of the most impressive dramatic experiences to be found on any stage. The settings in the vast proscenium openings are breath-taking, the costumes gorgeous beyond description. Technical equipment and production compare favourably with any in the world.

The plays, mimes, and dances are generally well-tried favourites known word-for-word, action-for-action. Their most important function has always been to act as media for the personalities and talents of outstanding actors. The idolatry given to English actors like Kean and Garrick was nothing compared with the worship of the matinee idols of the *Kabuki* theatre. Their every gesture on the stage was noted and compared with those of their predecessors, their behaviour and dress off-stage dictated the popular fashion.

Although no Westerner can fail to be impressed by the dazzling spectacle that this theatrical form provides, few can understand its studied grimaces and tortured poses. These are intended to express the emotional struggles of the actor and can move a Japanese audience to scenes of wild excitement. For all their artificiality they are extraordinary histrionical feats. The tradition of an all-male cast has survived and the skill with which slim, adult male actors impersonate female roles is completely deceptive.

The personalities and plays of *Kabuki* provided the colour-print designers with a vivid world of subjects peculiarly suited to their art. The popularity of the actors ensured a ready sale for prints depicting them in their successes. Many of the finest prints show either actors or the girls of the Yoshiwara. A social commentator of the time complains of the energy spent in endless sexual adventures, in continual experiment with luxury and extravagance, of the addiction to lust, drinking, gambling, profit-hunting, songs and dance, music and artistic accomplishments, etc. The explanation is that these were the only ways in which the *chōnin* could use their wealth and express their political frustration.

A description of one of the most popular *Kabuki* plays may help a Westerner to appreciate the actor prints. The classical version of *Chūshingura*, 'The Storehouse of Loyal Retainers' for example, which was written by three playwrights, Takeda Izumo, Namiki Senryū, and Miyoshi Shōraku, has remained a firm favourite with Japanese audiences. Any *Kabuki* troupe in financial difficulties immediately turns to *Chūshingura* to solve its problems—in the same way in which its Western counterpart puts on *Charley's Aunt* or a bedroom farce.

The play is based on an historical event of 1701 in which a lord, insulted by an avaricious superior in the *Shōgun's* palace, was goaded into raising his sword and wounding his insulter. For the serious crime of unsheathing a sword within the palace precincts, he was sentenced to commit suicide. His retainers banded together and, after a year's plotting, brought about the death of the original wrong-doer. Their mission achieved, they then gave themselves up to the authorities. The crime would normally have carried the death sentence, but they were permitted the honourable end of committing mass suicide and were buried in a temple. They rapidly became national heroes.

For political convenience, the authors placed the play they wove about this event in the Ashikaga period and changed the names. They added a great deal of romance, incidental drama, brigandage, intrigues, murder and suicide, plots and counterplots so that the audience is never deprived of tension and exciting climaxes. The speed of the action sweeps one along from castle to geisha house, from forest to battlefield, from one scene of violence to another. The play is designed to show the ultimate triumph of right over wrong and the various rights and wrongs in the main and sub-plots are skilfully interwoven. Forty-six of the forty-seven heroes belong to the masterless *rōnin* or 'wave-men' a class of fighting men which increased rapidly during the peaceful Tokugawa period. Some of them turned outlaw and became a serious social problem. But their code of honour, inherited from earlier times, remained a romantic ideal with the admiring Japanese population even if occasionally it had to suffer from their arrogance. One of the most eagerly awaited moments in the play occurs when a merchant, a commoner like most of the audience, speaks the famous words, " I, too, am a man among men " and, as a reward for his courage and loyalty to the cause, is allowed to join the band as the forty-seventh avenger.

The leading parts in this play are still considered as the test of an actor much as Hamlet and Macbeth are in the West. Each of the eleven scenes or acts has its dramatic moment which provided an excellent subject for a colour-print.

Actor prints flourished to the end of the 19th century but the finest appeared in the first half of the 18th century when the Torii masters including Kiyonobu I, Kiyomasu I, Kiyonobu II, and Kiyomasu II dominated the period.

A print by Torii Kiyomasu I, *Arashi Wakano as the Poetess Ono-no-Komachi, Dancing* (Fig. 144), produced about 1745, illustrates the actor prints of the Torii school.[1] It is hand coloured and further beautified by sprinkling metal dust on a gum base to create the impression of metal-work. It is typical of the so-called ' primitives ' and shows a large figure in bold, flowing lines with the body strongly curved. The heavy drapery with its large designs seems to weigh down the body, the face is plump but the features are small and very simply indicated. The stately, sweeping movement of these large figures, as they appear to move slowly across the paper, produces a pageant-like effect.

The greatest master of line in this early period was Kaigetsudō who was active in the first half of the 18th century. Only thirty-nine prints from the hand of this master have survived, or as some authorities say, from these three masters; for three different names appear on the prints after the characters for Kaigetsudō. However, they are so similar in style that historians generally treat them as the work of one man. Figure 145 signed Kaigetsudō Dōhan shows a courtesan, a typical woman of the Yoshiwara with her gaily decorated robes around her. Although in black and white, the print gives the unmistakable impression of colour. America is fortunate in possessing twenty-four of the surviving thirty-nine Kaigetsudō prints.

In about 1740 the invention of true colour printing immeasurably enriched the wood block technique. Instead of the hand-coloured prints, pale red and green were printed with blocks. The credit for this invention is given to Okumura Masanobu (1686–1764), though the technique was known before Masanobu applied it to prints. However, in doing so he gave the art a new lease of life. Masanobu, like many print designers, was a prodigy and his interests included poetry, stories, and book illustrations. His output was enormous and, in common with his contemporaries, he would copy the designs of others where it suited him and if he thought that thereby he could find a market. He was an excellent business man and ran a shop of his own to sell his prints. Stylistically these range from the powerful black-and-white of Kaigetsudō to a more gentle, graceful style of his own which is typical of the early two-colour prints and which was taken up by Harunobu.

The change in the *ukiyo-e* style from the statuesque of Kaigetsudō to the willowy, petite, more familiar Japanese female figure made famous by the prints is best seen in the work of Harunobu who died in 1770. Masanobu's pioneering in two-coloured prints led rapidly to the extension of the technique so that eventually as many as thirty different colours could be applied. *Girls Fording a Stream* (Fig. 146) by Harunobu is a representative example of his work in which everything centres on the sweetness and grace of the ensemble. Charming, slim girls, perhaps a little monotonous in their sentimentality and lack of

[1] J. Hillier, *Masters of the Japanese Colour Print*, London, 1954.

144.   *Arashi Wakano as the Poetess Ono-no-Komachi, Dancing* by Torii Kiyomasu I
(*ca.* 1720–1763).   Hand coloured print.   10¾ by 6⅛ inches.   British Museum.

individuality, pose decoratively against a few architectural or landscape elements. His work is always the apogee of good taste and gentility. Harunobu's genius lies in his appreciation of the possibilities of the polychrome print, his masterly use of colour and in his impeccable harmonies.

Despite their fertility, few of the great names who fill the world of *ukiyō-e* designing were able to live by their art. An over-night change of fashion could make their prints unsaleable. A famous courtesan might change her hair-style, a new actor could create a sensation. Above all, the innovations of a new artist might capture the public fancy and eclipse the products of his rivals. One of the greatest was Kitagawa Utamaro (1753–1806) who took over the leadership of the print movement in the early 1790's. His smooth, refined prints of tall, elongated girls with complicated hair-dresses were an immediate success and constitute his best-known work. More original, however, are his large heads which are masterpieces technically as well as artistically. His work covers a wide range; some of his insect prints show a close observation of nature and faultless draughtsmanship. One of his most successful series illustrates the life of *Kintoki*, 'The Golden Boy,' the son of a dead *samurai* who, according to folk-lore, was brought up by a wild woman of the mountains, *Yamauba*. Figure 147 shows this mad, wild woman suckling the child. The concentration and fierce emotion expressed in this print come as a surprise after the idealized portraits of Yoshiwara prostitutes in their costly robes attended by their equally elegant attendants. Utamaro seems to have enjoyed the opportunity that this series gave him to express the savage protecting instinct of the wild foster mother and to escape for a moment from his beautiful girls.

The appearance of such revolutionary designs may well have been due to the influence of a courageous publisher like Jūsaburō who backed and stimulated promising young artists. Many of the finest prints come from his *Tsūtaya* or 'Ivy Shop' and carry his stamp. Like discriminating patrons of art through the ages, he supported unknown artists in whose work he had faith. The production of a print involved a considerable financial investment and the backing of a new talent was a risk. Jūsaburō's enterprise was responsible for some of the best prints of the whole movement.

Without him, for instance, an artist like Tōshusai Sharaku, whom many critics consider the greatest of all the print masters, would never have had his chance. Everything about this artist is mysterious. His origins are obscure; he was possibly a comparatively unknown actor of the *Nō* drama. In the course of about ten months of one year, 1794, during which he was backed by Jūsaburō, he produced over one hundred actor prints which are unique in the whole of *ukiyō-e*. They were not a popular success at the time and did not sell. Jūsaburō was forced to cut his losses and discontinue his backing. Sharaku, after a brief but brilliant moment, disappeared without trace from the print-designers' world.

Sharaku worked on an heroic scale designing portraits of actors with such acute observation of personality that they seem at times almost cruel. It is understandable that his version of stage idols made little appeal to the public which was accustomed to idealized portraits of their favourites. They have been called caricatures but in fact they transcend our conception of caricatures. Figure 148 of the actor *Segawa Tomisaburō in a Female Role* shows how Sharaku synthesized the personality of the actor and the character he was portraying on the stage. The elaboration of the butterfly-shaped coiffure crowned with a huge comb and long hair-pins offsets the extraordinarily simple lines with which he captures the facial expression. The innermost secrets of personality are laid bare with a few expressive

145. *Courtesan with Cat* by Kaigetsudō (1st quarter of 18th century).
Black and White.   23½ by 13 inches.   Musée Guimet, Paris.

strokes. The fusion of simplicity and complexity, tenseness and relaxation, whiteness and colour, warmth and coldness produces a depth of character study unparalleled in the whole movement. Sharaku's portraits breathe the authentic atmosphere of the theatre in the same way as do the ballet pictures of Dégas and the posters of Toulouse-Lautrec. His sardonic humour completely transforms the actor print, imparting to it a new grandeur. Altogether these profound studies are one of the most baffling expressions of all Japanese art

Figure 149, a rarer study with the two actors *Nakamura Ganzō and Nakajima Wataeimon* in the frame, shows the artist in his most ruthless mood. With a few decisive lines he exposes the meanness and grossness of his subjects with a clarity which takes us back to some of the early sculpture. In a recent exhibition at the Musée Guimet, Paris, this print was aptly entitled 'The Moneylenders.' It is easy to see how Sharaku alarmed and infuriated his victims. His work is a splendid climax to fifteen hundred years of Japanese portraiture.

The first half of the 19th century, the last great period of Japanese colour-prints, was dominated by two outstanding designers, Katsushika Hokusai (1760–1849) and Ichiryūsai Hiroshige (1797–1858). Both produced a vast number of prints in large editions and it is generally their designs which swell the tattered piles of old prints in antique shops. Unfortunately, many of them were printed from old or re-cut blocks and colours even more harsh than their originals have helped to damage their reputation. Landscape was the

146. *Girls Fording a Stream*
by Harunobu
(1725–1770).
9¾ by 7⅛ inches.
British Museum.

147. *Yamauba and Kintoki* by Utamaro   (1753–1806).
15 by 10¼ inches.   Museum of Eastern Art, Oxford.

148.   *Segawa Tomisaburō in a Female Role* by Sharaku, 1794.
14¼ by 9⅜ inches.   Musée Guimet, Paris.

149.   *Nakamura Ganzō and Nakajima Wataeimon*
by Sharaku, 1794.
14⅝ by 9 inches.
British Museum.

150.   *Yoro Waterfall*
from the series *Waterfalls of the Provinces*
by Hokausi (1760–1849).
14¾ by 10 inches.
Museum of Eastern Art, Oxford.

東海道
五拾三次
之内
蒲原

151. *Kambara* from the series *Fifty-three Stations on the Tōkaidō* (about 1834).
By Hiroshige (1797–1858). 14¾ by 10 inches. Museum of Eastern Art, Oxford.

main preoccupation of these great artists and their works include some of the most original designs ever produced.

Hokusai lived with unimpaired energy to the age of ninety. He created many of his most inspired prints during his last twenty years, among them some of the *Random Sketches* and his great series of landscape views such as *The Thirty-six Views of Mount Fūji*. His gifts of improvisation are inexhaustible. In the Mount Fūji set nothing could be more unlike the jagged Chinese-style Kanō rocks than the gentle, symmetrical slopes of this most Japanese of all mountains. It made a magnificent *leitmotiv*, sometimes dominating, sometimes almost invisible, always seen from a fresh, unexpected angle. Some of the designs seem a little forced in their search for novelty but even these show an astounding fantasy and fertility of ideas. The well-known *Wave of Kanagawa* and *Mount Fūji in a Storm* are perhaps the best-known of this series and have frequently been reproduced. Both are violent, dynamic backdrops conceived in the broadest terms and vitalized by the tremendous power which bursts through them. Accustomed as we are to the modern artist's efforts to achieve originality, their daring and powerful draughtsmanship still impresses. His *Waterfalls of the Provinces* (Fig. 150) and his *Views of Famous Bridges* show how Hokusai does not so much study landscape as tyrannize it. In him one sees yet again the Japanese love of the grotesque appearing in 19th century landscapes as it did in the masks of the 8th century.

Hiroshige's output of landscapes was even greater than that of Hokusai; a rough estimate puts it at 5,460 designs. Inevitably many of them are hurried, crude designs dashed off to satisfy an avid public but a remarkable number are outstanding; his snow scenes are superb (Fig. 151). He is the master *par excellence* of light and atmosphere and his genius for depicting rain gives many of his designs a peculiarly pungent atmosphere. The landscapes of Japan were almost ransacked by his restless imagination. His prints are softer in feeling than those of Hokusai, readily understandable and often humorous, particularly when, as so often happens, he depicts puny mankind being buffeted by the giant forces of nature.

Apart from their large prints some of these designers welcomed every opportunity to show their skill in different forms. In addition to his landscapes, Hiroshige made a number of most pleasing designs for printing on such things as luxury envelopes. Figure 152 shows how he decorated a difficult area $2\frac{1}{4}$ by 7 inches. With a few delicate strokes and some gauffrage (embossing) he produced a *Monkey Trying to Fish the Moon out of the Water*—a gentle sketch none the less masterly for its unassuming aims and limited scope.[1] One is constantly struck by the evidence of the underlying taste and refinement of this burly Tokugawa society.

The same delicacy of sentiment is found in the *surimono* (lit: ' printed things ') which designers made to order to celebrate special occasions like birthdays or New Year's Days (Fig. 153). In these rarer small prints with their fine lines, muted colours, gauffrage, and profusion of sprinkled metal dust, the actual technique of print making reached its zenith.

In the mid-19th century, after two hundred years of prodigious activity and the vast output of countless artists great and small, the quality of the art of colour-printing decayed sadly within only a few years. It is difficult to understand why this happened. The restrictive measures of the *shōguns* can hardly have affected it. Garish European aniline dyes carelessly used created a horrible clash of strident tones, cheapened the look of the prints, and destroyed their line. A deterioration in the taste of the Edo public may have been a major factor but it is always difficult to determine the reasons for such a decline. Perhaps the mass production encouraged by the success of men like Hokusai and Hiroshige lowered the standards. Whereas a set of blocks once served for two hundred prints and was then discarded, towards the end they were made to serve for three thousand impressions with a corresponding loss of quality. Perhaps *ukiyo-e* simply exhausted itself—no talent or combination appeared powerful enough to impose its taste on the public and revive the art. Distinguished artists like Kuniyoshi produced some designs powerful enough to match the hard dyes but generally the rearguard of the movement was either sensational and coarse or weak and superficial.

It was possible to give here only the most sketchy outline of the print movement and to mention only a few of the outstanding artists who raised it from a folk-art to an art form of international significance. A number of competent artists are now trying to revive wood-block printing but, although their technique is in the best tradition, the spirit behind their artistry owes little to the *ukiyo-e* world of the Tokugawa period.

It is only a small step from the colour-prints to the textiles of the period. One of the most striking features of the prints is the beauty and extravagance of the robes worn by many of the figures. The courtesans wear dazzling *kimonos* with large, gay *ōbis* or ' waist bands '; the actors pose in bold, colourful costumes. As previously mentioned, an artist's success often depended on his keeping closely in touch with passing fashions. The colour prints, in fact, often acted as fashion plates; a quick comment on fashion, or on an innovation in dress or hair which appealed to the public could make the fortune of a print. We can now seldom distinguish the subtle changes which they reflect but in Tokugawa Japan the provinces eagerly followed and imitated the changing modes of the capital. It seems highly probable that some of the *ukiyo-e* artists also tried their hands at textile designing.

[1] See T. Volker " Hiroshige's Fūtō " in *Oriental Art*, Old Series, Vol. II, No. 2. 1949.

152. *Monkey Trying to Fish the Moon out of the Water*.
by Hiroshige (1797–1858).   Approx. 7 by 2¼ inches.
National Museum for Ethnology, Leiden

153. *Feeding the Chickens, Surimono*
by Eisen (or Yeisen). (1790–1848).   7¾ by 7 inches.
Museum of Eastern Art, Oxford.

Textiles and dress are dictated by the whims of fashion and they change more rapidly than any other form of the arts. Since they are also the most intimate and most widely-used of all art products, they reflect very closely the character of the times in which they are made. Thus, in Tokugawa Japan, their brilliance reflects the exhibitionism of the newly-rich. The sumptuary laws were largely directed against the elegant dress in which the merchants liked to see their wives and paramours. Yet laws against luxury are always the most difficult to enforce and tend to have the reverse effect of that intended. They merely emphasized the importance of dress and encouraged the quick-witted to evade the spirit without breaking the letter of the law. One can imagine how the public would have applauded the flouting or evasion of restrictions as reported in the prints!

As in all the crafts, it was the Momoyama period which laid the foundations for the textile designs of the Tokugawa period. The search for ever freer, bolder patterns is the keynote of the period. The restrictions on trade with China enacted in the 1630's increased the cost of gold and silver-thread used for the embroidery which had hitherto provided the finest costumes and threw the Japanese back on their own resources. The sumptuary laws of 1680 forbade the use of embroidery except for belts (*obis*) or the robes of actors and priests. Simpler means demanded bolder treatment. Thus the restrictions stimulated the development of new, eye-arresting methods for decorating textiles which dispensed with the need for embroidery in precious metals. The laws restricting embroidery also encouraged the creation of methods to produce the broad assymetrical patterns which are a feature of modern Japanese design. The wider market provided by the increasing numbers of wealthy people further stimulated these new techniques.

The most popular was tie-dyeing (*kō-kechi*) applied in a number of ways. This method could produce a small fish-egg pattern or a large over-all sweeping design with sharply-defined contours. The most characteristic textile feature of the period was the large patterns which swept like boldly conceived pictures from hem to shoulder. Smaller repeat-patterns were less popular. However, it was not until the textile workers perfected the resist process of pattern dyeing that these large designs could be economically produced. A rice-paste resist was invented about 1665 by Morikage but the credit for the perfecting of the process is given to a painter Miyazaki Yūzensai (active in the Genroku period, 1688–1703) after whom the process is named *Yūzen*. It is a relatively primitive method but in the hands of the Japanese, capable of producing splendid pictorial designs. The inspiration for the process may have come from the *batik* textiles which the Dutch introduced into Japan from the East Indies in the 16th century. But the way the Japanese developed it equals the manner in which they made the Chinese colour-print into the finest *ukiyō-e*. Figure 154 shows a detail of a short-sleeved garment decorated with scenes of the Yoshiwara on a brown background. The figures in this example were produced by embroidery which despite the restrictions, was sometimes added to these *Yūzen* textiles to increase their rich effects.

The art of weaving also progressed during the period, especially at places like Nishijin in Kyoto which still produces the finest Japanese silks. The Nishijin products were largely reserved for the use of the ruling households but this was only one of many silk-weaving centres throughout Japan each with its own speciality and renowned for its particular colours.

From 1800 onwards it became necessary to invent an even cheaper method of decorating cloth capable of mass-production. As one might expect, the craftsmen turned to wood

154. Detail of a short-sleeved garment
decorated by Yūzen dyeing and embroidery
to represent a scene from the Yoshiwara.
Tokugawa period. Nagao.
Museum of Art, Tokyo.

155. Four stencils. Late 19th century.
Each 8 by 14 inches.
Museum of Eastern Art, Oxford.

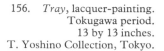

156. *Tray*, lacquer-painting.
Tokugawa period.
13 by 13 inches.
T. Yoshino Collection, Tokyo.

block printing techniques. These satisfied the demands for speed and economy but not for the popular large designs which treat the whole surface as a single picture plane. Perhaps the most ingenious technique used at the time was the stencil process. Stencils were made which are the finest produced anywhere in the world. The ingenuity and originality of the designs, to say nothing of the skill required to cut them, are typical of the imagination and care lavished on all the crafts. Figure 155 shows a number of these stencils cut at the end of the 19th century.

The technical perfection of Tokugawa art is seen in lacquer work perhaps better than in the other crafts. It seems to epitomize the taste of the period in the applied arts. A lacquer box with its many compartments, all tastefully decorated and fitting perfectly, the motifs repeated with subtle variations reflect the Tokugawa artistic atmosphere as accurately as a colour print.

Tokugawa lacquer-work, like its textiles, took inspiration from the innovations of the Momoyama period. The tireless search for what was new and original and the wealth available to back it created ideal conditions for a luxury art of bewildering variety which combined perfection of manufacture and originality of design. Every possible technique was employed to give lacquer objects the sparkle of jewellery and the scope and interest of painting. It is difficult to think in terms of ' art ' as opposed to ' craft ' when handling the products in this sensitive idiom. New techniques appeared and old ones were revived. One of the most interesting of the revivals was of the ' oil-painting ' type of lacquer decoration last seen in the painting on the Tamamushi Shrine (see p. 23). In this the lacquer-worker, like the textile designer and print artist, thought in terms of free brush-work and bold pictorial styles. Every artisan seems to have been a born painter.

Figure 156 shows a tray in the revived painted-lacquer technique. Its sides are in black lacquer and the background in red while the design is in yellow, green, and black. The tips of the waves are in silver, and the figure in gold. A boat, propelled by one small sail, forges upstream, so heavily laden with its wicker-baskets of rice that the stern is almost under water. Even the well-fed boatman, holding on to his wide hat as he leans against the wind, cannot keep the prow down and stop the waves lapping hungrily over the gunwales. A few branches of bamboo balance the boat and provide a second diagonal, thus avoiding any possible monotony in the composition.

The design unites the twin affections of the Japanese craftsman of the period—a love of nature and a close, friendly interest in human behaviour. He felt no need to force his designs into set patterns, the whole world was his pattern book.

The Japanese added to this love of nature and mankind a very sensitive appreciation of the inner qualities of the material in which they worked. This is a sensibility which Western craftsmen are only now re-discovering. In Japan it is seen at all times—in a tea-ceremony bowl as much as in a noble wooden sculpture.

The beauty of a fine piece of lacquer owes much to the mirror-like perfection of its smooth finish and high polish. Anybody who handles Eastern art objects of jade, procelain or lacquer develops a sense of appreciation through touch. This tactile sense is impossible to express adequately in words but it can quickly be gained by handling Japanese lacquer. The effect produced by setting simple, natural forms against the most refined material, though sometimes capricious, never jars. The Japanese have developed to perfection this combination of the rough and the smooth, the rustic and the sophisticated.

If the output of the colour-print masters was prodigious, it was easily matched by that of the potters. The Momoyama period products also laid the foundations of their art and throughout the Tokugawa period they produced a rich diversity of wares inspired by native and by many foreign examples which came into the country. So much so that the Tokugawa period is sometimes called by the Japanese " The Age of Pottery and Porcelain." One Japanese critic has estimated that there were as many as ten thousand different kilns and individual potters.

During these two and a half centuries the craft, both technically and artistically, reached full maturity. The Japanese showed the same powers of adoption and development as they had in the centuries following the introduction of Buddhism, and as they were again to show in the change-over to Western methods in the 19th and 20th centuries. A good example is the sloping-kiln technique. This is, in effect, a communal series of connecting kilns built up a hill side and fired simultaneously, a system which was brought over from Koera and is still used. The best craftsmen even now have first choice of position in the row of kilns. This technique resulted in a much greater productivity. The inventiveness of design, far outstripping the more conservative Chinese genius, found ample expression in ceramics. Eminent artists applied themselves to the craft in a manner which Western artists have only recently adopted. Clay was a means of expressing personality— a concept unknown to the Chinese. The works of potters known by name were highly prized. One of the most famous was the Kyoto potter Ninsei (active in the early Tokugawa period). Many of his works show a strong influence of lacquer wares in their designs and surface textures. Figure 157, his most famous piece, is a large jar with a design of cherry blossom on a mountain-side. The mists and contours of the mountain are done in white and gold, the flowers in red and blue. The black background is particularly reminiscent of lacquer. The decoration is set off by the buff clay. The strong shape is said to have been inspired by South Chinese wares imported during the Momoyama period.

The eclecticism of the Japanese artists in the choice of their material is a modern phenomenon, and gave their work a refreshing vitality. All material was one to their restless
seeking. Once again the small communities centred around a feudal lord provided patronage for countless small craftsmen. Their position was far more honoured and exalted than
that of their unnamed counterparts in the great factories of China.

The tea-ceremony continued to create the demand without which the arts of the ceramic
workers could never have blossomed. Its implements provided a wide range and ample
scope for ceramic ideas—not only in the tea bowls themselves, but also in tea-caddies,
flower vases, incense burners, and containers, rests for ladles and for jar-covers, bowls
for tea slops, ash containers, cake bowls and plates, plates for charcoal braziers, and other
wine and food vessels. In fact any vessel which could serve a useful function in the ceremony
was welcomed into the ceramic family and arrayed for admiration on the mats before the
masters. If the ceremony need a vessel there was a potter ready to give thought to producing
a ware of fitness and beauty. The combination of implements was dictated only by
experiment and taste. They were, for example, constantly changed according to the seasons
of the year. Successful innovations were always applauded. The juxtaposition of the
various pots was carefully thought out with a view to the harmony of the ensemble.

The appreciation of unusual wares and the love of variety created a fashion for preserving
examples of the craft from China, Annam, Siam. Chinese export wares of the Ming dynasty
which reached Japan via the Pacific islands, and even Dutch wares reaching the country
through Nagasaki were very popular. All fitted into the tea-room, were admired and
influenced the work of the native potters. The words *wabi* ('rustic tranquillity') and *shibui*,
which were constantly on the lips of the tea devotees, reflect the Japanese admiration of
restraint in their best ceramics. The 'life' demanded of the best wares is an extension of
the Japanese appreciation of individuality in all their art. It gives the work of the potters
an inner warmth which cannot be claimed for the Chinese products, in which perfection
and grandeur take its place. The downright eccentricity of some Japanese wares is but
the extreme expression of this trend.

The irregularities which, at first sight, seem to be the result of faulty technique were
often created on purpose and admired for the strength or vitality they impart. The knife-
cuts, thumb-marks, squeezed sides, mottled or running glazes, irregular foot-rims, lop-
sided shapes were felt to increase the interest of a vessel. These recur down the years,
though the potters took care in the best pieces not to turn these 'defects' into conscious
affectations. 'Beauty within simplicity,' 'unobtrusive grace' were the ideals of the
tea-ceremony wares.

It was, nevertheless, a vigorous age; the consumate skill and tranquil perfection found
in the finest Chinese wares generally escaped the Japanese potter. Where the Chinese
are assured and work steadily towards perfection, the Japanese are experimental and above
all restless. These are qualities which Western art has led us to understand. Equally the
Japanese are never the prisoners of their own techniques as were sometimes the Chinese,
especially in later times. Thus in Japan the art never died as it did in 19th century China.
It is as alive and as progressive to-day as it was two hundred years ago.

Some of the earlier kilns were mentioned in the chapter on the Momoyama period.
Figure 158 shows a bowl from one of the Karatsu kilns in the southern island of Kyūshū,
a great ceramic centre. It is a 'Painted Karatsu' bowl of a typically Korean shape with a
greenish-brown glaze and decorated with two sprays of freely painted strokes in black.

157. *Jar* by Ninsei with a design of Mount Yoshino. Tokugawa period. Height 9 inches. Seikadō Foundation, Tokyo.

158. *Bowl*, Painted Karatsu ware. Tokugawa period. Height 6½ inches. S. Idemitsu Collection, Tokyo.

Being nearest to Korea, the influence of Korean wares of the Yi dynasty (1392–1910) was even stronger here than on the mainland. The congealed glaze which reveals the body appeals strongly to the Japanese appreciation of contrasts. The design is in the best tradition of free-hand decoration which goes back to Korean, and possibly even to *tz'u-chou* wares of Sung China. The Karatsu kilns produced a wide variety of wares (Fig. 159) in addition to this type—plates with designs of fruit and flowers, *mishima* type wares with very small repeated inlaid designs in white (Fig. 160). Sometimes brush-marks or comb scratches swept quickly across the glaze produce a design of great vitality and freedom. The brush-mark effect was greatly admired and developed. Painting and scratching methods of decoration were often most cleverly combined. Thick, white glazes in imitation of Seto wares were sometimes used. These Karatsu wares have an infinite variety of shape and design combined with the simple strength demanded by the masters of the tea-ceremony.

Pottery remained popular throughout the period but an important innovation during these centuries completely changed the direction of the craft. This was the discovery by the Japanese of the nature of the raw materials and the technique of porcelain manufacture which had previously been unknown to them.

Japan, like Europe, admired the jewel-like hardness and brilliance of Chinese porcelain, but its inventors had guarded the secrets of its manufacture very closely. Koreans, who had worked in Chinese factories, finally revealed them to the Japanese. Thereafter, many Japanese pottery kilns quickly changed over to porcelain manufacture and a host of new factories began to produce it exclusively. Again the variety is so great and the output so widely distributed among the many active kilns that only the broadest identification is possible. Skilful copying of early wares by later potters adds to the problems of dating; the constant cross-fertilization of ideas between the various kilns adds to the confusion. Japanese experts themselves quite often frankly admit defeat in trying to establish the kiln which made a certain ware or the date when it was made.

The most famous kilns were those belonging to the Arita group near Nagasaki in Kyūshū. Korean style wares had been made there since the early 17th century, but historians credit Kakiemon I (1595–1666) with the invention of the technique of overglaze decoration towards the middle of the century. This spread rapidly to other kilns in the district. The Kakiemon family continued to work as potters throughout the period and is still active. The products of the various members of the family are extremely difficult to distinguish and they therefore pass under the generic name of *kakiemonte* or ' in the style of Kakiemon.'

The Arita *Kakiemon* wares are of milky white porcelain decorated in polychrome fashion with red, green, yellow, blue, and aubergine enamels, often enriched with gold. These inspired the potters of Meissen and Chelsea wares. Although modelled on Chinese wares of the K'ang-hsi period (1662–1722), the potters almost invariably show a decorative approach which can only be Japanese. The lobed dish in Figure 161 is decorated in enamels and underglaze blue with a most sensitive design of a woven hedge with a profusion of flowers growing from behind it. A butterfly hovers above them adding to the lightness of the composition. This refined decoration is characteristically Japanese. The whole surface is treated as a single unit—an approach inherited from the Momoyama period. The Chinese in their finest ceramics may show a more perfect technique but their designs often give the impression of having been constantly repeated. Japanese ceramics made for the home market have an air of being individual works of art, each one the result of as

159. *Jar*, Painted Karatsu ware.
Tokugawa period.
Height 9¾ inches,
British Museum.

160. *Bowl* on high stem.
Mishima type. Tokugawa period.
Diameter 6 inches.
Museum of Eastern Art, Oxford.

much thought as a painting. When a Chinese potter made a set the pieces were generally identical, whereas in a Japanese set each individual piece often has some small variation —it may be a different bunch of flowers, a butterfly in a different position, or a design reversed. The respective craftsmen seem to have been conscious of their public. A Chinese vase is made to be admired on its pedestal; a Japanese, to be studied in loving hands. The Chinese connoisseur expects his potters to demonstrate their skill; the Japanese, to transmit their personalities.

Apart from the dislike of repeat designs and the tendency towards pictorial treatment, the effect produced by Japanese porcelain is softer and more lyrical than that of Chinese wares of the same period. The Japanese excel in the successful combination of naturalism and abstraction, weaving both into tasteful harmonies. In their way, the finest of these *Kakiemon* wares can hold their own with the products of China in the 18th century.

The *kakiemonte* wares are only one of many groups made in the Arita district. Another large group are the Imari wares, so-called from the port of Imari whence they were shipped. The Dutch East India Company brought many of these late 17th century porcelains to Europe where they were in great demand as decorations for palaces and large country houses. So great was their success in Europe, that the Chinese copied them in order to share the lucrative market. Most of them are decorated in underglaze blue, iron-red, and gold, and many are little short of ceramic monstrosities. They deserve the bad name they have among modern connoisseurs, but we should remember that they were made entirely to satisfy a European taste which the Japanese had shrewdly assessed. Even to-day the Japanese will send cheap, shoddy objects to Europe while keeping the finest things for their own more discerning market. There is, however, a group of these Imari wares made for Europe and decorated with designs of Dutch ships and men which have an interest and charm of their own (Fig. 162).

The most beautiful of the Arita wares is the Nabeshima porcelain made in Okawachi near Arita. This kiln was established by the ruling family of Nabeshima in the beginning of the 18th century, to supply its own house with porcelain of the very highest quality. Few pieces were sold outside the family. The finest period of the kiln was the second half of the 18th century and the beginning of the 19th. Every care was taken to make these plates and dishes the ultimate of refinement and perfection. Blue-and-white and celadon wares were produced here but the most typical variety, for which it is justly famous, is coloured ware (Fig. 163). Here again the decorative approach is essentially Japanese, and strongly influenced by the very original textile designs of the period. The potters of Nabeshima were certainly inspired by the elegance and technical accomplishment of Chinese porcelains of the Yung-chêng and Ch'ien-lung period (1722–1796), but the Japanese colours are more diffused, the designs bolder and less mechanical. The scale of design is always broader and more sweeping than in the *kakiemonte* wares. Their soft, ' milky ' pastel shades seem almost luminous.

The Hirado kiln, also situated near Arita, flourished 1712–1843. This kiln is famous for its blue-and-white wares which at their simplest come remarkably close to the Chinese. The pure whiteness of the glaze gives them an added perfection. At times the potters of this kiln tried their hands at complicated forms which show one of the less attractive Japanese characteristics—an inability to exercise a mastered technique in simple terms.

Porcelain manufacture was not restricted to the island of Kyūshū alone. In East Japan on the mainland, a kiln was established in the 17th century at a village called Kutani

161. *Lobed Dish.*
Porcelain decorated in enamels
and under-glaze blue.
Kakiemon type.   Diameter approx. 5 inches.
S. Jenyns Collection.

162. *Plate* with design
of Dutchmen and ships.
Arita export ware.   Tokugawa period.
Diameter 9½ inches.
Museum of Eastern Art, Oxford.

P

163. *Plate.* Nabeshima porcelain.
Tokugawa period.
Height 2 inches, diameter 6¾ inches.
W. Cohn Collection, Oxford.

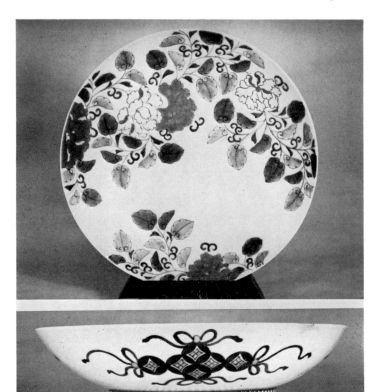

in Kaga province. It flourished for only about fifty years, and enjoyed a short revival in the 19th century. The *Kō-Kutani* or 'Old Kutani' enamelled porcelain from this site has a character all its own. Its strong designs and heavy grandeur of colour are not found either in Nabeshima or Kakiemonte wares. Old Kutani wares were made in many styles; pieces are found in Chinese style, in pure Japanese style, and in combinations of the two. A ewer in the Victoria and Albert Museum (Fig. 164) shows the typical freedom of brushwork, sweeping design, and originality which gives these wares their life and their appeal. The sturdy shape bridges the gap between the conscious roughness of the pottery tea-ceremony wares and the suave perfection of the technically accomplished porcelains of the late 18th and early 19th centuries. The rhythm, as powerful as any seen in Ming coloured enamels, is not gained at the expense of heaviness. The confident shapes and incisive brushwork remind one of much early European porcelain. If the Japanese potter could not always produce the lightness of his Chinese inspiration, he never forgot the need to satisfy the tactile sense which is so important to the Japanese ceramic lover.

No account of the Tokugawa wares, however brief, can avoid mentioning Satsuma. Satsuma is a generic name for Jōsa, Maeshima, Tateno, and Ryūmonji wares. Most Japanese wares brought by the public into the oriental departments of museums are late

19th century specimens of this type with ornate decorations in every possible colour over a creamy crackled glaze. Often, alack, their only admirable qualities are a remarkable dexterity of design and execution. The earlier pieces mostly copied Korean pottery in plain colours with amber, black or white decoration. The black over white glaze tea-caddies, most of which were made in the Tateno kilns, are highly prized. In later times fine pottery was enamelled over the glaze. Before the wares became too rococo Satsuma produced some fine pieces with delicate but brilliant designs on lustrous crackled glazes of great depth (Fig. 165).

The metal-work crafts shared the prosperity of the ceramic industry. A wide variety of objects from cast vessels and figures to iron kettles have decorations ranging from the most restrained to the most flamboyant. One sees the understanding of material, care in manufacture, and attention to detail—the norms of Japanese craftsmen in this period— as much in the sturdy reticence of the tea ceremony iron implements as in the extravagant

164. *Ewer*. Kō-Kutani porcelain.
Tokugawa period.
Height 8 inches.
Victoria and Albert Museum, London.

208

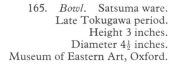

165. *Bowl*. Satsuma ware.
Late Tokugawa period.
Height 3 inches.
Diameter 4½ inches.
Museum of Eastern Art, Oxford.

gold inlay of the sword-guards. *Tsuba* manufacture especially attracted the finest metal-workers and absorbed their energies. The long lists of schools and masters can here only be represented by six which show some aspects of the diverse work of the period. They by no means cover the whole range of work produced in the medium.

Figure 166 a. is a typical iron guard with gold inlay. The inlay of delicately worked clematis flowers covers both faces and the slightly raised border and edge. The gold itself is in two slightly different tones to give added life and variety. The inlay itself is of the flat type (*hira-zōgan*) in which the iron background is cut to take the inlay with a slight undercutting to hold it in place. The whole surface is then rubbed flat. This *tsuba* is probably an early example of the type dating from the 18th century. The advance in technique on the Momoyama guards is very noticeable. The workers in this period seem to delight in overcoming technical difficulties. As in the prints every technical challenge was met and overcome.

Figure 166 b. is a brass guard of the *sentoku* variety which has gained an attractive chrome-yellow effect from a pickling process. It illustrates the characteristic Japanese use of figures, here applied in high relief and in various metals to produce a pictorial effect (*iro-e*). On one side of the guard (not illustrated) is a gnarled pine tree, part of which creeps over to the reverse side and under this branch are two seated figures. They represent the legendary Takeshi-no-uchi-no-Sukune, an aged minister of the warrior Empress Jingō (2nd–3rd centuries A.D.) receiving from a kneeling demon, the servant of the Sea God, the two 'tide-ruling' gems. The pine tree is engraved with a special tool which the craftsmen invented to produce in metal the effect of brushwork. It is signed Kigōdō Naoyoshi, and is probably Nara Toshinaga School work of the late 18th century. The design and workmanship are bold and confident; the various techniques are skilfully combined. No pictorial or sculptural effect was too difficult for simulation in these miniature frames of metal.

Figure 166 c. belongs to a group of miscellaneous iron guards decorated with gold inlay in a unique Japanese technique. This was developed to create in metal the impression of wash-drawing. The *nunome* or 'cloth-grain' method was used to inlay floral branches

A   B
C   D
E   F

KEY

166. *Four Sword Guards* in a variety of techniques.   Tokugawa period.
About two-thirds scale.   Museum of Eastern Art, Oxford.

which surround *kiri* ' paulownia ' badges. The branches spread freely over the edges in a manner typical of the late Japanese decorative sense. The background and design are by this means completely integrated. It is signed by an unrecorded artist Hakuman Nobutoshi, whose name is repeated in a double-gourd shaped seal. This is an example of what the Japanese call ' presentation work.' Such jewel-like guards were used by the *daimyōs* as presents for *shōgunal* officials and became popular as gifts between friends. They reflect the finesse of taste in the period and the high standards demanded of the craftsmen.

Figure 166 d. is a simpler, less ostentatious guard which appealed to the *shibui* side of Japanese taste. It is an iron guard pierced in such a way that the modelling is almost in the round. The design of two blades of rice in the ear skilfully surrounds the central area within a narrow border. It seems that there was no space, however awkwardly shaped, that the Japanese could not turn to decorative use. The *tsuba* is signed ' Myōchin Yoshihisa, Resident in Echizen.' The Myōchin School is one of the most famous. Its founders were originally armourers and the family took the name Myōchin in 1150. As *tsuba* makers they were eminent from the 16th century onwards and some members of the family worked as sword fitters for the *shōguns*. Their innovations were only surpassed by the number of other craftsmen who incorporated their ideas. The school was widely dispersed; the branch which made this particular guard worked in Echizen province until well into the 19th century, and all its followers signed themselves Yoshihisa. This example was probably made in the early 19th century.

Figure 166 e. and f. show the climax of technique and sensibility in *tsuba* manufacture. Both are made of *shakudō*, the alloy of copper and gold, and the backgrounds are punched with the minute *nanako* (fish-roe) dots. In ' f ' the edge is overlapped by a mass of leaves in relief inspired by the various autumn plants depicted on each face—chrysanthemum, asters, gentian, begonia, lespedeza, patrinia, and eularia. The flowers are richly encrusted in gold, with here and there a subtle touch of silver—including even tiny silver drops of dew on the leaves, minute details which only the most scrupulous inspection reveals. The extra-vigilant will often find such rewards in the craft work of the Tokugawa period. A grass-hopper and a cricket are incorporated into the design on the side illustrated. It is signed Terumasa (1704–1772) and is an unusually fine example from this justly famous master of the Omori school founded in the early 18th century.

The guard shown in Fig. 166 ' e ' has a plain edge richly gilt and decorated in bold *iro-e* work almost in the round. Two quail are shown below sprays of various autumn plants. The moon, partly clouded over, is in silver inlay with the *nanako* punching continued over its surface. The signature is that of Mokuyensai Ishiguro who died in 1838. The school to which he belonged was founded by Ishiguro Masatsune (1760–1828) and had a large following until the mid-19th century, its products being particularly popular with the *samurai*. The decoration of this guard is characteristic of the minute incrustation work on soft metals combined with the most delicate modelling of birds, fish, insects, trees, flowers, and blossoming hedges in which this school specialized.

After the mid-Tokugawa period, armour was less in use and some Japanese claim that the meticulous workmanship and minute detail of the later guards resulted in superficiality and triviality. These objects were as non-practical and frankly decorative as a piece of jewellery. Nobody would disagree with the fact that they have lost the powerful, practical lines of the earlier examples. Without doing so they could never have been raised to that level of beauty and fantasy which we see in so many of them.

Perhaps even more popular with Western collectors are the tiny carvings of the period. Here too the workmanship, despite its minute compass, often rises to heroic proportions. The vast reserve of sculptural talent which disappeared from the service of the temples after the Kamakura period dispersed itself in the design and manufacture of such objects as *netsuke*. These are small objects of many shapes used as buttons to prevent the end of a cord from slipping out of the *ōbi* or belt. At the end of the cord hung such things as *inrō* 'seal boxes' or portable smoking and writing implements. Like the *tsuba* they were made in their thousands and represent an output of unrivalled quality and quantity.

The origins of *netsuke* are obscure but they are said to have been made first in the 15th century. No examples from this early period exist and even 16th century specimens are extremely rare. The introduction of the habit of smoking by the Portuguese after 1542 increased the use of accessories hanging from the belt and hence also the need for *netsuke*. *Inrō* with *netsuke* to match became popular and many famous craftsmen such as Kōetsu (Cf. p. 162) turned their skill to making them. Many of the oldest *netsuke* are small objects of foreign origin which the Japanese adapted to the purpose and it is said that Hideyoshi brought some of these back from his campaigns on the mainland. Once accepted in Japan, the production of *netsuke* shared the enthusiasm of the other crafts. The names of 2,700 makers of the 17th to 19th centuries are recorded. The main centres of the craft were in Tokyo, Kyoto, and Nagoya but many smaller areas were situated throughout the whole of Japan also produced them.

The carvers generally, but by no means exclusively, used wood and ivory for their carvings. They also experimented with every possible material which came to their hands —horn, coral, tortoiseshell, mother-of-pearl, lacquer, pottery, marble, obsidian, and, of course, the various base and precious metals. All the decorative techniques found on metal and lacquer-work were adapted for the purpose and the choice of subjects was equally wide. Humans and animals form the largest group but landscapes, seals of Chinese form, curiosities such as telescopes, sundials, pistols, whistles, and firefly cages are also frequently found. An amusing group of 'trick' *netsuke* provided the carvers with a further opportunity to display their ingenuity. Some of these are human figures weighted in such a way that when knocked over they always return to an upright position, others have revolving eyes or protruding tongues. They carved chestnuts with worms which move, wasp nests with movable grubs, buds with movable seeds and cunning reversible masks which look like faces whichever way up they are held.

The shape most frequently found is that of the *manju* or Japanese bun, known in the West as the Japanese button. Masks modelled on those used in *Nō* plays formed popular subjects from the 17th century onwards, their most famous carver being Deme Yeiman of the mid-18th century, a descendent of a famous school of mask carvers. The *kagami-buta* type, in which a decorative metal disc is set in a circular frame of ivory or wood, gave the metal-workers an opportunity to participate in the production of *netsuke* and such eminent schools as the Myōchin made them.

The six *netsuke* illustrated here give only a glimpse of the infinite variety found in these masterpieces of liliputian art. Figure 167 b. *Dutchman Holding a Fighting-Cock* is an unsigned work in wood. It probably comes from a Kyoto workshop of the 17th century. A number of such surviving figures, not all of which are so unflattering to the Westerner, provide an amusing sidelight on the pleasures of the Dutch in Japan and on the Japanese view of the strange 'barbarians.' The *Oni* or 'Devil' mask in Figure 168 b. is also of wood

167 a. Netsuke, *Okame Yawning* by Hidemasa.   Osaka, Wood and Ivory.   18th century.
Height 5¼ inches.   British Museum.
b. Netsuke, wood, *Dutchman Holding a Fighting-cock*.   Height 4 inches.   British Museum.

168 a. Netsuke, *Ashinaga Yawning and Tenagu Sleeping* by Chikamasa.   Ivory.   Late 19th century.
Height 3¼ inches.   British Museum.
b. Netsuke, *Oni or ' Devil ' Mask*, Wood and glass.   *ca.* 1800.   Height 1½ inches.   British Museum.
c. Netsuke, *Fish* by Masanao (*ca.* 1800–1830).   Kyoto.   Wood.   Height 1½ inches.
British Museum.
d. Netsuke, *Bull and Calf* by Tomotada (active 1750–1800).   Ivory.   Length 2½ inches.
British Museum.

but with glass eyes.   Such devils often appear in Japanese art and are usually represented with a square head, two horns, sharp teeth, and malignant eyes surmounted by bushy eyebrows.   This unsigned specimen was probably made about 1800.   Figure 168 c., a skilfully modelled, plump *Fish* is signed Masanao who worked about 1800–1830 in Kyoto.   He is one of the most famous names in *netsuke* carving; his originality and fine carving influenced many successors and imitators.

Figure 167 a. *Okame Yawning* is a combination of wood and ivory possibly by the 18th century master Hidemasa of Osaka.   Okame's full name is Ama-no-Uzume-no-Mikoto. She is the goddess of mirth who, by a lewd dance, helped persuade the sun-goddess Amaterasu to come out of the cave into which she had fled so depriving the world of light. She is usually shown laughing, and her jovial figure, often scantily clad, is a popular *netsuke* motif.   Hidemasa's designs are always distinguished by simple lines and powerful modelling.

Tomotada (active 1750–1800) who carved the *Bull and Calf* in Figure 168 d. was, with Masanao and Yoshinaga, one of the three great masters of the 18th century.   His work has much in common with that of Masanao but he worked quite independently of him.

This animal group, made about 1800, is most typical of his carvings, and the composition was much imitated by later craftsmen. Many very sensitively carved animals are represented in *netsuke* and they are always a delight to handle.

The *netsuke* illustrated in Figure 168 a. is a more grotesque ivory group *Ashinaga Yawning and Tenagu Sleeping* by Chikamasa who worked from about 1830 into the Meiji period which began in 1868. His school is famous for its groups of animals and humans. The two mythical figures in the carving were said to have lived on the coast of China. The long-armed Tenagu was supposed to have caught fish while perched on the back of Ashinaga who could wade deep into the sea on his long legs. These few *netsuke* show just a few of the many sources to which the Japanese turned for fitting subjects for these tiny works.

It is not altogether unfitting to end this short survey of Japanese art with the *netsuke* of the 19th century. It opened with the Jōmon figurines of two thousand years before. The spirits which inspired the arts of Jōmon and Tokugawa times differed completely but it is not too far-fetched to see the same hand at work in both of them. Certain characteristics persist in an art of unusual continuity—through the earliest portraiture of the *haniwa*, the idealism of Nara, the mysticism of Heian, and the realism of Kamakura. With the *netsuke*, the Japanese carvers seem to have turned full circle, summing up as they did so the abilities of nearly two millenia.

By 1868, a combination of internal and external pressures had forced Japan out of her self-imposed seclusion and the ensuing contacts with the West brought a flood of European art, itself then entering a very stimulating revolutionary phase. In the turmoil this created, a number of distinguished and original native painters tried, often successfully, to preserve and develop their own *bun-jin* styles. Others studied in Paris and on their return either copied French styles or attempted the most difficult of all syntheses, that of Eastern and Western manners. Interesting and vigorous, though it was, we are not yet in a position to assess their work.

The second half of this century may well see a re-assessment and revival of traditional styles of painting in Japan. It is one of the functions of the artist to make us see things with new eyes; in this the Eastern modes, whose powers of adaption are unquestionable, have much to offer us in the West. A revival is already evident in new Japanese styles of calligraphy which are constantly appearing. Calligraphy is an essentially Eastern art not easily dominated by foreign influences and from calligraphy to painting is but a short step. In the course of this study we have seen Japanese artists repeatedly absorbing influences from China, which after a century or so they have made entirely their own. We may well see them do the same with the powerful influences from the West.

ALPHABETICAL LIST OF CHARACTERS
WHICH FORM THE NAMES OF THE MOST
IMPORTANT JAPANESE COLOUR PRINT
MASTERS[1]

馬	ba (Hokuba)
文	bun (Bunchō)
珍	chin (Chinchō)
重	{ chō (Chinchō) : shige
調	chō (Bunchō)
潮	chō (Shunchō)
岳	gaku (Gakutei)
川	{ gawa (Utagawa) : kawa
羽	hane (Hanegawa)
春	{ haru (Harunobu) : shun
廣	hiro (Kiyohiro)
菱	hishi (Hishikawa)
北	{ hoku (Hókušai) : kita
為	i (Iitsu)
居	i (Torii)
石	ishi (Ishikawa)
一	itsu (Iitsu)
葛	katsu (Katsushika)

勝	katsu (Katsukawa)
川	{ kawa (Hishikawa) : gawa
溪	kei (Keisai)
木	ki (Suzuki)
菊	kiku (Kikugawa)
北	{ kita (Kitao) : hoku
清	kiyo (Kiyonobu)
湖	ko (Koriusai)
國	kuni (Morikuni)
満	{ man (Shumman) : mitsu
麿	maro (Utamaro)
政	masa (Masanobu)
倍	masu (Kiyomasu)
満	{ mitsu (Kiyomitsu) : man
守	mori (Morikuni)
師	moro (Moronóbu)
村	mura (Okumura)
長	naga (Shigenaga)

西 nishi (Nishimura)

宣 nobu (Moronobu)

信 nobu (Kiyonobu)

尾 o (Kitao)

奥 oku (Okumura)

樂 raku (Sharaku)

理 ri (Sōri)

龍 riu (Koriusai)

朗 rō (Shunrō)

負 sada (Kunisada)

齋 sai (Koriusai)

扇 sen (Shunsen)

泉 sen (Yeisen)

寫 sha (Sharaku)

之 shi (Yeishi)

重 { shige (Shigenaga)
     : chō

飾 shika (Katsushika)

昌 shō (Yeishō)

章 shō (Shunshō)

春 { shun (Shunshō)
     : haru

俊 shun (Shumman)

宗 sō (Sōri)

鈴 suzu (Suzuki)

橘 tachibana (T. Morikuni)

戴 tai (Taito)

斗 to (Taito)

祐 suke (Sukenobu)

鳥 tori (Torii)

豊 toyo (Toyonobu)

歌 uta (Utagawa)

英 yei (Shunyei)

榮 yei (Yeishi)

美 yoshi (Masayoshi)

芳 yoshi (Kuniyoshi)

喜 yoshi (Nagayoshi)

山 zan (Yeizan)

¹ Reproduced from W. v. Seidlitz, Geschichte des Japanischen Farbenholzschnittes, Berlin 1897.

SHORT BIBLIOGRAPHY

Sir George Sansom. *Japan: A Short Cultural History*. London, 1946.

E. Conze. *Buddhism*. Oxford, 1951.

Staff of the Tokyo National Museum. *Pageant of Japanese Art*, 6 vols. Tokyo, 1952 onwards.

Langdon Warner. *The Enduring Art of Japan*. Harvard, 1952.
The Craft of the Japanese Sculptor. New York, 1936.

H. Minamoto. *An Illustrated History of Japanese Art*. Kyoto, 1935.

J. Buhot. *Histoire Des Arts Du Japon*. Vol. I. Paris, 1949.

R. Groussett. *Japon*. Paris, 1930.

Seiroku Nōma.
Takeshi Kuno. *Albums of Japanese Sculpture*. 6 vols. Tokyo, 1953.

Kenji Moriya. *Die Japanische Malerei*. Weisbaden, 1953.

Lawrence Binyon. *Painting in the Far East*. 4th ed. London, 1949.

Seiichi Taki. *Three Essays on Oriental Painting*. London, 1920.

Tōichirō Naitō. *The Wall Paintings of Hōryū-ji*. Baltimore, 1943.

Kenji Toda. *Japanese Scroll Painting*. Chicago, 1935.

A Drexler. *The Architecture of Japan*. New York, 1955.

T. Mitsuoka. *Ceramic Art of Japan*. Tokyo, 1949.

H. L. Joly. *Japanese Sword Guards*. London, 1910.

F. Meinertzhagen. *The Art of the Netsuke Carver*. London, 1956.
Oriental Art. 1948 onwards.

Basil Stewart. *Subjects portrayed in Japanese Colour Prints*.

L. Binyon and J. J. O'Brien Sexton. *Japanese Colour Prints*. London, 1923.

J. Hillier. *Japanese Masters of the Colour Print*. London, 1955.
Hokusai. London, 1956.

James Michener. *The Floating World*. New York, 1954.

E. F. Strange. *Japanese Colour Prints*. London, 1931.

Faubion Bowers. *Japanese Theatre*. London, 1934.

RECENT WORKS

Robert Treat Paine and Alexander Soper. *The Art and Architecture of Japan*. London, 1955.

Hugo Munsterberg. *The Arts of Japan*. London, 1957.

Yukio Yashirō. *2,000 Years of Japanese Art*. London, 1958.

INDEX